SCHOOL RULES:
OBEDIENCE, DISCIPLINE, AND E

M000288817

How much say should students have in shaping their schools' disciplinary cultures? Should they have the power to weigh in on contentious issues like favouritism, discrimination, 'no hats' rules, and zero tolerance? What if pupils disagree with their teachers and administrators on certain rules? Rebecca Raby reflects on how regulations are made, applied, and negotiated in educational settings in the accessibly written *School Rules*.

Through an in-depth analysis of codes of conduct and other original data, including interviews with teachers, administrators, and students, *School Rules* reveals what rules mean to different participants, and where it is that they becoming a challenge. Raby investigates students' acceptance or contestation of disciplinary regulations, and examines how school rules reflect and perpetuate existing inequalities and students' beliefs about young people. Illustrating the practical challenges and political and theoretical concerns of involving students in rule-making, *School Rules* can help teachers and administrators facilitate more meaningful rules and student participation in their own schools.

REBECCA RABY is an associate professor in the Department of Child and Youth Studies at Brock University.

REBECCA RABY

School Rules

Obedience, Discipline, and Elusive Democracy

UNIVERSITY OF TORONTO PRESS
Toronto   Buffalo   London

© University of Toronto Press 2012
Toronto Buffalo London
www.utppublishing.com
Printed in Canada

ISBN 978-1-4426-4110-5 (cloth)
ISBN 978-1-4426-1041-5 (paper)

Printed on acid-free, 100% post-consumer recycled paper with vegetable-
based inks.

Library and Archives Canada Cataloguing in Publication

Raby, Rebecca, 1968–
    School rules : obedience, discipline, and elusive democracy / Rebecca Raby.

Includes bibliographical references and index.
ISBN 978-1-4426-4110-5 (bound).   ISBN 978-1-4426-1041-5 (pbk.)

    1. School management and organization – Canada.   2. School discipline –
Canada.   3. Student participation in administration – Canada.
4. Democracy and education – Canada.   I. Title.

LB3011.5.R32 2012   371.5'10971   C2011-908277-2

University of Toronto Press acknowledges the financial assistance to its
publishing program of the Canada Council for the Arts and the Ontario
Arts Council.

  Canada Council   Conseil des Arts    ONTARIO ARTS COUNCIL
       for the Arts   du Canada   CONSEIL DES ARTS DE L'ONTARIO

University of Toronto Press acknowledges the financial support of the
Government of Canada through the Canada Book Fund for its publishing
activities.

In memory of my dad, Stewart Raby (1940–2009)

Contents

Acknowledgments

Research for this book was made possible through a research grant from the Social Sciences and Humanities Research Council (SSHRC) of Canada, two internal SSHRC grants from Brock University, and a number of Brock University Experience Works grants which support the employment of Brock students. While such funding was vital to support this project, it is the participants who have given the project its value, depth, and texture. I very much appreciate the time and comments of student and staff participants. Student focus groups, in particular, have left me with some quite memorable moments of this research! Staff participation was also made possible through support from two Ontario school boards who agreed to allow me to approach teachers and administrators through their schools.

Over the course of data collection and analysis, a number of research assistants participated in this project and I am grateful to them all: Megan, Beth, Julie, Jesse, Rachel, Sylvia, Beth, and Kristina. Julie Domintrek, in particular, was involved in this research for a very long time and eventually co-published several papers with me. During Julie's involvement with this project she graduated and became a supply teacher at the secondary level, adding a valuable 'hands-on' evaluation of this work. I am indebted to her fastidiousness, commitment, inquiry, and enthusiasm.

I would also like to thank a number of colleagues, friends and family who provided comments, discussion, and/or editing: two anonymous reviewers, Brittany Lavery, Miriam Skey, Kathryn Payne, Mary-Beth Raddon, Shauna Pomerantz, Jon-Eben Field, Nancy Cook, Hans Skott-Myhre, Zsuzsa Millei, Alison Lohans, Kristina Gottli, Julia Gottli, and my mom Helen McFadden. Finally, a special thanks to Holly Patterson and Levi Patterson-Raby.

SCHOOL RULES:
OBEDIENCE, DISCIPLINE, AND ELUSIVE DEMOCRACY

1 Introduction

I see nothing wrong in the practice of a person who, knowing more than others in a specific game of truth, tells those others what to do, teaches them, and transmits knowledge and techniques to them. The problem in such practices where power – which is not in itself a bad thing – must inevitably come into play is knowing how to avoid the kind of domination effects where a kid is subjected to the arbitrary and unnecessary authority of a teacher, or a student put under the thumb of a professor who abuses his authority.

(Foucault 2003, 40)

Most people are familiar with school rules in some regard, at the very least remembering the rules which governed their own school experiences. Some might be surprised at how many rules I discuss in this book are familiar, across differences in the political, social, and economic contexts within which rules are created, applied, and received. Others, such as students, administrators, and teachers, might know very well the rules I examine from their day-to-day experiences in schools. Various rules, strategies for enforcement, and processes of surveillance have also gained recent prominence through the media as school personnel seek to ensure student safety and compliance in a broader culture of fears of violence.

This is not a how-to book to assist school staff in improving student discipline or ensuring student obedience, nor is it a book that rejects school rules altogether, for rules can provide community, skills, and interpersonal guidelines which help diverse peoples to coexist. Yet while most will agree that some kinds of rules are necessary to a social system, what such rules aim to accomplish, what they should look like, who should make them, and how they should be enforced are all subject to debate, particularly when considering rules that govern young people. For instance, to what extent should schools regulate what students wear, their accessories, and even their hair colour? How far does the purview of the school extend beyond school property in the regulation of fighting, littering, or dress? Should consequences for rule-breaking be the same for all students, regardless of personal circumstances? Should students be governed by different rules than staff? And who should be involved in making these kinds of decisions? In this book I argue that rules are not simply common sense, and how they are understood by different people reflects their deeper beliefs about human nature, growing up, and social governance. Starting from this premise, this book is a critical investigation of school rules as they are created, embedded in codes of conduct, understood and applied by school staff, and negotiated by students.

Key Themes

Drawing on various sources of data and engaging with quite distinct bodies of literature described below, I examine school rules through four overarching themes. First, I consider that school rules, their creation, and the consequences for breaking them reflect a wide range of beliefs about young people (e.g., as irrational), human nature (e.g., as calculating), and the purpose of schooling (e.g., to produce employees). In this text I thus examine how school rules and their application reflect cultural, developmental, gendered, racialized, and class-based beliefs about young people that frequently reproduce inequality. Some of these beliefs correspond to those regarding human nature in general and others do not. I also consider how rules and their application are grounded in assumptions about what is acceptable behaviour in the school as an institution of containment, hierarchy, education, and preparation for future roles.

Second, school rules do not simply reflect beliefs but create them. As such, this book examines how the rules are productive. They produce language of responsibility that then comes to shape students' and teachers' self-understanding, for instance. What the rules say and how they are applied attempt to create certain kinds of students and future adults, often along the lines of obedience. They also attempt to produce the school as a particular kind of space, often one defined by hierarchical and ordered relations. These attempts are not simple or automatically accomplished, however, but frequently complicated and even contradictory.

Third, school rules are negotiated within the school through certain recurring sites of struggle, and even resistance, that are often discussed by students and staff. These sites of struggle in turn reflect and reproduce broader beliefs and inequalities. For example, the case of minor rules, such as those against wearing hats in school, draws attention to significant differences between students' and staff understandings of the rules, in part reflecting distinct understandings of the school and its geography, of changing mores within the wider society, and of what rules are for, consequently creating tension within schools around expectations and enforcement. Another area of struggle is, of course, around students' breaking of rules and other ways that students may challenge rules. Beliefs about the reasons for school rules and how they should be applied resonate with beliefs about young people and why they might break rules. This book examines how rule-breaking is understood by staff as opposed to students, whether rule-breaking can be considered a form of resistance, what other forms of challenge are used by students, and how staff respond to such challenges.

The final overarching thematic thread within this book addresses how rules are produced and the question of young people's involvement or participation in such processes. Related to the above themes, this emphasis asks how we need to think about young people in relation to democratic citizenship. Child rights advocates, researchers concerned with the development of citizens skilled in democratic participation, and others have expressed interest in developing students' consistent, real participation in the creation of the rules, as the production of school rules is commonly top-down and unfavourable to democratic citizenship. Typically, most teachers and students are outside of the process of rule-development, with students' views particularly absent. How do students respond to rules which they feel are unfair or irrelevant and how are such responses understood by staff? What processes are available for student appeal or input? Advocates for change have faith in student involvement and the consequent development of democratic citizenship. But, while attractive and laudatory, are such goals practical? Furthermore, might such goals simply serve to deepen students' complicity in their own subjection?

Data and Context

In addition to drawing on others' research into the topics of rules and discipline, this book engages with several different forms of original data, most of which concentrate on two quite distinct non-Catholic[1] school districts in Southern Ontario, Canada. Initially, between 2002 and 2003 I collected and analysed codes of conduct from two districts' secondary schools, one metropolitan and one more rural. Then with my research team, I conducted eighteen focus groups with secondary students in two similarly distinct regions, nine in each. 'Big City' refers to a large, multicultural, urban centre and 'Whitton' refers to a region that includes small cities, towns, and farmland. These focus groups were conducted over the summers of 2004–6 and were organized with an interest in talking to a diverse range of young people. Participants were primarily located through service organizations. We also conducted interviews with teachers and administrators in both districts. Twenty-one in-person interviews were conducted with teachers and administrators in Whitton and ten phone interviews were held with teachers and administrators in Big City. All interviews and focus groups were transcribed, coded twice for themes by two independent coders, and then codes were recorded into NVIVO (a form of qualitative software) for organizational and analytic work with the developed codes in order to isolate the various themes and patterns that are examined in this book. Please see Appendix A for a more detailed discussion of data collection and analysis.

In Canada, education is a provincial responsibility, and so each province has its own policies and curriculum. School rules in Ontario are shaped by 1) provincial legislation, 2) school board policy which reflects, but can also build on, provincial legislation, and 3) specific rules created at the level of the individual schools. These three political and administrative layers together guide school personnel. The period of time during which research for this book was collected was one that saw significant changes introduced at the provincial level. Data collection began several years after the introduction of the *Safe Schools Act* in 2000 by the then Conservative government and the stated goals of this Act have remained unchanged. They are to increase respect, responsibility, and safety in Ontario's schools (Trépanier 2003). The Act includes roles and responsibilities for school boards, parents, volunteers, teachers, and administrators as well as students. The 2000 *Safe Schools Act* included provisions for schools to introduce uniforms through a vote of parents, and a *Code of Conduct* that was interpreted by many as a zero tolerance policy because it required suspensions and expulsions for specific rule infractions, such as fighting. The latter, however, did include two mitigating circumstances for staff to consider: if the pupil cannot control his or her actions or foresee the consequences to them, or if the pupil is not a threat to any person. The *Safe Schools Act* allowed teachers to give suspensions, a right that had previously only been held by the principal.[2] New strict discipline schools were introduced for students who had been expelled.

While most features of the *Safe Schools Act* received little public attention, popular criticism of the zero tolerance portion of the Act began to grow soon after its introduction. In particular, the new policy was seen as linked to a rise in suspension rates, and it was felt to disproportionately affect students who were visible minorities or who had learning disabilities (Bhattacharjee 2003; Gabor 1995). In response to these criticisms, in 2006 the new Liberal government introduced a series of town hall meetings and a policy team to review the *Safe Schools Act* and its application. This review resulted in a series of recommendations and, ultimately, an amended *Safe Schools Act*, 'Safe, Caring and Restorative Schools,' which was enacted at the beginning of 2008. This new Act drew on the language of 'progressive discipline,' which emphasizes the promotion of positive student behaviour and allows principals to determine the most appropriate consequences for student misconduct, rather than requiring a flat 'zero tolerance' approach.

The new policy maintained a list of offences that could lead to suspension or expulsion, but it also expanded the mitigating circumstances that must be taken into account before a student is suspended or expelled, to include considerations such as the student's age, family situation, and special needs. Offences which could result in suspension were expanded to include cyber-bullying and other forms of bullying occurring off school property, and the length of suspensions was decreased to no more than twenty days. Furthermore, the new Act required schools to offer some kind of educational support program for students suspended or expelled for more than six days and limited teachers' ability to suspend to one-day suspensions. Beyond suspensions and expulsions, the new Act recommended that schools consider a much wider range of preventative and progressive alternatives, including peer mediation and anti-bullying initiatives. Both versions of the *Safe Schools Act* are discussed further in chapter 5.

This book's analysis is complicated by these significant legislative changes that occurred over the course of my data collection, an issue I address in Appendix A. However, the changes have also offered an opportunity to consider the effects of overarching legislative changes on the 'ground,' in terms of how students and staff understand and experience school rules.

Research Literature

Classroom Management

A wide range of research literature tackles questions related to school rules through quite distinct lenses. The literature most directly engaging with questions of student discipline is in the area of classroom management, which includes theorizing about classroom management practices, advice manuals for teachers, and research studies. According to most of those working in this area, school rules and their enforcement ensure a degree of order and safety necessary for learning to take place. School rules are also closely linked to teaching young people the norms and values of their society (Noguera 2003), a position which reflects a philosophy advocated by early sociologist Emile Durkheim (1973) who believed school discipline to be key to teaching morality. Classroom management approaches also tend to draw on psychological approaches (particularly developmental stages) to understanding young people (Millei and Raby 2010).

A number of scholars discuss schools of thought on classroom management. Porter (1996), for example, reviews various approaches, considering their underlying assumptions and their strengths and weaknesses: these include the more traditional limit-setting approaches of researchers such as Canter and Canter and Fredric Jones, applied and cognitive behaviourism, neo-Adlerian approaches, humanist approaches, and William Glasser's control and systems theory. Others favour more 'hands on' tools and advice (e.g., Sprick 2006; Lewis 1991), although these, too, tend to draw on one or more of the above schools of thought. Advice manuals focus primarily on the specific initiatives that teachers and administrators can undertake in order to better address student discipline (Gottfredson, Gottfredson, and Hybl 1993) and to therefore facilitate a learning environment (Brophy 2006).

Such advice texts also draw on numerous research-based studies in classroom management. For example, scholars have found that students are more inclined to support the rules if they are invested in the school through having good relationships with teachers, wanting to get good grades, thinking rules are fair, and having a sense of belonging (Wald and Kurlaender 2003; Stewart 2003), while overly strict or lenient discipline have both been found to increase student drop-out rates (Ferguson et al. 2005). Similarly, Gottfredson, Gottfredson, and Hybl (1993) link misbehaviour to a series of what they understand to be individual features such as being male, having low grades, being anti-school, having negative peers, possessing poor social skills, and challenging adult authority. Yet they also cite classroom level causes, such as unstructured classrooms and a general school environment of punishment, unfairness, inconsistency in rule enforcement, and a lack of resources. Most studies find that avoiding problems through interactive, engaging, and supportive teaching styles, teaching social skills, and drawing on positive reinforcement are ideal methods for maintaining classroom management (Jones and Jones 2007). In contrast, classroom management based on rigid rules, student passivity, and compliance are anathema to abstract thinking, active learning (Brophy 2006), and effective classroom management (Jones and Jones 2007). Finally, within this area of research we can include the evaluation of policies such as school uniforms to determine their effectiveness in terms of safety, discipline, and academic success (Shannon and McCall 2003; Stanley 1996).

In Brophy's review of the history of classroom management, some clear patterns in classroom management research become evident. Methodologically, the focus tends to be on observational research and, to a lesser degree, hypothesis-testing. The focus also tends to favour research at the elementary school level. Often the focus is on the classroom itself, so that the role of administrators is left to the side, and other school spaces and activities, like extra-curricular activities, receive less attention. Classroom management research does not address the rules *per se* so much as the process of attempting to maintain classroom discipline. Furthermore, the work in this area tends to pay more attention to teacher styles than to issues of identity or morality within discipline processes, although some researchers also address wider but vital social issues such as social inequality (Skiba and Rausch 2006; Jones and Jones 2007).

The classroom management literature is well-researched and provides important guidance in terms of disciplinary strategies, with a clear focus on fostering a positive classroom environment which students feel is fair and intellectually engaging. It also generates some questions which inform this text. Classroom management is often centred on order. How central is order to our understanding of schooling and how does this goal inform the development and deployment of rules? Should order be of primary importance? Also, what is the relationship between classroom strategies and the blanket rules developed by such governing bodies as provinces and school boards – to what extent do such broader rules complement or contradict ideal strategies for the classroom?

While the classroom management literature directly informs analysis of tensions between context and consistency and strategies for addressing cultural differences in the classroom, its concentration on classroom dynamics often lends it a more micro-sociological and psychological focus. In contrast, my approach here focuses more on the school than the classroom and more on the actual rules and student and staff negotiations of them than on teacher temperaments or styles. Furthermore, I have indicated that some critical approaches ally themselves with classroom management (e.g., Skiba and Rausch 2006; Jones and Jones 2007); I concentrate more on the relevance of structural inequalities and the contested nature of rules themselves than tends to be the case in classroom management.

Moral Education

'Moral education' is another related approach that examines school discipline processes, with an underlying focus on the development of morality in children. A key author in this area is Larry Nucci (2001) who has conducted a number of cross-cultural studies to examine children's understandings of morality and how they distinguish it from convention. He argues that we have an innate and early sense of morality based on ideas of care, justice, and rights, which transcends specific cultures and religions. Convention, on the other hand, involves social mores which are localized to the governing rules of specific contexts. In addition to morality and convention, he argues, there is a third domain which governs what is considered the considered the personal realm, including free association and personal appearance.

Work in moral education addresses education in terms of discipline as well as curriculum, with children's interpretations of the rules and their enforcement linked to their understandings of these domains (Nucci 2001; Goodman 2006a; Smetana and Bitz 1996). According to this approach, children tend to expect rules grounded in morality, such as 'no bullying,' as well as conventional rules that do not encroach on what they consider as their personal domain. From this perspective, researchers such as Nucci have importantly argued that teachers should discipline with these domains in mind, providing rationales for rules and involving students in moral discussions and decision-making around rules. In her work on moral education, Goodman is concerned that schools tend to conflate moral and conventional issues by listing rules as if they are all of equal importance and treating all rule violations similarly. She also introduces the 'derivatively moral' (e.g., rules such as those against lateness that are given moral attributes under certain interpretations) to discuss some of the murkier areas of school discipline. Children interpret enforcement as more legitimate when teachers emphasize the effects of an act, or the rationale for the rule, rather than simply saying 'don't.' Brophy (2006) cautions that moral educators are concerned that when discipline becomes simply a case of following rules no matter what, obedience itself becomes the moral imperative, rules proliferate inappropriately, and young people fail to learn about morality. The area of moral education thus raises specific, relevant issues regarding how rules are presented to young people and how students morally engage with them. A deeper discussion of moral education can be found in chapter 3.

While the moral education approach to understanding school codes of conduct is useful, particularly as students themselves create such domain distinctions between rules, it is also one that should be used with some caution. While Nucci argues for an innate, cross-cultural sense of morality, he also finds that children in more traditional societies and lower classes are more likely than others to moralize conventions. He further points out that perceptions of morality are affected by power and hierarchy; those who have more power in society are more likely to moralize social beliefs that advantage them, including beliefs around class, gender, and race.[3] These distinctions are not central to Nucci's work and yet they are important reminders that understandings of morality and convention are culturally distinct and ideological. As those working from the perspective of critical pedagogy observe, both these facets come to bear on an analysis of school rules and their application.

Critical Pedagogy

Researchers in critical pedagogy argue that the organization of schools, including school discipline and the assumptions behind it, is not benign, but rather is shaped by class, race, and gender inequalities. In their now classic text, Bowles and Gintis (1976) contend that schools sort students into future occupational and economic roles, such that they are groomed for certain kinds of work, with the effect of reproducing existing class distinctions. Oakes makes a similar argument in her analysis of the negative effects of streaming in high schools (1985). A key part of the critical tradition argues that for most students entering school, there is a trade-off that allows for discipline to be accomplished: students obey the rules and follow staff authority and in return, they receive an education (Noguera 2003). Yet for those students who are being sorted 'to the bottom' and find that education brings little hope of improvement for their lives, this trade-off does not succeed and there is little incentive to follow the rules. The disruption this provokes has, in fact, been reconceptualized as resistance to the middle class biases of the school (Willis 1977).

Those working in critical pedagogy argue that schools, in turn, add to the marginalization of this group of students through responses such as detention and suspension, most commonly punishing minorities, males, low achievers, those with learning disabilities, those in foster care, homeless youth, and those who come from a low socio-economic background (Noguera 2003). Robbins (2008) joins many in thoroughly criticizing zero tolerance policies in the United States, for example, for perpetuating class- and race-based violence against poor and minority students who are more likely than others to be suspended or expelled. Suspensions in turn commonly reproduce academic marginality when students lose instruction time (Skiba and Rausch 2006). This is not to say that teachers are conspiring to marginalize minority and working class students. In fact, teachers are commonly drawn to the profession specifically because they want to address inequality through education. Yet they end up caught in a system where they must focus on control (Robbins 2008).

The hidden curriculum also communicates to students certain values that reproduce inequalities (Wotherspoon 1996; Lynch 1989; McLaren 1989). For example, Pierre Bourdieu introduced the concept of cultural capital (Bourdieu 2001; Bourdieu and Passeron 1977) to suggest that schools reward dominant values and consequently those students who are most familiar with these values. From this perspective, many school rules are understood to be based on vague, middle class, culturally dominant language and values, contributing to the reproduction of inequalities through marginalizing certain students (Raby 2005; Lynch 1989; Jay 1997), and ultimately fostering a climate where certain students are more likely to drop out (Bowditch 1993; Fine 1991).

The work in critical pedagogy is vital when considering school rules, for this work destabilizes assumptions that rules are simply common sense or that schools operate outside a broader social, political, and economic system that in fact includes unequal class, race, and gender relations. Those working in this area are adamant that any examination of school discipline must consider these more structural questions, challenging those working within the educational system to think beyond the more immediate context of managing a classroom or a school. It also argues for social change towards greater equality both within schools and beyond. Critical pedagogy is not enough, however. There are other, related processes at the level of subjectivity[4] that are involved in the creation and application of school rules that strive to construct certain kinds of individuals and future citizens. Governmentality studies provide a powerful tool to analyse these processes, one that allows us to consider the ways that student investment can be enlisted at the most intimate level of the self.

Foucault and Governmentality Studies

School rules and how they are talked about both reflect and produce discourses[5] of adolescence and beliefs about human nature which can be examined through the work of Michel Foucault, who was interested in how knowledge is produced through relations of power. Foucault examines power relations at the most micro levels (e.g., between a student and a teacher) and how they link together to reproduce forms of domination but also to produce new knowledge and subjectivities (Foucault 1978a, 1978b). The attempt to create certain kinds of students, workers, or future citizens can similarly be examined through Foucault and others' discussions of governmentality (Rose 1990, 1999; Tait 2000). Nikolas Rose, a key figure in governmentality studies, defines governmentality as 'all endeavors to shape, guide, [and] direct the conduct of others' (1999, 3). From this perspective, government extends far beyond the state to include wider processes of governance through the school, the family, and other organizations and institutions. Unlike sovereign power, which attempts to maintain legitimate authority through top-down, hierarchical applications of power (Kelly 2003), governance is conducted through trying to guide people's freedom (Rose 1999) and mobilize self-governing persons interested in making rational choices and minimizing risk (Hannah-Moffat 2000).

Drawing on such studies, dress and discipline codes can be seen as sites of knowledge production (e.g., about the 'respectable' student or the 'problem' student), the internalization of discipline, and the creation of docile citizenship. Rather than resorting to direct social control, such neoliberal governance practices conceptualize people 'as subjects of responsibility, autonomy and choice, and seek to act upon them through shaping and utilizing their freedom' (Rose 1999, 53–4). Millei (2010) cautions that while various approaches to classroom management attempt to increase student freedom through emphasizing self-discipline and negotiation between staff and students, ultimately these strategies are about deepening control through an emphasis on the self. Furthermore, the current emphasis on developing self-discipline does not mean that more 'top-down,' sovereign forms of rule have disappeared. Foucault saw punishment, discipline, and governmental processes working together, a system we now see in the uneasy relationship between demands for both obedience and cultivation of self-discipline evident in many school codes of conduct (Millei and Raby 2010). A governmentality studies perspective enjoins us to investigate the rules as they produce beliefs, categories, and self-regulation. In this book I will engage with this approach to investigate the rules in terms of what kind of present and future individuals they seem to be attempting to create, as well as the ways the rules are deployed by staff to suggest both governance through responsibility, autonomy, and choice, and demands for obedience. I also reflect on whether a call for increased student participation in rule-making is a problematic form of governmental tactics.

Sociology of Childhood and the Importance of Student Voice

Finally, there is a growing body of work in the sociology of childhood (James and Prout 1990; Jenks 1996) now developing to also examine adolescence (Lesko 1996a; Adams 1997; Best 2000). This research focuses on the categories of childhood and adolescence as socially constructed within historical and current contexts, attending to intersecting locations of race, class, gender, and sexuality, contexts that also influence the perception, experience, and application of school rules (Ruck and Wortley 2002; McLaren 1989). Methodologically, many of these researchers advocate young people's participation in research about themselves (Christensen and James 2000).

Research examining students' own views on school rules is somewhat limited (Ruddock and Flutter 2000). Classroom management research investigates how young people feel within their classrooms, but not necessarily how they feel regarding the rules. Some pertinent discussions with children have informed moral education, as I have discussed. Others have specifically investigated students' views on how the rules are created, finding that some students feel disenfranchised from their schools and would like greater involvement. For instance, Devine's ethnographic research with primary students in Ireland found that children wanted a greater voice in the organization of their school (2002). At the secondary level, through interviews with students in Saturday detention, American researcher Sue Thorson found that they would like greater communication with administrators about school rules and attention to the context of disciplinary situations (1996). Similarly, through interviews with students conducted in small-town American schools, Schmuck and Schmuck (1989) found that while students are generally invested in their schools, they feel that their school councils are impotent and they are frustrated with teachers who are seen as disrespectful, too stern, harsh, or permissive, and who play favourites. Students on the margins are less likely to experience school rules as fair. Two quantitative Canadian studies found that non-White students, in particular, perceive an unequal application of school discipline (Ruck and Wortley 2002; MacDonell and Martin 1986). These findings are supported by Bhattacharjee's submission to the Ontario's Human Rights Commission on Ontario's *Safe Schools Act* (2003) and by Ferguson et al.'s investigation of early school leaving in Ontario (2005). Both Thorson (1996) and Schmuck and Schmuck (1989) emphasize the value of listening to young people's experiences and they join others in advocating students' deeper involvement in legitimate decision-making within the school (Ruddock and Flutter 2000).

Another related dimension within the sociology of childhood is an understanding of children as social agents and social participants (James and Prout 1990). While children may have different skills from adults, they are considered here as competent in a way that is frequently underestimated (Smith 2002). This position is reflected by those researchers and advocates interested in children's participatory rights. Children's entitlements to participation rights have been championed by various activists and researchers, some directly focusing on young people's participation rights in schools (Alderson 1999), including their governance (DeRoma, Lassiter, and Davis 2004; Effrat and Schimmel 2003; Schimmel 2003). Children's rights have also been enshrined in the *United Nations Convention on the Rights of the Child* (CRC), which states that children have the right to free expression and consultation on decisions that directly affect them. Within this convention, there is some tension regarding participation rights, however (Archard 2004). While children are to have a say in matters that directly affect them, their participation rights are limited by what adults, including teachers and principals, consider to be in the best interests of the child, including their best interests based on their rights to protection (e.g., security) and provision (e.g., in terms of education or health care). To what extent should young people have a say in the organization of their schools? How might such participation be envisioned? One goal of this book is to consider calls for student participation in light of the sociology of childhood, critical pedagogy, and governmental perspectives, and to offer some alternatives for how this has been done in some contexts.

Balancing Perspectives

Much of the focus of critical pedagogy emerges from a modernist tradition with an emphasis on social structure and an understanding of power and coercion that sees it as something held by certain people or groups and applied against others. To a large extent, the new sociology of childhood focuses on rights and student voice in a way that also draws on this modernist tradition. Governmentality studies, in contrast, resonate with a post-structural approach focused on micro and shifting power relations, the creation of subjectivities, and the production of knowledge. To some critics, a governmental approach is more interested in explaining the processes of government than in evaluating them. In contrast, I concur with O'Malley, Weir, and Shearing (1997) on the potential for those in governmentality studies to weigh the effects of power relations within a broader context of social relations that include the inequalities and dominations so fundamentally addressed in critical pedagogy. These distinct lenses are useful for examining school rules, their intent, and students' engagement with them. The difficult tension between these perspectives cannot be overlooked, however, and consequently provides an underlying current to this text.

One place where this tension between more modernist and post-structural positions is apparent is in the area of student response to the rules, for students will experience, receive, understand, and engage with rules in unexpected and challenging ways. Resistance has been a pivotal concept for a number of youth scholars, particularly for those working in critical pedagogy and cultural studies (e.g., see Willis 1977; McRobbie 1978; Giroux 1983; Hebdige 1979) and several examining how young people resist schools' attempts to discipline their bodies (e.g., see Simpson 2000; Lesko 1988; McLaren 1993). It is also a concept that is understood quite differently based on one's theoretical commitments (Raby 2005), as modernists tend to assume an essential subject, and opposition between those with power and those without (Scott 1990), while post-structuralists assume a constructed subject, and examine how resistance is diffuse and responds to multiple relations of power (Muñoz 1999; Butler 1990; Foucault 1978b). Young people's engagements with dress and discipline codes can be understood and explored in relation to these quite distinct approaches to resistance, with consequent implications for understanding their agency. This area of theoretical investigation is found in chapter 8.

Potential Readers

It is hoped that this book will be valuable to a wide range of readers, including those studying sociology, anthropology, and education. There are three groups of people who may find this book particularly relevant, however: pre-service teachers, in-service teachers, and administrators (including policy-makers).

Pre-service teachers may be feeling some trepidation about entering the classroom, not only in terms of knowing and teaching the curricula but also in terms of classroom discipline. Not coincidentally, many 'how-to' books on classroom discipline specifically address new teachers. Such worries are also linked to image. Pre-service teachers may be concerned about making a good impression through being seen as in control of their classroom space; they also may feel when starting to teach that they must enforce all the school rules in order to ensure a good relationship with administration. These concerns can lead new teachers to focus on the top-down creation and application of fixed rules. Other new teachers may be excited about alternative classroom and school management strategies, including increased student involvement. I invite pre-service teachers to use this book to reflect on some fundamental questions about school rules and school discipline, and to use this reflection to inform their future practice. What assumptions do they personally hold about rules, discipline, and young people and where do these come from? How might codes of conduct be understood and experienced by different stakeholders in the school, including students? What might be some challenges to teachers who are either hoping to reinforce the *status quo* or hoping to do things differently? Those entering the teaching profession can also more broadly reflect on how they understand the role of a teacher in terms of pedagogy and how this becomes linked to discipline. This book encourages such questions. It also places importance on building relationships with students and listening to their views as a disciplinary and pedagogical strategy.

In-service teachers will also likely find material in this book thought-provoking. Seasoned teachers may feel confident in their teaching but would like to think more deeply about how rules are developed and applied. Some may be contemplating ways to better engage with, and mentor, their students. Others may have strong feelings about certain rules in their school and how these are (or are not) enforced by others. Current teachers may be bringing specific moral or ethical dilemmas that they have faced when engaging with school rules, between consistent application and attention to context, for instance. The material and questions presented in this book might suggest alternative ways of thinking about these dilemmas; it might also create more. This book encourages teachers to reflect on their past and current practices to consider how their assumptions about their students inform their presentation, interpretation, and enforcement of school rules, and how these interpretations in turn shape their relationships with students and other staff members. Teachers are also encouraged to reflect on whether they do, or should, educate students about their rights, not only didactically but through students' participation.

Most school administrators have a particularly important role to play in the creation and application of school rules, even when school board and provincial policy shape their practice. Administrators set the tone of the school, prioritize certain rules, and are the key people to introduce alternatives and innovations. School administrators are likely to be policymakers. As this book explores, rule policies and processes for their creation can be shaped in ways that empower or disempower teachers and students, promote or discourage cooperation, and foster or hinder innovation. School rules and how they are enforced shape school climate and culture. Is an administrator focused primarily on strictness and order? Is attention to context blurring into favouritism and discrimination? Is an administrator concentrating on consistent application of the rules no matter what, or are they concerned with the diversity of a student body and the context of students' lives? Different approaches will shape what kinds of classrooms teachers feel they can have, and also whether students and teachers are comfortable sharing their ideas or concerns. It is hoped that school administrators, as well as policymakers within school boards and governments, will find this book compelling for its review of relevant literature, its presentation of current data, and its discussion of many difficult questions related to school rules. For those who have concerns with the current system, this book provides evidence to suggest that their concerns are well-founded, but that there are also ways to imagine things differently.

Organization of the Book

The following two chapters will focus on the rules themselves. What they are, what values they reflect, and what kind of students the rules seem intent on assuming and/or creating. How do students know about the rules and, in turn, how do they engage with them? In these chapters it becomes clear that students largely accept the rules as a familiar, inevitable backdrop to their daily school routines. Participants were far more likely to talk about, and sometimes dispute, more 'minor' rules, such as those regulating dress, than about the more 'major' ones, such as those against weapons. As a result, most of chapter 2 will focus on the former, with a particular interest in the 'no hats' rule. The rule against hats or headgear came up in almost every single focus group and interview; this issue ties in with a number of broader tensions between students and staff regarding school rules and foregrounds many issues that emerge throughout the rest of this book.

Chapter 3 then moves into examining the 'bigger' school rules, specifically those addressing issues such as fighting, weapons, violence, and possession of drugs. Those working in the area of moral education argue that these rules tend to be based on morality rather than convention, suggesting their relevance across contexts. Yet within our focus groups there was not a *full* consensus on these issues. Fighting and carrying weapons were both justified within a few focus groups of more marginalized students. The distinction between morality and convention becomes similarly murky when we consider the spectre of the repeat offender and certain other staff (and student) attempts to elevate conventional rule violations to moral ones. Interestingly it is through appeals to safety that seemingly minor rules often get redefined as deeply significant. Finally, this chapter examines the specific case of suspension as a controversial consequence to rule-breaking, a practice which most students and staff found illogical and many academics have found unsuccessful and deeply unfair to those marginalized students who are the disproportionate recipients of its use.

Chapter 4 reflects on the underlying beliefs behind school rules – what rules are for, in terms of both the present and future. It focuses primarily on staff views, examining them in light of wider literature on discipline and student governance as well as conceptualizations of young people and what they will become. There is also a lesser engagement with some student views and their reactions to staff logic and philosophy behind school rules. This chapter highlights the conflicting viewpoints of teachers, administrators, and students in their underlying views of the rules.

The most overarching concern to arise in my interviews with staff as well as my focus groups with students was tension between context and consistency, which will be examined in chapter 5. Many staff sought to maintain a consistent application of rules across teachers and administrators, although some also disagreed with certain rules, or felt that occasionally exceptions should be made. Many staff recognized that sometimes students should not all be treated the same, when distinguishing 'first time' from 'repeat offenders,' for instance. Students, however, attentive to diverse contexts across the school and students' lives, felt that rules and their consequences should allow for greater diversity. At the same time, they felt that school staff should take more care to avoid discrimination and favouritism among students. Ultimately, this chapter foregrounds the difficult tensions between staff, and between staff and students, on the question of consistent enforcement of school rules. This issue has also arisen at the more provincial level through legislation such as the *Safe School's Act*. Ultimately, concerns with context and consistency reflect staff and student philosophies of human nature and adolescence, as well as issues of discrimination.

Chapter 5 notes how students perceive an unequal application of the rules across student populations; chapter 6 subsequently focuses specifically on how the rules and their enforcement reflect and reproduce inequalities that arise through cultural differences and racialized discrimination. Such perceptions of discrimination were particularly acute in Big City where all student groups discussed racism within the school system. This concern is supported by much of the recent literature on zero tolerance policies and work in critical pedagogy on cultural and class distinctions in experiences of school rules and their enforcement. This chapter is thus devoted to questions of discrimination, cultural difference, and inequality, particularly through reward of cultural capital.

Chapter 7 shifts the focus to sexuality and gender, areas most directly addressed when respondents discussed written dress codes and their application by teachers and administrators. This discussion concentrated mostly on girls' dress. Specific examples from the rules suggest the assumption of a middle class aesthetic regarding girls' dress. Female students themselves are also concerned with girls' dress as they evoke the fine line between 'cute' and 'too sexy,' illustrating students' investments in some of the dress codes. This chapter also considers gendered patterns in how rules are enforced, and sexual harassment policies, including rules against any kind of touch in schools.

Most frequently students accept the rules, but they also break, and sometimes overtly challenge, them. Chapter 8 thus looks at when students break the rules and what they think about rule-breaking, contrasting this data with teacher and administrator observations about rule-breaking, particularly as seen within certain constructions of adolescence. When do we consider such rule-breaking as deviance and how might it be understood differently through the language of resistance? A case will be made that it is important to recognize student conflict with the rules as more than simply knee-jerk defiance. This chapter also discusses challenges to the rules in the form of informal negotiations with teachers and organized student dissent.

Few written rules suggest student involvement in their creation or possibilities for appeal. Students themselves experience the rules as top-down givens and they find it nearly impossible to imagine their own participation in the creation of these rules. Teachers and administrators express some interest in student participation, although ultimately with the goal of increasing student compliance. Chapter 9 contrasts this seeming impossibility of students playing a more active role in the creation of school rules, with a number of practical examples of such involvement from other schools in North America. This chapter will consider the relevance of rights discourse and the *United Nations Convention of the Rights of the Child* for ensuring student participation. I will also reflect on rights, student participation, and engaged citizenship by drawing on governmentality studies: are such strategies merely deepening student governance or are they emancipatory?

Schooling is mandatory, occupying a significant portion of our childhood and adolescent days. This book asks readers to consider the processes through which these days are governed, where these processes come from, what they assume and reproduce about young people, and how staff and students engage with them. Ultimately, we need to consider what school rules and their enforcement convey to young people about who they are, who they will be, and how power and authority work. Too frequently, rules are negative, framed around obedience to authority, petty, and unfairly applied, leaving students with rule-breaking as their only way to negotiate those they disagree with (Raby and Domitrek 2007). While I engage with diverse perspectives, this book concludes with an argument for attention to 1) the politically charged nature of school rules and the dangers of authoritarianism, 2) the need to address intersections between school discipline and the perpetuation of social inequalities, and 3) the value of increased student involvement and local school autonomy in the creation of school rules.

2 'No hats!' and Other Conventional Rules

I: No hats?
ALL: Bad rule.
I: Why is this a bad rule?
JEEZY: Because you should be able to wear a hat if you want to [. . .] Like what if one day you come and your hair is not looking all proper, you know, [you] have a hat to cover it or something, you know? But then again, there are some schools that let you wear your hat still.
JIMMY: Isn't that disrespectful, wearing a hat?
[. . .]
ASHLEY: Mm-hmmm.
JIMMY: Yeah, well you're not really supposed to wear your hat if you're in a classroom, like it is disrespectful.[1] (Big City FG 6)

What are the rules? How do students know about them? And what do they, and staff, think about them? Research for this book included eighteen focus groups with students and thirty-one interviews with teachers and administrators. In all this data, despite a broader climate in which violence in schools is often a top concern, the 'no hats' rule received the most comment and the most controversy. Other similarly conventional and more 'minor'[2] rules were also frequently discussed and debated, much more frequently than major rules, e.g., against either weapons or drugs. This chapter reviews some general patterns I have identified in terms of the rules, their dissemination, and how they are received by staff and students, but the primary focus will be on these more disputed rules, particularly the 'no hat' rule – an especially interesting one to examine as it gives rise to so many issues that will be examined again in relation to other rules and later chapter topics. In this chapter, I raise concerns about school codes of conduct. In doing so I am not suggesting that all codes of conduct should be abolished or that they are all made to oppress students but I do want to complicate these pervasive, normative sets of rules that are often assumed to be easy and logical.

The Rules

Many schools and school boards now post their codes of conduct on-line, so it is fairly easy to view them and to realize that there is a common pattern across North America. Through my in-depth examination of over seventy schools' codes of conduct across two districts of Ontario, Canada (one urban, one non-urban; see Appendix A), this pattern quickly became evident, although there are some subtle but important differences between schools and regions.

Many codes of conduct begin with some kind of preamble which frames the rules in terms of wider philosophical goals such as rights, responsibilities, obedience, and self-discipline (Raby 2008b). Many codes of conduct then list various school rules, either by theme or alphabetically, often through a series of 'no's' that emphasize what students should *not* do. The rules I reviewed commonly focused on the expectations for students rather than staff, with little mention of how the rules came about. While rationales were sometimes presented alongside the rules, this was surprisingly rare.

Here is quite a typical list of areas addressed through school rules. See Table 2.1 below for information on how closely schools followed this kind of code.

- Academic stipulations: Policies addressing regular attendance, punctuality, and the procedures that students must go through if they are late. Importance of doing homework. No cheating or plagiarism.
- Harassment concerns: Usually discussed under respect for others and provisions against bullying. These concerns also link in to issues of fighting and bringing weapons to school. The more urban codes I examined also emphasized respect for diversity.
- Dress code policies: No winter jackets, non-religious headgear, or hoods in the school. Some schools allow hats but not in assemblies or during the national anthem. No beachwear or other distracting clothing (e.g., 'spaghetti straps'). No gang wear, colours or activity.

No ripped or torn clothing. No clothing promoting hatred, advertising tobacco, alcohol, or drugs. No jewellery such as spiked bracelets, dog collars, or heavy chains that could be used as a weapon. No backpacks. Some schools have uniforms.[3]

- Other general rules addressing the following areas:
  - ○ Hall conduct during class time, where students should be during spares and where students should and should not eat and drink.
  - ○ Appropriate language (no swearing, verbal abuse, etc.).
  - ○ Students identifying themselves to school staff, identity cards (in urban schools), and unauthorized visitors.
  - ○ Prohibitions on smoking, alcohol, and drugs on school property and at school events.
  - ○ Students' behaviour during the national anthem and when listening to announcements.
  - ○ Electronic devices such as music players, pagers, and cell phones which are usually either prohibited or limited to certain times and places (i.e., during lunch in the cafeteria).
  - ○ Consideration for school property and respect for the personal property of others. Some urban schools also mentioned concern for the environment and/or recycling programs.
  - ○ Stipulations against gambling and extortion (in urban schools).
  - ○ Snow-throwing (banned by a small number of schools).
  - ○ Rules of conduct for assemblies, sporting events, field trips, dances, and the parking lot.
  - ○ Rules governing computer and internet use.
  - ○ Rules against public displays of affection (non-urban schools).

Codes of conduct that I collected in the more semi-rural region tended to have more homogeneity across rules, with some schools even sharing identical codes of conduct. Also, codes of conduct that I collected in this region tended to reflect greater concern with 'appropriate' dress and public displays of affection (such as kissing) and were more likely to provide a detailed list of dress requirements. They also placed a greater emphasis on responsibility, restraint, and student civility. The urban school codes, on the other hand, recognized the greater cultural diversity of their student populations and often addressed harassment based on ethnicity[4] and race. For instance, they commonly indicated that religious headgear was exempt from the 'no hats' rule. They also addressed homophobic harassment. At the same time, urban codes

Table 2.1 Frequency of dress and behaviour code details

Specific codes	Non-urban codes (n=21)		Urban codes (n=45)	
Dress codes				
Business/Work appropriateness	2	9%	9	20%
References to 'good taste' and 'common sense'	16	76%	20	44%
Concerns that sexual messages are conveyed through clothing	19	90%	24	53%
Dress to be neat and clean (no torn or ripped clothing)	18	85%	14	31%
Students must wear uniforms	2	9%	8	19%
Behaviour codes			(n=43)[1]	
Punctually linked to success in future work	9	38%	6	14%
Respect for self, others, property and authority	9	42%	9	21%
Respect for the majority, but not all the categories of self, others, property and authority	11	52%	31	72%
Respect for self in reference to sexual behaviour	4	19%	2	5%
Respect for Canada	0	0%	11	26%
Students must wear ID badges	0	0%	13	30%
Rules addressing discrimination, harassment/bullying	12	57%	31	72%
Rules addressing racism	0	0%	25	58%
Rules addressing homophobia	0	0%	12	28%
Public display of affection prohibited	8	42%	0	0%
Reasons given for specific rules?				
Yes, comprehensive	6	28%	5	12%
Yes, partially	2	9%	9	21%
No, or only sparsely	8	38%	29	67%

[1] The urban dress codes draw on 45 school codes, behaviour codes draw on only 43.

suggested a greater concern with security issues related to gangs and school intruders. They were thus more likely to use identification cards and uniforms. Urban codes were also more likely to include reference to Ontario's zero tolerance policy, which was in place at the time the codes were collected, listing automatic consequences for breaking certain rules.[5] Finally, alternative secondary schools were only collected

in the urban area. Some of these have quite distinct school rule policies, usually with fewer, more flexible rules. These regional differences are linked to different student populations, local traditions, and
school board policies. Yet despite these differences, it is quite striking
how much similarity in codes there is between, and also beyond, these
regions.

It was also striking that when we conducted interviews with teachers
and administrators, the majority of them felt their school's rules were
good and in little need of change. The rules were considered as simple
'common sense,' obvious, or reasonable 'givens' to be followed.

IRON (Whitton teacher): No, I'm not in the mood for discussing. The rules
are very simple, they're straight forward, they're in the handbook. What's
the problem? So that's my feelings for it. You wanna give me a hard time?
Then we'll take it to the next level.

MIKE (Whitton vice-principal): [The rules are] not like, I don't think, really
hard. Like they're common sense type things.

SARAH (Big City teacher): [Parents are] listened to and they would have
input, but quite frankly most of the rules are pretty straightforward,
I mean [pause] you know, 'no cell phones,' 'no hats,' 'no coats,' those are
the big ones, you know, it's . . . can't swear at your teacher. [laughs]

Yet the rules may not be as obvious and logical as many staff believe,
for they reflect values, including certain economic, class, and cultural
assumptions. Further, focus groups with students suggest that there are
a number of places where they dispute and complicate the 'common
sense' of the rules.

Values behind the Rules[6]

One place where we can recognize that rules are value-laden is in their
overt linkage to acceptance of authority, particularly in preparation for
certain kinds of future work. This pattern was prevalent in the codes of
conduct I examined. First, some codes of conduct stressed that students
must respect authority.

Treat everyone with respect and accept authority. (Edison Secondary, urban)

> Throughout life you will have to respect the authority of people who, because of their position, have been given the right to impose authority. (Sir Alfred Secondary, non-urban)

Sometimes this respect was specifically framed in terms of respect for law or for employers. Second, particularly in the non-urban region, some rules emphasized the need for punctuality as preparation for future employment.

> Punctuality is a good habit which will be expected of you, both in your personal relationships and on the job. (Avenue Secondary, non-urban)

> Students are expected to be on time [. . .] to develop both on-the-job and personal relationships. (Joseph Fretts Secondary, urban)

Third, a number of schools, particularly those that were less academically focused, framed the school as a place of business to explain dress codes. As stated by Jerome Flynn Institute (urban), '[We have] general workplace dress expectations. For this reason, students should ask themselves "Is this appropriate for a general workplace environment?"' Schools were similarly defined against the street to emphasize the professional, business-like environment of the school:

> Dress should be appropriate to an academic setting, [creating a] separation between street and school . . . (Fleet Secondary and This Town Secondary, non-urban)

While the street is considered as a place of peer-centred freedom, the workplace is assumed to be contained and controlled,[7] although this distinction fails to address ways in which the street may sometimes itself be a place of work.

The link between school rules and future work may seem unproblematic to many: Isn't the school meant to prepare young people for the workforce? Isn't the school a place of business? Yet through these rules, we see attempts to construct students as *certain kinds* of workers (and citizens): obedient, punctual and restrained in dress, rather than innovative, independent, or defiant in the face of inequality. Furthermore, scholars in critical pedagogy, particularly those studying hidden curriculum (e.g., see Bowles and Gintis 1976; Lynch 1989; Wotherspoon 1996) argue that streaming students into becoming certain kinds of workers often reproduces their class backgrounds. It is therefore likely not a coincidence that technical school codes I reviewed were more likely than others to frame the school as being like a workplace in this sense. Codes of conduct are not neutral when they reference future work then, they assume a certain kind of workplace and certain kinds of ideal workers. In contrast, as I will examine shortly, students are less likely to see the school as a place of business – for them it is a mandatory setting where they live out their practical and social everyday lives before their future work.

The rules can also be interpreted to reflect and produce dominant, middle class morality, with their emphasis on respectable, sexually restrained dress. For example, dress codes often draw on vague, moral language:

> Students should be clean and neatly dressed in a manner which maintains the good moral tone of the school. (General Secondary, non-urban)

> . . . good common sense, good taste, decency and socially acceptable attire. (Quarry View Secondary, non-urban)

In these latter examples, one must ask whose standards of 'good taste,' 'common sense,' or 'socially acceptable' apply? The language of 'good taste' is slippery and flexible, presuming a previous, shared knowledge of what it means.[8] Some researchers argue that such assumptions of good taste are really middle class ideals. For example, in her research on teachers' perspectives on class discipline in Australia, Robinson (1992) found that students and teachers in middle class areas tended to prefer young women to behave in ways that reflected their own middle class values even when these values were not relevant to those girls who had working class backgrounds. She observed that working class girls were more likely to challenge the 'good girl' image, and this was seen by the teachers to negatively affect the positive image of the school. In another instance, Archer, Hollingsworth and Halsall (2005) suggest that marginalized youths negotiate their disadvantage by accessing a sense of worth through style, which often includes clothing that clashes with what is seen as preferred by dominant groups. One example they give is of working class sexualized dress style being framed by the school staff as anti-educational. Because of their dress, these young people are thus labelled 'trouble' and 'anti-educational' in school, adding to their educational marginalization.

Similar concerns are raised in regards to culture and race. In an attempt to deal with gang activities proliferating in schools, most school policies ban any indicators of gang affiliation (including bandanas) out of concern for safety. Ann Bodine is concerned with the gang and violence rhetoric used to defend dress codes and uniforms because she feels that references to gangs are often 'perceived as code for "ethnic minorities"' (2003, 51), adding to problematic stereotyping of minority males as dangerous. This pattern can alienate young people who are drawn to gang style dress and who then see this style (and therefore themselves) condemned (Bodine 2003), a situation illustrated in Garot and Katz's ethnographic study of a small, public, alternative school on the American west coast (2003).

Alan Hunt defines moral regulation as 'practices whereby some social agents problematise some aspect of the conduct, values or culture of others on moral grounds and seek to impose regulation upon them' (1999, xi). Moral regulation is evident when people's activities are governed through references to moral principles which are framed as normal and, in turn, internalized. Such processes also negatively categorize those who fail to comply with such practices. From this perspective, we can consider certain school rules as moral exhortations which are embedded in dominant culture. What is considered problematic behaviour or attire is not shared by all, and can reflect class-based values and cultural differences. It can also reproduce social inequality.

> More powerful groups, like the middle classes, tend to enjoy a greater synergy between their own life-worlds and those of dominant societal institutions and structures, and hence benefit from a privileged ability to know, understand and play the 'game.' (Archer, Hollingworth, and Halsall 2005, 220)

When a student's background is distinct from the class and cultural expectations embedded in school rules, he or she may not share what is understood by 'good taste,' have trouble negotiating these rules, or find the rules more frequently used to critically evaluate his or her dress and behaviour.[9] Similarly, other students are more familiar with, and invested in, the dominant values that are embedded in the school curriculum and that reflect their everyday ways of being. These students are thus more likely to thrive in the institution.

We see an example of this in Rollock's (2007) semi-structured interviews with staff and students at a United Kingdom inner city secondary school. Rollock draws on the work of Pierre Bourdieu to argue that teachers have authority in the school to define what is given value. In this instance, teachers' ideas about student success included a certain presentation of self that clashed with 'Black street culture.' As one teacher commented, when students 'haven't got their Nike on' they become better students. Rollock argues that students embodying Blackness and masculinity were thus seen as less legitimate students.

Codes of conduct are developed within a cultural context that they in turn reflect and reproduce. There is often strong logic behind these codes of conduct, in terms of safety, of guiding students, or of what an educational environment is supposed to look like. This logic is understood by many as obvious and fair. Yet what might first seem neutral or basic assumptions often reflect dominant beliefs and the moral regulation of some by others. Codes of conduct can thus be seen as attempts to not only homogenize or mask student diversity (Gereluk 2008; Leck 2000) but to preserve dominant ideals.[10] As an outcome, what might seem and feel like an equal disciplinary treatment of all students actually favours some over others.

What Students Know and Think of the Rules

I: OK, how do you know all these rules?
THE FLAG: Because/
BEE: They make you read them out of your agenda the first day of school.
DEZZ: Yeah, it's like the code of conduct basically.
I: You read them out loud?
[Yeahs]
DEZZ: I had to write them down for us. (Whitton FG 7)

While some school safety committees or other rule-review bodies include minor student representation, by far most students are presented with the rules as non-negotiable. The rules are usually conveyed to students through an agenda or handbook that lists the rules and that they receive at the beginning of the year. Most staff then review these rules in assembly or in classes; a few schools even require that students and/ or parents sign the handbook to indicate that they have reviewed them. Beyond this initial introduction, schools post or announce reminders, particularly in response to specific breaches in discipline and at the beginning of the second school term. While many staff and some students felt that such promotion of the rules is sufficient, other students I talked to noted that sometimes the first they heard of certain rules was through a reprimand.

In our focus groups, students enthusiastically discussed a wide variety of rules, often debating them among themselves or identifying similarities and differences in rules and their enforcement across schools, classrooms, and teachers. For the most part, the 'big' rules, such as 'no weapons,' received little comment – they were considered 'givens.' Students were particularly invested in rules which they saw as addressing their own safety or disciplining students who they perceived as making life difficult for everyone else. Some students were frustrated with others who broke rules repeatedly, as they felt this undermined more legitimate reasons for rule breaking, e.g., being late because of a missed bus, or wearing a tank top in hot weather. Overall, many followed most of the rules without being particularly aware of them. By high school, students have been in the schooling system a long time and the backdrop of rules has become normal.

The language of the written codes of conduct frequently filtered into students' discussion of the rules, suggesting familiarity. For example, students talked about self-respect and self-control in ways that seemed to fit very closely with the language of the rules. The language of the conduct of codes was also evident when students referred to the role of the rules in preparing them to become future, adult employees, and the importance of punctuality and safety.

LIZ: [re: dress codes] . . . They're trying to prepare you for the real world!
BEE: Yeah people are judgmental and they're just trying to tell you that the clothes that you're wearing, as soon as you walk outside, what do you think? These people are talking behind your back. And you don't want that.

LIZ: If you went to a job interview, would you wear like a short little mini skirt to let your butt show? (Whitton FG 7)
I: Why is it important to be punctual? Just out of curiosity.
JIM: So you don't disturb the class and so you're able to learn everything. (Whitton FG 4)

BIBI: I think [the 'no hat' rule] is perfectly fine. It's for safety issues, it's for surveillance and safety, making sure that your students are protected while they're under there, while they're attending school, and it's a liability issue too for schools . . . (Big City FG 3)

These examples suggest that often students have internalized the rules and the rationales behind them. Despite moments of controversy students frequently agree with the rules.

Such acceptance can be understood as indicative of their successful governance, their incorporation into present and future systems of hierarchy, their appreciation for the regulation of their peers, and their recognition that diverse needs must be weighed within an institutional context such as a school. Students were more likely to accept rules when they seemed logical, practical, and in the interests of students as a whole and of themselves personally.[11] Yet despite these places of agreement and the repetition of school rules over their years of education, students also frequently debated and criticized 'minor' rules, broke these rules, and lamented how much their enforcement takes up school time.

Dress Codes and Other 'Minor' Rules: Sites of Conflict

A Montreal school faced public criticism for indefinitely suspending a girl who dyed her hair blue (Gatehouse 1998) and a Halifax high school confronted student and parent anger in its attempt to ban hooded sweatshirts (Moore 2007). An Edmonton high school dress code banned cut-offs, short shirts, 'unnatural' hair colours, and industrial chains, among other things – with mixed student response (Thomson 1998), while Ontario students complained about their school dress codes regulations, including those against bandanas (Reid 2002). Meanwhile, many Canadian newspaper and magazine articles wrestle with broader questions of appropriate dress for school, and weigh the merits of uniforms. Articles include concern about provocative rather than professional dress (Runions 2002; Thomson 1998), student rights to free expression (Bonilla 2001), and even adult fears associated with their desires to regulate student dress (Page 2002). Dress codes are the 'hot points' of school rules: they stir up debate and frequent reports in the popular press, with particular concern about female students 'revealing too much'.

Dress codes are favoured by most principals and many parents. As Wendell Anderson (2002) reviews, in the United States dress codes (and especially uniforms) are thought to improve safety by decreasing gang violence, identifying intruders, and preventing students from hiding weapons, to improve academics by allowing students to focus on their education over fashion, and to improve school spirit through decreasing peer pressure and encouraging students to invest in their schools. These assertions are more likely to be supported anecdotally than empirically, however (Gereluk 2008). Anderson also reports on student protest against required features of dress codes and uniforms, as some students feel that they stifle free expression and are merely a surface solution to deeper issues of inequality, violence, and insufficient school funding.

In this book's study, while all participants were clearly informed that this research was about school rules, many first assumed that the focus was going to be on dress, even though school rules address so much more. Similarly, when I told people I was researching school rules, most immediately assumed the focus would be on dress. This is striking because compared to other potential trouble in schools, dress would seem, at first, a relatively minor concern. But student dress is a significant point of tension in the schools. It is the regulation of dress that seems to take up the most focus of rule-makers who often see dress as symbolic of so much else. As Garot and Katz explain, 'The logic of school control of student appearance is to insist that educational culture trump youth culture on school grounds' (439). The regulation of dress most rankles students, who are particularly likely to challenge rules related to dress. A seemingly minor set of rules takes on enormous significance for staff and students alike.

Certainly, almost all the school codes of conduct I reviewed included a dress code, and several had a uniform policy. These dress codes tended to include the kinds of details set out at the beginning of this chapter. Upcoming chapters discuss these details in relation to race and gender but in this chapter I will focus on rules against hats or other non-religious headgear. The 'no hats' rule was one of the most controversial issues discussed in our data collection and it represented many of the broader issues and tensions related to participants' views on other school rules.

'No hats'

The 'no hat' or 'no headgear' rule is common to most schools and tends to refer to all forms of headwear, including bandanas, hair-bands, baseball caps, and do-rags, with the exception of religious headwear. The 'no hat' rule seems most violated by boys, who are more likely than girls to wear baseball caps. Consequences for violation include being asked to remove the hat or confiscation of the hat, and in cases of repeat offenders, possible detention or suspension for defiance of authority.

This rule is usually grounded in traditional etiquette (Thornberg 2008b) although sometimes it is also explained as a rule related to safety. School staff and some students I talked to explained the 'no headgear' rule in terms of respect, safety, and academic integrity. Yet these reasons were rarely outlined in the school codes of conduct themselves. For example, when I was studying codes of conduct, the 'no hat' rules were ubiquitous, yet only explained in four of the non-urban school codes and three of the urban ones. The non-urban codes cited the easy identification of intruders; urban codes cited safety or respect. Usually the rules simply state that no hats are allowed on school property.

Removing your hat, either upon entering a building or interacting with someone in a position of authority, is a cultural tradition[12] and one which some participants, both students and staff, greatly valued. Many teachers felt that it was a sign of respect for students to remove their hats in the school.

> SIMON (Whitton teacher): They need to learn etiquette and respect. The hat rule is not sufficiently reinforced. No hats should come through the door.

> LAUREL (Whitton teacher): It's a case of when you walk into a building, I mean it's just that, you take your hat off to show respect for [pause] other people within the building and everything and that's, that's gone back for years. It's not something new.

For one Whitton teacher it even symbolized much broader respect for authority in the school:

> JOE: And I like that rule cuz it's a simple one and it reminds students that, you know, they don't run the school. The school is run by somebody else and it's just, it's just a simple thing and it teaches them about respect and authority. You know the rule could be 'no grey socks.' It doesn't matter. Just the point is as soon as they walk in the door they know it's a different place.

Joe's comment is a particularly stark outline of how rules are often about hierarchy and obedience.

Students also recognized the tradition behind the 'no hats' rule, citing the need to remove your hat during the national anthem or at the dinner table. Yet while some students accepted this tradition, others were unconvinced due to the cultural specificity and breadth of this rule. Mike (Whitton FG 1) noted that the tradition is culturally specific to Christianity and thus should not be required by all. Indeed the one group which entirely agreed with the no hat rule was the Big City Catholic school group where 'you are used to going to moments where you have to be reverent' (Vee, Big City FG 8). Similarly, in Big City FG 2 an interesting discussion involved one student explaining to another why in her culture it is disrespectful to keep a hat on in her house, leading the group to see the value of this rule as 'debatable' because it depends on culture. Several other students accepted the tradition of removing one's hat for the anthem but felt it should not extend to every moment, or throughout the entire school; they felt that hats should be acceptable in the hallways, but not in the classroom, for example. This tendency for students to distinguish between areas within the school was quite common with regards to their views on other rules as well, especially those addressing the use of cell phones or portable music devices (see Domitrek and Raby 2008).[13] Dickar (2008) discusses this distinction between areas of the school by conceptualizing school hallways as a thirdspace in which students negotiate between their street, peer, and community cultures on the one hand and the academic culture of the school on the other. This analysis illustrates how students may be more likely than teaching staff to distinguish between regulating the hallway and the classroom. Dickar's analysis also suggests that the emphasis on the no hat rule is primarily about requiring boys to remove a symbol of masculine street culture. By putting their hats back on when they are not supposed to, she argues, boys are attempting to regain status and respect. Hats thus become fraught with meaning as they symbolize power, status, respect, gender and obedience.

Yet the no hats rule is often cited in terms of safety instead of respect. Some staff and students explained that hats can hide people's identities, so a ban on hats would better allow school personnel to recognize intruders. A few mentioned that hats could be used to hide weapons or notes for cheating. While teachers referred to such safety issues, few students were convinced by this argument. One student felt that there are ways to both wear a hat and show your face, and another contended that this issue is sufficiently addressed by having identity tags. Similarly, Annabel (Big City FG 3) argued that the logic that you can hide a weapon under a hat just did not 'make any sense because you can hide weapons in your clothes.'

Overall, while some students accepted the 'no hat' rule, most were critical of it and dismissive of the rationales given behind it. Hats were

described as 'part of our clothing' (Steven Whitton FG 1), complement-
ing an outfit, reflecting a style, or covering up for 'bad hair.' Further,
students felt that it was illogical to include such things as headbands
and do-rags in the ban. Many just did not think wearing hats is such a
big deal, a feeling that arose with remarkable consistency, and indicating a student acceptance of those school rules most relevant to safety
and education:[14]

NICOLE: . . . Like how is wearing a hat such a blasphemous thing? (Whitton FG 4)

BETTY: It's not preventing you from learning! (Whitton FG 5)

FERNANDO: I don't think it's fair at all because what are hats gonna do?
(Whitton FG 8)

JULIE: Hats don't do anything, it's not like [they're] gonna fire a gun. (Big
City FG 2)

MARIAN: What's a hat going to do? (Big City FG 4)

QUEEN: I don't, personally, I don't think it's fair, cuz what's a hat going to
do? You're not gonna get hurt . . . (Big City FG 5)

Finally, Big City FGs 1 and 6 drew attention to the issue of inconsistent
enforcement, with a student in FG 6 suggesting that racism plays a role
in this inconsistency, with White students less likely chastised for wearing a hat than Black[15] students – an issue more deeply addressed in
chapter 6.

Enforcement of the no hat rule was an issue of contention among
teachers too; some resented that policing the hat rule takes up con-
siderable energy and others were critical of their colleagues for failing to consistently uphold this rule. Those who were frustrated that
other teachers failed to police hat-wearing felt it created inconsistencies
and put the onus on them. As well as fostering antagonism between
teachers, the 'no hat' rule triggered conflict between staff and students,
with students frequently challenging the no hat rule and their failure to
comply then interpreted as defiance, therefore escalating disciplinary
moments.

BARB (Whitton teacher): . . . it does become a power struggle and it's just, you know, it's one more thing. And it's such a simple action but those kids who are looking to make a point and to [pause] trump you with power it's such an easy way to get that power or think that they have that power . . .

IRON (Whitton teacher): . . . if I ask a kid to take their hat off and they do and then I turn around and they put it back on again, I march them right to the office. To me, that's called 'defiance.' So I think defiance deserves suspension. I believe that it's a suspendable act.

Despite these conflicts and enforcement challenges, two thirds of teachers and administrators were supportive of the 'no hats' rule for reasons of respect and safety.

In contrast, about one third of the teachers were either against the 'no hats' rule or ambivalent about it, feeling that the issue reflected generational differences or that there were more important things for them to do than expend so much energy battling with students about their hats.

DYLAN (Whitton teacher): I'm working up in resource so a kid that's been kicked out of three classes, having a really, really rough time, you know, if he's sitting there with his hat on, I really don't care.

BARB (Whitton teacher): . . . there's so many other things that they should be getting torn down for, you know, other than wearing a stupid hat.

LURALEEN (Whitton teacher): I don't want to fight that rule anymore. I want to talk to kids about what is safe and what is healthy.

While these teachers accepted the link between removing hats and showing respect, they argued that the no hat rule receives too much emphasis, with other issues far more important to address. A few teachers also suggested that the tradition of removing your hat out of respect no longer makes sense to students who are used to wearing their hats every day, in a wide range of circumstances. As Bill (Whitton teacher) argued, hats are 'just a part of them and they don't think of it,' suggesting that perhaps certain rules need to change with the times.

Clearly, there are a number of clashing views that arise in response to the rule against hats. There is a significant lack of consensus about the rule, its rationale, and its enforcement, contributing to stress and conflict within schools. Many of the issues raised about hats, from questions of practicality and enforcement to respect, power, safety, consistency, and context, are emblematic of controversies surrounding many other school rules as well. Such controversies include cultural and gendered assumptions embedded in school rules, beliefs about the reasons for having rules, questions of enforcement priorities, the relevance of context and consistency, and distinct stakeholder positions. Do students have legitimate concerns about rules such as this one? What does it mean if students usually think about the school and its rules differently from how teachers and administrators do? How do teachers' and administrators' views on hats reflect broader, differing orientations that distinct staff might have towards school discipline more generally and certain students specifically? And how are these differences negotiated? Finally, when students break such rules is this about habit, practical need, defiance, or resistance? The following chapters tackle these questions in much more depth.

Other Controversial Rules

In addition to the 'no hats' rule, there were others that arose repeatedly across student focus groups as sites of dispute. Table 2.2 indicates which rules were most contested by students. This table reports on the results of an activity in which we asked participants to distribute various individual rules into one of three piles: good rules, bad rules, and controversial or debated rules. Rules were also sometimes placed in the controversial pile if they were considered unenforceable or if there was a notable difference in group opinion around them. As evident from this table, rules related to dress, including references to appropriate dress (e.g., no spaghetti straps), no hats, and no heavy coats, were subject to debate and critique. Students also took issue with rules governing how they negotiate the school space, such as those against carrying backpacks, addressing lates or 'skips,' eating anywhere except the cafeteria, and in the regulation of personal electronic devices such as cell phones. The remaining portion of this chapter will examine some of the issues students raised around these more controversial rules, the role of parents, and teachers' and administrators' responses to student concerns.

Nearly all of the students had broken a minor rule at some point in time and, most often, had broken it for what they considered to be a practical reason. Practicality was a significant theme emerging from

Table 2.2 Focus group categorizations of the rules

A snapshot of what Whitton students thought about the rules[1]

Rules	Good rule #	Controversial rule #	Bad rule #
No fighting No bullying No weapons No vandalism No sexual harassment No drugs/alcohol	6	0	0
No littering	5	1	0
Must be punctual Respect teachers	4	1	1
Must attend class	3	3	0
No clothing advertising alcohol, drugs, violence, racism, or obscenity	3	2	1
No spreading rumours	3	0	3
Respectful clothing	2	4	0
No offensive language	1	3	2
No heavy coats in class No shoving or horseplay	1	2	3
No spaghetti straps or short skirts No public displays of affection	0	5	1
Uniforms No gang type clothing No hats No ripped/torn clothing No walkmans, pagers, or cellphones	0	4	2
No backpacks in class	0	2	4
Eating only in cafeteria	0	1	5

[1] Note that this data is drawn from focus groups 4 to 9 only and there was a police officer in the room during focus group 9.

A snapshot of what Big City students thought about the rules[2]

Rules	Good rule	Controversial rule	Bad rule
No weapons No vandalism No sexual harassment	9	0	0
No drugs or alcohol No bullying	8	1	0
No shoving/horseplay No fighting No offensive language Respect teachers	7	2	0
No littering[3]	7	1	0
No clothing advertising alcohol, drugs, violence, racism, or obscenity	6	3	0
Must attend class	6	3	0
No gang clothing	6	2	1
No spreading rumours	4	4	1
Must be punctual	4	4	1
Respectable clothing	2	5	2
No hats	2	1	6
Eating only in cafeteria No heavy coats	1	3	5
No public displays of affection No electronics	0	7	2
No backpacks	0	2	7

[2] Note that some of the students' parents were in the room during focus group 4.
[3] One group did not sort the 'no littering' card into a pile.

students' stories of rule-breaking. Based on practical needs, many students argued that it should be acceptable to:

- Wear coats in cold classrooms.
- Carry backpacks to transport heavy books or when breaks do not allow for time to get back to lockers to switch books.
- Eat in class or in hallways on breaks, especially when lunch is scheduled at an awkward time[16] or when the cafeteria is too small.

- Skip class when other important assignments are due or there is a test to study for.
- Have cell phones for emergency calls.
- Listen to music to help concentrate during seat work.
- Wear hats on bad hair days.
- Go to the bathroom when needed.

Having to eat only in the cafeteria was seen as particularly frustrating:

> TINA: . . . you can't even like, like if you get something at break, like you can't even have – you're not supposed to have like a snack at break while you're walking in the hall. If you have to go to the cafeteria and eat it then, like you're late for, like it doesn't make sense. It's frustrating.
> I: It's not practical?
> TINA: Yeah. (Whitton FG 4)

While students recognized the rationale behind this rule – that it contains spills and garbage – they felt that students should be able to eat when and where they need to. Participants also resented rules that made them feel as if they were 'four years old,' such as needing to ask permission to go to the bathroom. As such, the students we talked to were critical of students who used bathroom breaks for reasons other than going to the bathroom, such as going to see friends, which would then cause teachers to crack down legitimate bathroom use.

Students similarly argued that attendance is not always a straight-forward issue either, as sometimes 'you just shouldn't be in class,' e.g., in circumstances where students have significant assignments due in other classes or when they are emotionally unable to participate. As Allison (Whitton FG 9) describes in the latter case:

> I think there's a point though. Like you might be at school and say [pause] something really shitty happens. Like you're not gonna want to go to class in tears [. . .] like I had a friend who was going through a lot of family crises. She went to class and just walked out, because she could not deal with it. Every time you looked at her, she's in tears. She obviously was supposed to either be in the guidance office, outside or in a washroom with a friend comforting her. I think that when you come to a point like that, you don't want to be in class. Sure you're missing out on your education and that's really shitty but – I just realized how many times I've said that. [laughing]

Finally, while some readers may not feel this is a case of practicality, several participants talked about skipping classes due to boredom and the perception that the class is a waste of time:

> STEVE (Whitton FG 3): [. . .] right now I would skip three days in a row, like fourth period, because I've been in school for three days and one of those days I've written something on a piece of paper, one of those days out of three [inaudible] and I just can't believe it, I can't stay there, so when fourth period comes along and I know my teacher's not there and he's sick and they tell us, you know, 'just stay here and waste an hour and come back and sign yourself in so you don't skip,' right you know, at the very end, and it's like 'no I cannot waste another hour of my day.' So I leave.

In this case, the school is seen by some students as failing to provide a stimulating environment where learning can occur. Though only mentioned by a few participants, this link between attendance (and other disciplinary issues) and the need for relevant, stimulating pedagogical practices is upheld in research on classroom management (Hoy and Weinstein 2006).

As the interviews with teachers and administrators took place after the focus groups, we had the opportunity to follow up on these student comments by asking staff whether they concurred that students sometimes have legitimate, practical reasons for breaking school rules. The eighteen staff respondents who spoke on this issue all cited circumstances wherein practical reasons might be legitimate, suggesting the need for flexibility around context in the everyday application of rules. For example, Whitton staff members Barb, Gemini, Jen, and Joe all felt that there were times when it is acceptable for students to eat in class as long as the students clean up after themselves. As Jen explained, 'I know I'm hungry quite often and teenagers are always growing and whatever and [food in class] doesn't bother me as long as they're not being gross about it.' The challenge of the 'no backpack' rule also received some sympathy, particularly when there is little room in lockers or students have limited time. One Whitton administrator mentioned changing a rule on skateboards in order to accommodate students using them as a primary means of transportation. Teachers and administrators were willing to bend rules or to strategize with particular students to address practical concerns (e.g., by moving a student's locker to accommodate a particularly difficult timetable). Staff similarly acknowledged that some students also have personal crises to deal with that may lead them to break rules, such as skipping class. As Bill (Whitton teacher) noted, 'There are reasons that rules can be broken and we need to be aware of that sometimes.'

That said, half the staff participants doubted most practical reasons students might cite for breaking rules, suggesting that these concerns only really affect a small minority of students. To these staff participants, the rules are good ones and 'practical' reasons are really excuses.

ROBIN (Whitton vice-principal): Well, 'it's hot outside so I'll wear a strap lace top' or whatever the case might be. Baloney.

I: So it seemed like a lot of their reasons [for breaking rules were] for more practical reasons. So what do you say to that [chuckles]?
GLENN (Whitton teacher): Yeah. I say a *small* percentage of them, yeah!

These participants' responses drew attention to the challenges staff face in distinguishing legitimate from illegitimate reasons for rule-breaking, decisions that often draw on teachers' subjective interpretations of students and situations, and their personal views about discipline. Some teachers recognized practical reasons for lateness, for example, while others did not. Several respondents indicated that the reputation of a student made a difference as to whether a practical excuse was accepted or not. For example, one teacher felt that if a student is cold one day then they can wear their jacket but that they would be less sympathetic to someone who is always cold. Iron also raised the challenge of balancing practical with safety concerns. The 'no backpacks' rule is to address safety issues, for instance,[17] so is safety then compromised when backpacks are allowed in specific cases? Finally, Teacher X, for whom the consistent application of rules is vital, suggested that practical rule-breaking indicates needs for structural change; eating in the halls would not be an issue if the school introduced a breakfast club, for example. This question about accommodating the context of a rule infraction versus consistent enforcement of the rules defines chapter 5.

In marked contrast to the teachers' and administrators' frequent support for all their school rules, students felt that some of the more 'minor' rules, such as those against hats, did not make sense and even saw them as simply a means for authority figures to control them. Many felt various rules to be illogical and therefore unnecessary:

QUEEN: And at our school and the way that they, like, tell us no littering, if you come inside with like, like gum or something, then they think you're going to spit it out, so they make you go [pause] like if you're already at your locker, they'll make you go outside and find a garbage can outside and spit it out outside. I don't know, I just don't know why they won't let us spit it out inside, or throw stuff out inside. (Big City FG 5)

Other rules students found hard to define. Participants asked, 'what exactly is "gang-related clothing?"' This was a particularly likely question among the Whitton students who did not seem to feel that gangs were really a problem in their region but worried that certain students would be targeted for breaking this rule, even though they were not clear on what it meant. Some Whitton students reported being told to remove pink and tie-dyed bandanas they had worn as fashion accessories, for example, because they were 'gang-related':

NICOLE: . . . I've been kicked out of class before for wearing a bandana. [3 second pause]. It was like pink or like yellow or something and I was like 'yes I'm [in] the sunshine gang!' (Whitton FG 4)

They also noted that any clothing could be 'gang-related' in some sense, and that this rule was therefore based on stereotypes and teachers' or administrators' perceptions of particular students. Such confusion is not unique to Whitton students. In their ethnographic work of an American, inner city high school, Garot and Katz (2003) found that while adults tend to think appearance norms for gangs are clear, actual gang-related clothing draws on ever-shifting significations such that even young people in areas with a high degree of gang activity are not always sure of what is considered gang dress.

Even a rule that was generally supported by students – 'no weapons' – was seen to be exaggerated in its application:

LILY: Um, in our cafeteria, um when we're like, if we buy like um pasta or something, they don't even give us plastic knives any more and then if we [pause]. Like my mom, if she gives me like steak or whatever for lunch, she'll always pack a knife. So I'm always so scared to take it out, but I'm like how do you eat it without a knife? I'm like trying to break off pieces with my fork and I'm like, it doesn't work. (Big City FG 8)

VEE: But there are so many things you can get inside the school that can hurt a person. If you want to hurt a person you can find something, you can go to the tech room, go to the arts room, you can get anything. Get a, like a metre stick, and whack someone! (Big City FG 8)

Similarly, as I will discuss in chapter 7, while students agreed that limits are needed in areas such as public displays of affection and dress, they were concerned that such rules can be applied so widely that any little infraction results in a consequence. In these various instances, rules were seen as irrelevant, ill-defined, or too broadly interpreted.

All participants observed that the policing of more minor rules requires significant expenditure of time and energy on the part of teachers and administrators. In one focus group, where students were in a school with uniforms, they wondered if the principal's primary job was to stand around looking for minor rule violations. Generally, students did not question people getting in trouble for violating the big, 'must have' rules; rather they questioned why so much time is spent telling students to take off their hats, take off their coats, go home to change, or to tuck in their shirts. To many students, it seemed that sometimes the policing of such minor infractions dominates the time administrators spend with them, creating an image of administrators as concerned only with the rules and ultimately uninterested in students' lives.

Clearly there are some significant differences between student and staff perceptions of many rules and their enforcement, illustrating that the rules are not quite as simple as some staff believe. These differences in orientation to certain rules point to why students and staff both report so much conflict around the regulation of certain rules and raise the question of student voice. There seems little formal room for students to discuss the challenges certain rules may frequently pose for them and little avenue for students to raise these concerns except individually.

What Parents Know and Think of the Rules

While this book focuses primarily on the views of students and staff, there is also a third set of relevant stakeholders in the school with regards to school rules. While parents come into occasional points of contact with regards to school rules, students suggested that their parents are largely uninformed, which the students generally seemed comfortable with. Apart from those parents who are involved in the school through parents' or school council, most parents end up being involved in their children's engagement with the disciplinary apparatus of the school in three ways. First, a number of schools request that parents sign the student handbook where the code of conduct is listed in order to acknowledge that they have read it. One goal of this approach, as Whitton vice-principal Robin explained, is to 'create a bit of a partnership' with parents, although Robin also noted that usually only about a quarter of parents sign and some even refuse to sign. Nonetheless, when students later get into trouble, staff refer back to parental knowledge of the rules in order to support their disciplinary actions.

Second, contact with parents is a point in the discipline process, either in cases of suspension, or sometimes sooner, to notify parents and in the hopes of garnering parent support for the discipline process. When students were asked about what their parents knew of the rules and what they felt about them, many emphasized that parents only really became involved and knowledgeable when contacted by the school because the student was in trouble, in cases of absences, lates, and suspension, for instance. It is important to note here that for most parents then, the first personalized contact they have with the school is often in regards to a negative situation rather than praise or positive feedback.

Third, either in response to being contacted or in response to other disciplinary issues, parents would contact the school. Some parents are supportive of the school, but staff spoke with frustration about many instances when parents would simply defend their children. They found themselves having to convince a parent that something is serious or to justify a consequence. Whitton vice-principal Blair explained how negative this could sometimes be:

> I mean I call, or a teacher calls, home. Ninety per cent of the time, we have to defend and explain more often. Um, you know, 'Well, OK so he said that to the teacher, what did the teacher say?' [. . .] And sometimes it's legitimate. But sometimes it's [pause] not. Sometimes it's – you're not helping your kid and we can't work together and if the home and the school aren't working together [. . .] what they're learning is wrong. They're learning that you can divide and conquer and get away with it. And I don't know if that's a good message either. But I don't like the old way where the school is always right either because the school wasn't always right.

Several staff also spoke about the problems parents themselves face. Some parents were concerned about a suspension, for instance, because they would not be home from work to provide supervision.

Students similarly cited cases when their parents would argue their case with the school. Twelve students mentioned situations where a parent, almost always a mom, successfully supported them: e.g., in complaining about a teacher who called a student an 'airhead,' in a case of being late, around dress, and so forth. Parents were important resources for defending their children, both in cases that were described by the student as unfair and also in cases where the student felt they needed to skip out or come to school late. There were a few instances where parental support was not seen to be as effective, however – this was notable in a case where two quite marginalized students were living with their grandmother. A note from the grandmother was once disregarded, as was a note from the mom. Furthermore, other students said that their parents would not intervene, either because a student was about to graduate and should 'suck it up,' or most commonly because their parents supported the school either in the case of a specific rule or, as nine students described, their parents just supported their school's decisions in general.

Distance and misunderstanding are easily fostered when parents' primary form of involvement with the school is when their child is in trouble, particularly when home and school represent quite distinct cultural backgrounds. With the 2008 provincial policy of 'progressive discipline' this pattern is noted as it recommends more positive dialogue between parents and schools. In 2010 the Ontario government also introduced new legislation requiring that parents of victims always be contacted as well as parents of students who are suspended. These strategies are intended to bring parents into a greater partnership with schools but at the time of data collection, most parents were really quite peripheral to the creation and application of school rules until students were really in trouble.

Too Many Rules?

As I have illustrated, there is a significant distinction between student and staff views of school rules. Students I talked to were critical of many of the 'minor' rules, particularly ones addressing deportment, and they found school staff excessively focused on minor rule infractions. Students recognized distinctions between specific classroom contexts, areas of the school, and times of the day, and they felt that these distinctions should be accommodated rather than schools having blanket rules. Students understood the importance of context around addressing rule infractions but they at the same time were critical of favouritism and discrimination.

In contrast, teachers and administrators tended to see the current rules as good and, for the most part, fairly enforced. They were particularly adamant that dress codes are important. While some teachers shared students' recognition that the school is made up of distinct spaces and that the school day is divided by types of class time and free time, many teachers and almost all administrators spoke in favour of blanket rules and the importance of consistency in enforcing them, a position reinforced by the application of uniform provincial and school board policies on rules.

Clearly, there was a large gap between student and staff views, quite likely exacerbating conflicts between students and staff over rule infractions themselves, conflicts which then foster frustration for everyone in the school. These findings resonate with those reported elsewhere. In their review of research on teacher and student perspectives on classroom management, Hoy and Weinstein (2006) express concern about this difference between teacher and student views. Findings suggest that teachers commonly focus on student behaviour. They seek respect for authority, student cooperation, and student compliance in the classroom. Students, on the other hand, value relationships with teachers. They seek respect, trust, patience, communication, clear limits, and some degree of choice. Marginalized students in particular seek more personal caring. Teachers feel that they must manage and control students, particularly when they are feeling under threat (Lewis 2001), yet students resent feeling managed or controlled, particularly at the secondary level. The authors argue that these divergent views lead to a circle of growing distrust in which teachers are more likely to show personal interest when the students are engaged and students are more likely engaged when teachers show personal interest (Hoy and Weinstein 2006).

Most students and staff agree with the bulk of the school rules and their enforcement, but these are important places of disagreement that are frequent sources of conflict. In the meantime, school rules are often morally laden and reflective of dominant values, often autocratic and generally negative, with the reasons behind them weakly communicated. In the following chapters some of the tensions reported here will be investigated in more depth. For example, staff views on the rules reflect deeper philosophies regarding rules, rule-breaking, adolescence, and the role of the school, philosophies also reflecting the wider social, political, and economic context beyond the school. Similarly, student frustrations arise in part from perceptions of favouritism and inequality.

3 Big Rules and Big Consequences

Presumably, the most important school rules are the ones that ensure the safety of students and staff, such as rules against fighting, bringing weapons to school, or bullying; and such rules are likely to be supported by students (Smetana and Bitz 1996; Thornberg 2008b). Perhaps because they are 'obvious,' these kinds of rules did not receive the bulk of my participants' attention and were for the most part considered 'givens.' This chapter will consider arguments within moral education (Goodman 2006a; Nucci 2001) to explore this distinction between such 'givens' and the more controversial rules discussed in the previous chapter. The subsequent discussion will take up four further issues: first, the 'no fighting' rule, a rule that is commonly framed as a 'must have' but that was questioned in two of the more marginalized focus groups of students in this study; second, repeat offending, for it is commonly through repeat offending that more minor, or conventional, rule violations become elevated to moral ones; third, the elevation of conventional rules to moral ones based on students' future selves or self-respect; and fourth, safety, another key concern that can shift a rule from being considered minor or personal to serious and protective. The final section of this chapter addresses consequences to significant rule-breaking, with a primary focus on the frequent and yet problematic use of suspension.

The 'Must Have' Rules

Participants generally agreed with most rules, particularly those seen as 'major' rules addressing school safety, facilitating education, or preventing illegal activities. When we asked students, 'What rule do you follow and why?' sometimes such a 'major' rule would be mentioned, but mostly participants did not actively think about how they follow these 'major' rules – they were considered basic and obvious.

> EMILIA: Um . . . I can't think of one [rule] I follow.
> I: Have you ever brought a weapon to school?
> EMILIA: No! I follow that rule! [laughing] (Whitton FG 5)

Sometimes these more significant rules were so assumed that they were not even mentioned when we first asked students which rules they had in their school. When presented with these rules on cue-cards, students agreed with many without question because they were considered basic and thus generated little discussion:

> FERNANDO: 'No drugs or alcohol.' That's a given.
> MOE: That's fair.
> FERNANDO: That's a given. 'No bullying.'
> MAURICE: That's another given.
> FERNANDO: Yeah, it's a given.
> MOE: It's a given but it'll still happen.
> FERNANDO: Yeah. 'No vandalism.' That's a given.
> MOE: Given, but it'll still happen. (Whitton FG 8)

In Whitton, all groups that participated in the cue-card distribution exercise agreed with 'no fighting,' 'no bullying,' 'no weapons,' 'no vandalism,' 'no sexual harassment,' and 'no drugs/alcohol.'[1] In Big City, the majority of participants in all nine groups agreed with 'no weapons,' 'no vandalism,' and 'no sexual harassment.' There were also rules which the groups generally considered good but that seemed hard to define or enforce (as Moe pointed out above) such as 'no drugs or alcohol' or 'no shoving/horseplay' and were therefore placed in the 'debated' pile. Overall, these 'big' rules were seen as necessary to keep the school safe, prevent discrimination, and generally ensure school is a pleasant place for students to spend their day and to learn. For the most part such rules have been categorized as moral rules (Goodman 2006a).

Moral versus Conventional Rules: Lessons from Moral Education

As students Tina and Nicole astutely observed, there are different categories of rules and problems arise when these distinctions are not acknowledged:

TINA: . . . if there's so many rules people get fed up and don't know which ones are more important almost like [. . .] there's so many rules and say you get the same punishment or similar punishment for breaking totally different rules, then you kinda look and say 'well what's the point?' I dunno, so I think actually it can work against/

I: . . . so if you have lots of petty rules then maybe people won't recognize the importance of the bigger rules?

TINA: Yeah like/

NICOLE: One girl at my school got suspended for wearing a short skirt and not changing. Then another kid got suspended for the same amount of time for smoking pot out in the smoke pit [. . .] It's like, you know, serious legal offending crime and then a school rule.

I: Right, right.

NICOLE: There's like a law and then there's a rule.

TINA: That, that, yeah exactly. (Whitton FG 4)

These students are also critical of consequences that seem disproportionate, providing a nice illustration of the complexity of the rules and how young people engage with them. Moral educators in particular are interested in how young people and adults think about, explain, and categorize rules, similarly complicating assumptions that children simply internalize all rules equally or that all rules are of the same importance.

Larry Nucci's work in the areas of child development and moral education examines how children distinguish between moral, conventional, and personal domains. Instances of *moral* infraction are ones which would be wrong even without a specific rule. Nucci draws on Elliot Turiel to define morality as referring to 'conceptions of human welfare, justice, and rights, which are a function of the inherent features of interpersonal relations' (2001, 7) – indeed, he cites cross-cultural studies to suggest that there are certain actions, related to how people treat others, that are consistently considered right and wrong, regardless of local customs and distinct religions. In contrast, *conventional* rules are contextual, supported through consensus or authority.

What distinguishes them . . . is that in the case of morality, the source of the rule is a reflection upon the effects of the act, whereas in the case of convention, the status of the act is a function of the presence or absence of a governing rule. (Nucci 2001, 13)

Finally, the *personal* domain covers areas of individual choice, such as freedom of expression or association. Its parameters are cultural and children are much less likely to accept rules as legitimate that attempt to regulate the personal domain (Nucci 1981), as indicated in the previous chapter.

Nucci's data suggests that children's conflicts with each other tend to centre on moral violations while adults are more likely to conflict with children over conventional violations, both in the school and the home. Nucci argues that this is, in part, because children are more likely to have moral disputes when they are not being witnessed by parents but also because adults and children prefer that children solve moral disputes on their own, especially as children get older. He contends that these patterns suggest that moral issues reflect intrinsic issues, such as 'no hitting' that even young children understand, although he cautions that adults should not abandon children to sort out moral issues on their own, hence the need for moral education.

Nucci is particularly interested in how the moral, conventional, and personal play out in schools. For example, he argues that children evaluate school rules through these domains. Children appreciate rules associated with moral issues, such as 'no hitting' and 'no theft,' and see them as legitimate because they resonate with a deeper moral order which they accept. Like the participants in my own study who wanted teachers to better address instances of bullying, Nucci's participants wanted to see teachers supporting these rules. Children also understand the need for schools to have conventional rules and generally accept such rules as long as they make sense to them (Thornberg 2008b) and do not encroach on their personal domain, particularly as students age into adolescence (Smetana and Bitz 1996). Just as children will accept certain kinds of rules over others, Nucci finds that there are conditions under which children are more likely to see teachers' enforcement of rules as legitimate: when teachers emphasize the effects of the act (e.g., hurting another) rather than simply commanding them (e.g., 'don't hit'); when teachers' responses correspond to the domain of the rule-breaking (e.g., not moralizing a conventional issue or reducing a moral situation to a conventional one); and when consequences fit the rule transgression. Students will challenge rules as they develop their own moral compasses, so Nucci argues that the best response is not punishment but logical consequences,[2] discussion with students on morality, and student involvement in decision-making around school rules.

Joan Goodman (2006a) draws on Nucci to similarly address the role of morality and convention in school rules and their associated sanctions. Ultimately she finds that most American school codes of conduct problematically fail to distinguish between morality and convention, a pattern illustrated in British schools as well (Rowe 2006). First, as I also found in examining school codes of conduct in Ontario, schools tend to conflate moral and conventional issues by listing rules as if they are all of equal importance. Second, often rehabilitative solutions are initially used in response to non-moral violations, such as lateness or eating outside the cafeteria, but then in cases of repeat offences, responses escalate to punishment for non-compliance. In this way all offences can become moralized. Commonly Goodman found that there is also disagreement among staff about what constitutes a moral issue in itself. Some may see lateness as a conventional wrong, for instance, while others may elevate it to a moral issue of order and respect. These murky areas Goodman calls the 'derivatively moral' (rules given moral attributes under certain interpretations). Rather than resorting to the derivatively moral, Goodman argues that codes of conduct need to be kept to a minimum, with clear distinctions between conventional and moral violations, appropriate domain-related consequences for each, limited interpretations of insolence, and student involvement in dispute resolution.

Also working from within moral education, Thornberg (2008b) has examined what students at the primary level in Sweden think about school rules and the rationales behind them. Most students in Thornberg's study understood and accepted relational rules, such as 'no bullying' and 'no fighting,' rules categorized into the moral domain. Most students also accepted protecting rules, which were seen to address issues of health and safety, depending in part on students' own assessment of the actual risk. Finally, Thornberg suggests that convention actually covers two quite different kinds of rules: structuring rules and etiquette rules. Structuring rules organize a space, outlining where and when students may talk or eat, for example. Students felt that these rules prevented disruptions of school-related activities, sometimes provided protection, and helped to smooth relations. It is interesting to note that students invested in the pedagogical project of the classroom were most likely to accept these rules. Etiquette rules, in contrast, are the rules that reflect customs or traditions and the ones that students were most likely to consider arbitrary and pointless. Students did not see the reason for rules against wearing hats indoors, for example, or rules against swearing (as long as it is not at others). Etiquette rules resonate with Nucci's category of the personal domain and were the least valued by Thornberg's students.

This distinction between categories of rule infraction, including the moral and conventional domains, provides a useful lens through which to interpret the data collected for this book. As I have illustrated, students in this project tended to distinguish between more controversial, 'minor' rules and the more acceptable, 'major' school rules which generally reflect the moral domain. This was particularly the case when they discussed actions which harm others. In fact, many felt that rules against bullying should be better enforced within schools,[3] a concern that the provincial government has more recently addressed by considering bullying a suspendable offence and introducing various anti-bullying initiatives (Ontario 2008).

We can thus take some important lessons from those who have researched school rules through the lens of moral education: that rules should not be treated as if they are of equal importance because they are not, that young people thoughtfully engage with the rules and should be provided more meaningful opportunities for such engagement, and that we need to be very cautious when suggesting that young people should follow the rules 'just because.' Yet Nucci's emphasis on domains as important to moral education also downplays important distinctions between students which have been emphasized by other scholars, notably those working in the area of critical pedagogy. Nucci (2001) argues that there is cross-cultural consistency in understandings of moral rules but notes more briefly that this consistency sometimes shifts, with lower class children more likely to see conventions as rigid and members of more traditional societies 'more likely to "moralize" their conventions' (95) and thus to see them as unalterable. Nucci further contextualizes the potentially inherent nature of morality when he introduces questions of power and hierarchy. Dominant members of society are inclined to moralize social beliefs that advantage them. What are assumed to be intrinsic moral interests may therefore really be those that reflect dominant interests.

Also, Nucci observes that sometimes student resistance to the rules arises from student identification with an alternative social system, or a 'resistance culture.' As an example of this, Ferguson (2000) suggests that some Black students oppose 'White middle-class values' embedded in certain kinds of academic and social behaviour, Paul Willis similarly emphasizes class-based resistance (1977), and others have analysed subcultures such as goth through a lens of resistance (Siegel 2005). Rather than questioning or shifting schools' social conventions, however, Nucci suggests that to counter such 'resistance culture,' students need to be drawn into the schools' own social convention through discussion and input. These examples are reminders that understandings of morality and convention can be culturally distinct and ideological, factors Nucci plays down in his book. I will now turn to examining several cases that arose in my research which similarly complicated distinctions between moral, conventional, and personal domains. These illustrate how values and justification are also potentially linked to marginalization and suggest that even the 'big' rules may not always be so clear-cut.

No fighting[4]

There were some young people, mostly but not exclusively from the focus groups with street and other marginalized youth, who were more likely than others to have broken the 'bigger rules.' For these students, such rule-breaking was often considered justified through a variety of explanations. In Whitton FG 2, four or five members pursued a lively discussion about fighting, which they uniquely framed as an inevitable, and for some even useful, form of conflict resolution. Because fighting is inevitable and simply moves off school property when stopped, they felt the 'no fighting' rule to be impractical and the wider group seemed to agree.

I: [. . .] so OK, there's fighting anyway, so do you guys think it's a problem, this fighting?
ALMOST EVERYONE: NO!
BECKY AND LINDSEY: It happens anyway [people talking over each other].
I: So do you guys think it's good that people fight?
JAMIE: It's not good to fight but it happens [people talking over each other]. [. . .]
MALE VOICE: There's not going to be anyone – no one can stop us. If people really want to fight each other they are going to do it/
GIRL VOICE: Yeah, yeah, yeah.
MALE VOICE: Whether they do it right there and then or save it for later [people talking over each other].
JAMIE: Yeah man/
AMY: Even after school/

JAMIE: The school can put a fight on hold but as soon as you get on the bus, you leave the school property you are getting it anyway.[5]

Two of the discussants had been suspended at some point for fighting and were perhaps trying to justify their actions by suggesting that fighting is 'just life.' Yet more broadly, as with many street youth, many of the youth in this group were marginalized within school (Transitions Committee 2003): they had all at some point been suspended or expelled (e.g., for fighting, skipping out, and 'flipping out' at a teacher), they had all attended more than one high school (one as many as eleven), half of them talked about their dislike of school, and several mentioned instances in which they felt teachers discriminated against them. Further, in their immediate context, these youth were economically marginalized and disproportionately prone to victimization (Gaetz 2004). Arguably, for some, fighting is therefore their area of strength, one considered practical within their peer culture and life circumstances.

Many of these characteristics also described the second group to recognize the need to fight, Big City FG 1, which was held in a drop-in centre for inner city youth. While most of the members seemed to accept the 'no fighting' rules, it was described as 'not the fairest,' in part due to the demands of self-defence:

MICHAEL: When someone fights you, you still have to self-defend.

[. . .]

JJ: Yea, that's what principal[s] don't get, they don't get it. Like when you get attacked [if] you don't fight back, you get beat up.

Similar approaches to fighting are described by Thorson (2003). These debates around the 'no fighting' rule underscore the ongoing relevance of social context in how school rules are conceptualized. As Vee, from Big City FG 8 suggested, rather than simply scaring students with suspension and informing parents, you 'have to go to the root cause. Why are these people fighting in the first place? Because they want to defend themselves, because they think that they're worth nothing, you know?'

Ferguson (2000) and Dickar (2008) (among others) examine the relevance of masculinity to fighting, echoing much other work in studies of masculinity. In the schools they studied, fighting was the expected, masculine way to solve a problem (for both boys and some girls)[6] rather than weakly going to an adult. Fighting can be about ritual, skill, a masculine expression of emotions, a defence of hegemonic masculinity, and self-defence. In this context fighting is not deviance but normative – a position also reinforced when parents support fighting. As Janice in Whitton FG 1 explained, 'My parents say if someone starts a fight you do something about it, like not a verbal fight, like if someone punches you, you punch them back.' These examples illustrate that a distinction between convention and morality is not always transparent. In these instances students identified situations where they felt it necessary and even moral to hit someone else, situations specific to their immediate lives in which verbal forms of conflict resolution may be less accessible or successful. If moral educators and school administrators fail to engage with the perceived legitimacy of fighting in certain contexts, they will fail to address fighting in school. My position here is not to argue that fighting should be accepted in schools but rather that simply saying 'no fighting' is insufficient without recognition or discussion of why or when young people fight and consideration of what alternatives might be available for students that would address why and when they fight.

The Repeat Offender and Defiance of Authority

As Goodmen suggests (2006a), the second example to blur a clear distinction between convention and morality is the repeat offender. When students repeatedly break a conventional rule, they come to be defined as repeat offenders, with consequences that can then become more severe as repeat offenders are no longer simply breaking rules but are deemed insolent or defiant. Indeed, in interviews with teachers and administrators, certain students who repeatedly broke the rules were routinely cast as such 'problem students.' For many staff members, frequent re-offending around rules such as 'no hats' or lates would shift a conventional offence to 'defiance of authority,' a blurry, moral category of infraction particularly subject to interpretation, yet nonetheless embedded in some codes of conduct and considered worthy of suspension.

> IRON (Whitton teacher): And I use the word 'defiance.' I say, 'They defied me, I asked them to take their hat off and as I turned around they put it back . . .' And then they try to say, 'Oh I was getting something out of my pocket' and I says [unbelievingly] 'yeah.' So I think defiance deserves suspension. I believe that it's a suspendable act.

Understandably, staff become quite frustrated when faced with a repeat offender and a number of staff members talked about how they would respond more harshly to a repeat offender than they would to a student breaking a rule for the first time, even to the point of arguing for their suspension, as Iron does. In such instances teachers may be drawn to more authoritarian techniques also because they feel that the situation is getting out of control (Porter 1996). Codes of conduct, particularly in Whitton, often mention the importance of respect for authority and emphasize obedience. In this way, minor rule-breaking can become major rule-breaking with significant consequences when teachers and administrators are faced with certain students' incorrigibility.

Goodman (2006a) is concerned that when a student repeatedly breaks a rule and is then charged with insolence, 'a sometimes immoral act can be converted into a categorical moral offense' (221, italics in the original). She argues that we need to be careful when creating such categorical moral offences because it is so easy for these judgments to extend to every possible circumstance and to therefore significantly blur conventional violations with moral ones. Goodman is concerned about the unlimited expansion of moral interpretations because if all rule violations can be defined as insolence or 'defiance of authority,' then discipline is reduced to discipline for its own sake. She argues that such overpolicing in turn creates more discipline problems because it reduces conventional and moral issues into requirements for blind obedience and therefore fails to provide students with moral education.[7]

Other Elevations of Convention to Morality

If students are more likely to accept rules that they interpret to be addressing moral issues, it is not surprising that staff, and some students, also justified some ostensibly conventional rules through appeals to morality. Such a tactic was achieved, for instance, by applying future meaning to present rules: rules that might otherwise be considered ones based on personal etiquette, such as dress codes, or based on conventional organization of time and space, such as punctuality, were framed as preparing students for their future in the 'real world' of work and the education required for this work. In this way conventional rules could be imbued with much deeper significance through the moral imperatives of guidance and industriousness. Reflecting the language of the codes of conduct, almost all staff members discussed future employment as a rationale behind their enforcement of certain rules. As Dylan (Whitton teacher) said, 'I think we fall back on [the idea that school prepares students for the real world] when we're trying to teach kids what it's going to be like when they get a job.' Students similarly accepted the language of punctuality based on their preparation to be future workers:

> SMEGAL: Must be punctual.
> BRENDAN: That's a good rule.
> KRISSY: That's a good rule if you're late. I'm always late, I'm trying to work on that.
> SMEGAL: That's a good rule, why?
> BRENDAN: Because, like if you had a job and you were late every day, [you] would be fired.
> KRISSY: They don't take that at work. (Big City FG 9)

Similarly, appropriate dress was framed as an issue of future employability, although more so as an issue of mutual and self-respect, reflecting moral judgments.

> ROBIN (Whitton vice-principal): The bottom line is that if it's a string halter or something, it's not appropriate for school. It's not appropriate for business and as a result you're not wearing it alone, you'll have to wear something over it.

> NICOLE: For me it's disturbing. Like 'great, you're wearing a thong, show it to your boyfriend, show it to someone who cares.' (Whitton FG 3)

> MARJORY: I like the dress code ones a lot 'cause I don't appreciate the girls wearing like . . . [group agreeing] the midriff and the thong. I don't like seeing that. (Whitton FG 4)

Staff and student engagement with 'appropriate' dress for girls is examined in depth in chapter 7, yet it is important to note here the moral evaluation of girls who were thought to dress too provocatively. Here what many might consider a more personal domain becomes moral through reference to future work, social harmony (not being forced to look at something one doesn't want to), and appropriate gender and sexuality.

Goodman tackles the potential expansion of morality through her category of the 'derivatively moral,' discussed above, when rules are given moral attributes under certain interpretations. She distinguishes the derivatively moral from intrinsic morality. Clearly the determination of what is derivatively moral is rife with ambiguity. For example, one teacher in my study encountered an incident where a student forged a sick note, an action which Goodman suggests is a breach of morality. As the teacher pursued the issue, however, he learned that the student had forged the note in order to go to the doctor for birth control without the permission of her parents. He felt that this was a situation where the larger question of access to birth control justified the student's lie and under the circumstances, he did not see her forgery as immoral. Similarly, while almost every focus group we conducted agreed that fighting is always bad (a moral issue), two groups were clearly more ambivalent.

Fighting, repeat offending, and provocative dress are all examples which muddy the apparently clear distinctions between the realms of the personal, the conventional, and the moral with regards to school rules. In the case of fighting, certain students suggested occasions when the 'no fighting' rule is not quite so clear-cut and seems to sometimes play an acceptable role. Similarly, a number of staff comments illustrated how, through repeat offences, conventional rule violations come to take on moral meaning as offences are redefined as defiance of authority. Finally, among both staff and students certain rules were framed in terms of future expectations and roles and/or the morality of public dress, reflecting class and cultural values about employment, gender, and sexuality. These examples complicate Nucci's suggestions that morality is inherently clear, indicating that some of the conflict over rules within schools is about cultural, subcultural, and/or class differences. These complications indicate how difficult rule creation and enforcement can become, as well as the importance of providing a convincing rationale for specific rules. Clearly, according to many students' comments, they are not always convinced.

Elevating Rules through Appeals to Safety

Finally, even quite minor rules can be elevated in importance when explained in terms of student and staff safety. Safety was frequently the primary justification given for school rules, reflecting the current 'post-Columbine,' 'risk-society' climate of fear in which school staff must constantly be on the lookout for dangers and threats (Gallagher and Fusco 2006; CBC 2008; Robbins 2008). Commentary on school safety arose across focus groups and interviews. For many vice-principals and teachers across both regions under study, school safety is paramount.

LOUIS (Big City vice-principal): My priority number one is safety, number two is student achievement because kids can't achieve if they don't feel safe.

JACK (Whitton vice-principal): I'm entrusted in this school [. . .] first and foremost around safety and then learning. Everything else is a bonus, is a perk, you know what I mean?

I: Mmm, hmm. But you think that [. . .] a safety issue [. . .] supersedes certain things/ Gemini (Whitton teacher): Absolutely. It should supersede everything else.

A number of students similarly felt that the safety of the school is vital, especially for a small minority who stated that they did not feel safe. Safety, and feelings of safety, in schools is certainly important. But the problem with a risk society is that no one ever feels completely safe and in such a context, safety concerns can become a flexible justification for almost any school rule, surveillance procedure, sanction, or denial of rights. Blankenau and Leeper (2003) provide a disturbing example of this in their interviews with 273 principals in Nebraska. They found that most principals saw only limited drug problems in their schools and deemed drugs searches as ineffective. Yet most of the principals used such searches anyway due to pressure from outside sources to make the schools seem safer, particularly where there were large numbers of racial minority students. The principals, parents, and even courts also supported the searches because safety is considered to trump individual rights. Blankenau and Leeper are concerned with the hidden curriculum here: students learn that it is consistently reasonable to waive privacy protections.

The participants in my own study overwhelmingly agreed that a safe school is desirable, but debate arose around what that entails and what breaches of privacy and personal autonomy are justified in the name of safety. Students tended to accept rules if they considered them to legitimately address issues of safety. For instance, several Big City groups felt that what makes a rule fair is if it prevents injury, and they therefore accepted rules against horseplay, rumours, fighting, and harassment. Similarly rules against weapons were supported across all focus groups. In Thornberg's research with elementary students he similarly found that students value such protecting rules, although he also found that this depended on students' assessments of actual risk (2008b) – e.g., there was dispute over whether running in school halls is really all that dangerous.

Within my research, rules such as those against hats, backpacks, coats, cell phones, and personal music players were subject to significant debate, with staff commonly explaining them through the language of school safety and students either unconvinced by such safety claims or redefining them (e.g., by claiming that cell phones provide safety). While teachers and principals were by no means unanimous on all rules, many bolstered disputed rules through appeals to safety. For example, four staff members commented that personal music players can be dangerous because students will not know what is going on in the event of an emergency.[8] Meanwhile most students felt that they should be able to listen to music on their own time and when doing private seat work in class. Heavy coats and backpacks were explained as safety issues, as well. Students had been told that heavy coats were linked to gangs, that they could hide weapons, or that they are a tripping hazard, but they were largely unconvinced and felt that sometimes they wanted to wear coats, especially if they had classes in a cold portable. Whitton staff too suggested that backpacks are dangerous because students can hide things in them, such as weapons, and because they are a tripping hazard, particularly in technical classes. Students also cited these explanations but again were less convinced. They tended to make fun of the 'no backpack' rule except in the specific instance of science classes. Of course, hats came up here, too, because one reason given for banning hats is that it exposes school intruders, again to much debate.

Gallagher and Fusco (2006) observe that through the climate of risk, there is little discrimination between big and little infractions; behaviour that is relatively non-threatening is criminalized and framed as a threat to security. They also find that fears about safety in schools often foster boundaries between legitimate students and illegitimate intruders. This fear is evident when certain dress code stipulations and the need for identification tags are discussed as necessary for identifying intruders, suggesting that any possible problems come into the school from the outside. My interviews indicated such generalized concerns for safety, as staff are responsible for ensuring student safety and are working in a social context where risks are perceived to be everywhere (CBC 2008). Also, by redefining etiquette rules such as 'no hats' as protective ones addressing school safety, staff may hope to increase students' commitment to them. In fact, one Big City teacher noted that she will sometimes refer to safety as an excuse for a rule even if she is unconvinced herself.

Concern with safety supports not only certain rules but also many expensive tactics of surveillance, from metal detectors to cameras and biometrics, that are supported by a profitable industry (Gallagher and Fusco 2006; Kennedy 2004; Robbins 2008).[9] The haunting spectre of Columbine has been used to institute such tactics in schools across the United States and also in some Canadian schools. In my data collection, it was used to support rules against heavy coats and gang affiliated clothing but also instruments of surveillance such as security cameras and even metal detectors. As Maggie (Whitton FG 1) explained,

> About the metal detectors and stuff I think that should be enforced
> [. . .] I think last year they found a gun on someone at School X and then at
> School Y they found like a bunch of knives on people. Like, you know, just
> to make the kids feel safer.

Other students argued against metal detectors. Kevin suggested that 'instead of spending all the money on metal detectors why don't they spend the money on improving the quality of life of students so stuff like that happens less?' Matthew was critical of how schools had become more obsessed with safety and security 'in the wake of the school shooting and September 11.'

Matthew similarly felt that dress codes cannot prevent students bringing weapons to school:

> I find it really weird, because they get scared about guns and stuff and then
> they tighten the dress code rules, but that has nothing to do with it, anybody
> who is bringing a gun to school is not going to be worried about breaking
> other rules, you know, they are breaking the biggest rule in the book!

Students generally tended to be more concerned about enforcement and safety in regards to major rule infractions. For example, two students found that specific instances of student violence in school were not adequately addressed, and two others cited Columbine to express their concerns that harassment is often ignored by teachers even though it can lead to 'psycho shootings.'

Clearly, appeals to safety or student protection provide another complicating factor to muddy distinctions between the moral, conventional, and personal domains, particularly when safety is referenced by some to explain rules that to others are considered purely personal. Staff comments that emphasize safety indicate their responsibilities and concerns with risk, yet also resonate with the wider 'risk' or 'suspect' society which provides a context for the militarization of schools (CBC 2008; Robbins 2008), ubiquitous top-down rules, and problematic appeals to blind obedience. Kupchik (2010) found this pattern to be very strong across four distinct American schools in his ethnographic research on school security, arguing that schools 'teach to the rules' in overreaction to possible threats to students. Policies created to prevent violence, for instance, lead to punishments for a wide range of misbehaviour rather than prevention measures. One example of this pattern is the introduction of police officers to school campuses. Kupchik suggests that police can provide valuable advice to a school's administration, legitimize safety initiatives, assist in potentially violent situations, and provide back-up for unpopular school policies. Yet he also argues that police officers are inclined to interpret misbehaviour as criminal behaviour, to escalate misbehaviour into criminal behaviour through their reactions, and to respond only with punishment rather than considering personal, emotional, or other problems a student may have. Ultimately Kupchik argues that when police officers become the norm within schools, it brings a criminal justice approach into an educational institution. As with other security strategies, including metal detectors or security cameras, issues with police officers in schools create a quandary for educators who want to limit surveillance and policing in schools and yet who also wish to effectively address safety issues and be seen as taking security seriously.

Consequences

A challenge of having many rules is that once a rule is in a code of conduct there must be some kind of consequence if it is broken. However, what such a consequence should look like is also subject to debate. Moral educators such as Goodman (2006a) distinguish punishments from guidance. Goodman is concerned that punishment involves moral condemnation and a presumption of willfulness, with students having chosen an action and then being punished by the group for choosing an action that is considered antisocial or dangerous. This punishment is then thought to logically deter future misconduct by the student and by other students who have seen the punishment occur. Many developing new discipline programs for schools have attempted to move away from the language of 'punishment' and towards that of 'consequences,' however (Goodman 2006a; Kohn 1996).

Consequences are thought to guide students, recognizing that students are learning appropriate behaviour for the future. Consequences are also meant to correspond in a meaningful way with an infraction. For example, the consequence of wearing a hat to school is that it is confiscated but the student is not punished for wearing a hat by also getting a detention. Kohn (1996) argues that for students, there is little difference between punishments and consequences, however, as they tend to interpret consequences like confiscation as punishment. He is also concerned that consequences often get framed as the student's choice – they *choose* to either follow the rules or to suffer the consequences. Kohn considers this a false choice that allows teachers or principals to absolve themselves of their disciplinary roles. Within governmentality studies this emphasis on student choice can be considered part of the potentially problematic process of developing student subjectivities invested in their own self-government (Millei 2011; Raby 2010c). A third response to rule infractions is correction, an instructional approach that can potentially involve joint problem-solving, for example, and which often comes before consequences.

In this book I refer to consequences, as this is the language used by most staff participants, although only a minority of the people I interviewed actively distinguished consequences from punishments in a meaningful way. The most common consequences for rule infractions presented in codes of conduct, staff interviews, and student focus groups were confiscation, notification of parents, detention, and suspension. Of these, the most controversial was suspension, a tactic that dominates the following discussion, particularly as it is the primary consequence in cases of more significant rule violations.

Most schools apply a standard set of consequences in response to rule-breaking, consequences often outlined in student handbooks and reflecting guidance from the province and school board. As will be discussed in chapter 5, amendments to the *Safe Schools Act* in 2008 introduced the formal language of 'escalating consequences' to describe the process of increasing consequences with repeated rule-breaking. For dress code and other minor violations students are usually first asked to correct the behaviour. They may be asked to change their shirt, take off a hat, or return a back-pack to their locker, for example. As a next step, for certain in-class issues such as talking during lessons, many teachers will keep students for a detention which they themselves supervise. While not all teachers agreed that detentions are the ideal consequence for rule infractions, many felt that they successfully address minor transgressions because they impinge on students' social lives and thus deter them from repeat violations. Detentions were commonly used at both the classroom and administrative level, with teachers supervising in-class detentions and formal detentions occurring either in the office or sometimes even in a detention room. During detentions, students may be expected to do homework, clean-up work, or simply sit still. Detentions were also frequently considered an early step in a series of escalating possible consequences – repeat detentions or missed detentions might thus earn students a suspension.

When faced with more serious discipline issues, teachers will send students to the office where vice-principals frequently spend some time talking to the student and sometimes intervening to address a practical problem. Vice-principals may also use detentions, contact parents, suspend, or even in rare cases, expel a student. Some schools have also introduced alternative sanctions such as community work placements. Most commonly, consequences were discussed by staff and students as punishing deterrents (e.g., detentions or suspensions), guidance for the future (e.g., through meeting with parents or community work), or safety tactics (e.g., suspending a dangerous student). Students were frequently accepting of such consequences. They felt that they should be held accountable for their actions, but that compassion should be exercised and the circumstances of particular situations taken into account when consequences are being administered.

Suspensions

> . . . marginalized youth cannot be punished/suspended into becoming engaged (School Community Safety Advisory 2008, 6).[10]

Short of police involvement and imprisonment, schools' most severe consequence for rule-breaking is expulsion, a consequence which was coordinated through transfers between schools in Big City but less formally organized in Whitton. As is commonly the case in North American schools (Fenning and Rose 2007), suspensions were much more likely to be used than expulsions in both regions, with Big City's rates much higher than those in Whitton, but both regions lower than the provincial average,[11] and were consequently discussed at great length among students and staff alike. Overall in the province of Ontario, rates of suspension shifted from 5.11 in 2000–1 up to 7.28 per cent in 2002–3 and then down to 4.54 per cent in 2007–8. There was a general rise in suspension rates between 2002 and 2005 and then a drop between 2005 and 2008. Commentators suggested that this rise was a result of the *de facto* zero tolerance policy that was in effect at that time. Secondary school students, male students, and students with exceptionalities are disproportionately represented in these suspension rates across the years (Ontario 2010).[12] In 2007–8, for example, 58 per cent of suspensions were at the secondary level, 76 per cent of suspensions were of boys and 21 per cent were of students with exceptionalities.

There are several common forms of suspension. In-school suspensions usually require that a student is removed from his or her regular classes in order to spend a series of days in a separate space such as a classroom, detention hall, or office. These kinds of suspensions were less familiar to my participants than out-of-school suspensions, which require that a student be off school property for a series of days. The suspensions might sometimes involve community service but most commonly a student is expected to stay home and do homework while banned from the school, although with the amended provincial *Code of Conduct*, students have had to be provided with alternative provisions for their education when suspensions are over six days (Ontario 2008). The amended *Code of Conduct* also indicated that suspensions remain the expected consequence for certain behaviour such as swearing at staff, fighting, and drug or alcohol violations. As I have already mentioned, suspensions are also used in order to address repeated violations of more minor rules, including things like dress codes.

Some staff I interviewed, notably five out of the seven administrators as well as some teachers, supported the use of suspensions. Those agreeing with suspensions felt them to be effective because they cut students off from their social connections, motivate students to behave, and clearly indicate to other students that certain rule violations have significant consequences.

BARB (Whitton teacher): They want to be there – they don't want to go to class, but they want to be there to socialize and . . . so you're taking that social activity away from them.

PATRICK (Whitton teacher): Not only does that student have to absolutely know that their behaviour was unacceptable or endangering safety is unacceptable, but also, like at Maple we had 800 sets of eyes watching to see what was going to happen to that student.

LOUIS (Big City principal): And you know what? When kids hear that so-and-so got into a fight and automatically got five days, you know what? That gets around real quick. And the word gets around that so-and-so got suspended for the uniform, um, you know what? The ripple effect counts a lot more than the actual consequence.

Whitton vice-principals Chicago and Mike also emphasized that suspensions provide a 'get tough' approach to dealing with problem kids, thus reinforcing school principles. Despite these arguments, however, only five respondents wholeheartedly supported suspensions. Others felt some ambivalence or that they had little choice due to policies or in the face of what they felt to be limited options. As Robin (Whitton vice-principal) stated, in response to persistent opposition to authority, 'I have to suspend.' Indeed, most felt that suspensions should be a last resort and, if given, schools should make an effort to ensure that students are not simply wasting time by ensuring that they are doing homework or community service.

The possibility of in-school suspensions was also attractive to some, although generally prevented by a lack of staff and space resources.

DYLAN (Whitton teacher): Like I said before, I don't like suspensions. I wish we had like an alternative – I wish we could almost have kids off-site but learning somewhere. Or like a detention room within the school. Then if you don't go to that, then, you're choosing to remove yourself for a couple days suspension.

MARIA (Whitton teacher): I think that an ideal situation would be an in-school suspension where – I guess they used to have at this school – where the students had to come for the whole day, they're in a room, they have to bring their lunch, they weren't even allowed to have their social hour with their friends, they had to do work all day from 8:30 to 2:30 or whatever, and uh, allowed for bathroom breaks out of the room and that's it. And they *hated* it.

The few participants working at schools that did have in-school suspensions seemed to appreciate them, although several noted that ultimately, in-school suspensions cannot entirely replace out-of-school suspensions because the latter must be used when students do not cooperate with the former and/or when students have been violent.

> IRON (Whitton teacher): Now, if they're going to defy the vice-principal and the principal . . . well they're not listening to us in the building [. . .] So what has happened is that the students have put us in a position where we have no control over them, therefore, we have to get them out of the building. So I don't think suspension's ever going to disappear.

Also, at least three teachers suggested that in-school suspensions simply allowed friends to hang out in another venue, perhaps fostering more trouble. Both Gregory et al. (2006) and Ferguson (2000) describe schools in which in-school suspension rooms simply became known as spaces of punishment and time wasting.

Other staff members and many students felt that suspensions, particularly out-of-school suspensions, are illogical, especially when used to address truancy.

> I: So what do you think of that, being suspended for skipping?
> JAMES: I think it is stupid, like that's the whole point. I don't want to be at school so why the hell would they suspend me, thank you!
> I: So did you like getting suspended?
> JAMES: Well, I just think it's retarded [sic], like I liked it cuz I never liked school myself, but some people do right? I like some parts of school, like I like history and stuff like that but I'd never [inaudible], I don't know I just think it's stupid that they suspend people, man, maybe in-school suspensions, that's the best way to go. (Whitton FG 2)

> BIBI: Yeah, I don't understand how they justify, like, for skipping classes or being late so many times they suspend you, like obviously . . . if the kid doesn't want to be there in the first place and you're suspending them then they're going to be completely happy and say 'you know what, I'm happy I don't have to go to school.' So I think it's better if you encourage students to go to school than to discourage them, right? (Big City FG3)

Many groups pointed to this lack of logic behind out-of-school suspensions and in two Big City schools in-school suspensions were specifically reserved for cases of truancy.

Staff opposed to suspensions were concerned that students are sent out into unsupportive homes and/or community environments where they will be unsupervised, and that they are likely to fall behind in school.

LURALEEN (Whitton teacher): Kids are *our* problem. We need to keep them here. That's how I feel about it. So I didn't want those kids sent home, or suspended [. . .] The best way to take care of them, the best way to make sure they're not doing drugs is to make sure that they're here.

BILL (Whitton teacher): Because we're recognizing that it's uh – if you're home, [inaudible] you don't have your time on task. So you're missing out on opportunities to learn and I think that's the most important thing.

Dylan (Whitton teacher) was also concerned that suspension rarely includes any kind of follow-up with the student. These reservations are echoed in much of the literature on suspensions.

Skiba and Rausch (2006) review research on the effectiveness of out-of-school suspensions and while they acknowledge the need to ensure school safety, they raise a number of important concerns. At the most basic, suspensions undermine academic achievement and exacerbate the alienation of those students who are frequently most academically weak and excluded (Bowditch 1993; Noguera 2003). They argue that out-of-school suspensions and expulsions are risky because they exclude students from their education and undermine these students' bonds with the school. Drawing on American data, Skiba and Rausch argue that problem students are frequently those who have experienced neglect and abuse in their lives and are most likely to be suspended. Robbins (2008) observes that it is the poor and minority students who are most likely to be suspended. Yet research consistently finds that despite their unequal application and significantly negative consequences, suspensions are commonly used and are not reserved for the most serious offences, such as fighting, but are also used for things like attendance, abusive language, disobedience, disrespect, and general classroom disruption (Fenning and Rose 2007).

Finally, concerns about suspensions connect to those about students dropping out of school, students who again tend to come from more disadvantaged backgrounds and to be in non-academic streams (Davies 1994). Such students are more likely to be absent a lot, to clash with teachers, and to be Black (Bowditch 1993). Dei's (2008) research with dropouts found that while some talked about dropping out or fading out, others suggested being pushed out for either interpersonal or structural reasons, such as the teacher not liking them or a hidden curriculum that thwarted their success. Bowditch similarly found that while dropping out is usually seen as a problem arising from issues internal to a student's life, school policies and procedures encourage disciplinarians to use suspensions and transfers to 'get rid of' students they deem 'troublemakers,' making 'push-outs' a more appropriate term (1993), an understanding of the dynamic that is powerfully reflected in Michelle Fine's ethnography *Framing Dropouts* (1991). Katz (1991) provides a stark example of this process in her ethnographic study of a largely Latino school in the southern United States where teachers were overtly encouraged to suggest that their weaker students simply stay home and eventually drop out in order to maintain the school's reputation for high test scores.

Teachers' and administrators' perceptions of the value of suspensions are mixed. For some, exclusion from the school body is a useful consequence that is easily accessible and provides a powerful statement to the offender and to other students. For others, it is a technique that further marginalizes students who are already ambivalent about school. Nonetheless, few staff seemed able to envision other options, suggesting the weight of tradition upon them, lack of resources, and broader commitment to suspension at the school and provincial board levels. Suspensions also resonate with 'get tough' rhetoric that often appeals to some teachers and parents, and more broadly to voters. As the only vice-principal to speak out against suspensions, Blair noted that her position was 'hard to sell sometimes to staff because when the kids are rude to them they want, they want a concrete [consequence].' However, Skiba and Rausch (2006) do not find that suspensions improve student behaviour. Indeed, the strongest predictor of later suspensions is earlier suspensions. Further, both students and teachers have reported that increased suspensions foster a negative school climate, perhaps because suspensions are ultimately about individualizing problems and excluding the most marginalized students from the school community. Generally schools with high suspension rates have lower student achievement overall despite the general economic or racial backgrounds of students in the school (Skiba and Rausch, 2006).[13]

Navigating Big Rules and Consequences

The rules outlined in codes of conduct can look straightforward, and consequences for breaking these rules familiar and necessary. These protocols and procedures are the ongoing backdrop for students and staff in schools, making them hard to question. This is particularly the case for those rules that address significant issues such as violence. Such situations seem very clear: infractions are serious and need serious consequences. Not surprisingly then, the 'big' rules tend to be uncontested by students, staff, and also some researchers, particularly when compared to the more conventional and personal etiquette rules discussed in chapter 2. The ramifications for breaking these rules also seem clear-cut, especially when codified within provincial or other legislation: breaking big rules should have big consequences. However, closer examination of these rules and consequences illustrates that even these are quite complicated, creating significant challenges for educators concerned about social justice. Morality is not intrinsic and the 'major' rules are not always understood in the same way by all, despite the serious consequences of breaking them. Goodman's concept of the 'derivatively moral' is also useful for illustrating how there are many occasions when serious consequences, such as suspension, are applied to less clear transgressions, as in the case of repeat offending, instances of 'defiance,' and minor rules that acquire added weight based on students' current and future welfare.

Using suspensions to remove students from class frequently seems like a logical choice for staff to make in response to difficult student behaviour. Indeed, it can be a significant relief for beleaguered teachers. It can address concerns regarding the safety or education of other students and it may 'send a clear message' to other students. The research literature is clear on the topic of out-of-school suspensions, however: they negatively affect the most marginalized students, with long term consequences for their academic success. Clearly when considering major rules, their creation and presentation, and the consequences for breaking them, educators and policy-makers must grapple with the mixed and sometimes clashing responsibilities of the school: guiding students towards pro-social behaviour, ensuring student and staff safety, fostering a community of learners, and striving to provide equal opportunities to all. The choices staff make in the face of such demands also reflect certain conceptualizations of students themselves, a more theoretical side to questions of school rules and their enforcement to which I now turn.

4 The Rules and Their Underlying Beliefs

LIZA: Because I think if there wasn't a rule to begin with, there'd be like all sorts of [inaudible] and then people would just, I don't know, they'd be like crazy, do stupid things and be like 'that's totally OK,' like whereas if there's a rule, they'll do it and they'll be like 'Oh, maybe I shouldn't have done it because it's bad.' (Big City FG 2)

The raison d'etre of discipline or classroom management is almost always to secure children's compliance with adults' demands [. . .] there is not a whisper of inquiry into whether these are reasonable demands, or how it must feel to be a student in a place where one's own preferences don't count for much. (Kohn 1996, xii and 15)

What are school rules intended for? How do we expect young people to respond to them? People's beliefs about what kinds of rules are needed in secondary school, how these rules ought to be enforced, and why it is that students break them invariably reflect deeper, underlying beliefs – beliefs about safety and discipline but also about adolescence, growing up, and human nature. These beliefs can reflect investments in perpetuating age-based (and other) inequalities, or they can challenge such hierarchies; they can provide leeway for young people's developmental location or they can emphasize human rationality. While not always consistent, the beliefs and goals underlying school rules also have material consequences (particularly in the lives of students). This chapter invites readers to reflect on their own beliefs about young people, discipline, and rules through first exploring philosophies of discipline and how these are reflected in codes of conduct and staff comments; the second section of this chapter then focuses on underlying beliefs about age and human nature.

What Is Discipline and Why Do Students Need It?

Various scholars have argued that rules reflect morality (Thornberg 2006; Goodman 2006a; Nucci 2001), social hierarchy (Raby 2005), preparation for future roles as differentiated workers (Apple 1995; Bowles and Gintis 1976), and certain understandings of citizenship (Effrat and Schimmel 2003). They also reflect significant and logical preoccupations with safety, as discussed in the last chapter. Relevant to all of these positions is the concept of discipline. Expanding on Goodman (2006a) there are several ways to conceptualize discipline:[1] 1) as mastering a discipline; 2) as providing order needed for learning; 3) as an independent good; and 4) as cultivated self-discipline.

The first is to see discipline in terms of following rules of practice, training, diet, and so forth, or *mastering a discipline*. Here discipline is about learning in and of itself. From a Foucauldian perspective this form of discipline can be considered as enabling. Parkes (2010) draws on this conceptualization of discipline, for example, when talking about mastering a martial art. Through this kind of discipline, the body becomes not docile but efficient and capable. He recognizes, however, that within martial arts, the process is voluntary and with a clear endpoint, a distinction from much schooling. Watkins (2010) draws on both Emile Durkheim and Foucault's later work to argue that discipline can be both enabling and constraining, depending on family routines and teachers' pedagogical practices. Discipline can build skills and become a resource for agency[2] as habit can be a 'pliable, generative phenomenon' (83). Watkins thus suggests that there are certain kinds of pedagogical discipline that can foster productive techniques rather than simply ensuring control or enslaving the mind.

While mastery is integral to schooling, this pedagogical understanding of discipline seems to play little overt role in current approaches to school rule-making. Rather, school rules are understood to allow learning to take place, as reflected in the second approach to the term: discipline as ensuring *the order necessary for* learning, a position widely reflected in classroom management literature (Hoy and Weinstein 2006), school rules, and in staff and student comments about them. Indeed, the need to maintain some kind of classroom order for learning to occur is a cornerstone of almost all theories of classroom management (Porter 1996; Lewis 1991). This imperative is linked to teachers' legal responsibilities to ensure students' safety and to manage large numbers of students, but also to certain beliefs about what learning should look like, with quiet, ordered, studious students indicating successful teacher control. The need for rules to ensure order is a position on discipline reflected in explanations for rules regarding safety, punctuality, and personal electronics (e.g., cell phones), for instance.

A third orientation towards discipline frames it as an *independent good*. 'With this rationale any rule will encourage restraint, delayed gratification, inhibition, and moderation as does the very act of submission. And any resistance or disobedience signals insufficient restraint' (Goodman 2006a, 215). From this position, discipline is valued as submission to authority in and of itself. In examining teachers' beliefs about classroom management, Hoy and Weinstein (2006) found that in addition to emphasizing order, most teachers at the secondary level embraced a 'custodial' or 'traditional' perspective which foregrounds such authority and obedience, with misbehaviour interpreted as a personal affront to the teacher and good behaviour learned through rewards and punishments.[3] Male teachers, in particular, are found to emphasize this approach, which Robinson (1992) attributes to the linkages between authority, control and hegemonic masculinity. From this approach to discipline, students should obediently accept teachers' authority, the power inequalities embedded within the school, and the age distinctions between adults and children, partly in preparation for the wider power imbalances they will need to negotiate in the wider society. Within such a custodial perspective, children are believed to have an inclination to misbehave and consequently school staff and other adults must guide them onto the right path – self-discipline is thus learned through the habit of obedience.

Finally, researchers critical of such emphasis on obedience to authority often prefer non-interventionist or guidance approaches towards discipline, such as those proposed by Gartrell (1998), Kohn (1996), or Porter (2003). These focus on developing self-discipline through a degree of cooperation with students; some even challenge the very concept of discipline because it implies control (Millei 2007). Instead, a guidance approach advocates students and teachers working towards shared ends, with the teacher taking the role of a facilitator or guide. These approaches emphasize cooperation, learning from experience, personal responsibility, communication, and democracy and are usually more popular at the primary level (Hoy and Weinstein 2006; Lewis 1991). Such non-interventionist approaches are inclined to consider children inherently good and/or deserving of fundamental rights in need of respect (Porter 1996). Guidance approaches face a challenge, however, in freeing students from control while maintaining classroom order. This condundrum is reconciled through attempting to indirectly shape students' desires to become certain kinds of people, therefore fostering self-regulation and indirect control (Fendler 2001; Pongratz 2007; Millei 2011).[4]

Perspectives on Discipline in the Data

Before more subjectively weighing the advantages and disadvantages of each of these approaches to discipline, I will take a moment to discuss how these conceptualizations play out in policy and practice. What forms of discipline do codes of conduct seem to reflect? What forms are embraced by the staff I interviewed? Codes of conduct reproduce the goal of ensuring school and classroom order necessary for learning. Within this structuring, however, the philosophies embedded in these codes of conduct reflect a tension in terms of how such goals will be achieved by combining quite distinct approaches to discipline. Preambles to various codes of conduct often emphasize self-discipline by drawing on terms such as responsibility, while the specific rules are framed in the context of obedience and order.

A quarter of the codes I studied included a fairly direct, opening gesture towards self-discipline:

> [The code of conduct serves] to promote a school environment conductive to effective learning and the development of self-discipline in all students, trust and mutual respect. (Smithson Secondary, non-urban)

> Our purpose is to assist young people to become self-disciplined, self-directed individuals who take responsibility for themselves and their education. (Huntington Collegiate, urban)

This emphasis was particularly concentrated in the semi-rural area. Usually the goal was students' *future* self-discipline, although almost all schools indirectly referenced present self-discipline when discussing responsibility. About 70 per cent of the non-urban schools and 60 per cent of the urban ones stressed responsibility wherein students are expected to take responsibility for themselves, their actions, their environment (including school property), and their learning. On the one hand, this can be seen as an example of a guidance approach, as an attempt to 'responsibilize' students towards their own self-management. On the other hand, in many instances the form of responsibility being emphasized is passive, evident only when students follow the rules (Raby 2008b).

Indeed, despite framing the rules with gestures towards self-discipline, the codes of conduct widely presented *specific* rules in ways that underscored obedience and passivity in the face of top-down punishment – as a long list of non-negotiable prohibitions, often without explanation. A similar pattern was found by David Schimmel in his examination of thirty secondary school conduct codes from several American states (2003) and Ramon Lewis's (1999a) Australian study of three hundred codes of conduct from secondary and primary schools. Furthermore, half of the non-urban school codes and one third of the urban ones clearly stated that students are expected to obediently follow the rules through declarations that students are to accept consequences when they are given. As one school code states: 'When disciplined, a student will be expected to be courteous and obedient.' In these ways, self-discipline is framed through obedience and an absence of autonomy (Archard 2004), a custodial approach disguised as a guidance approach. Such a position is reflected in many school and school board policies which state that students shall 'accept such discipline as would be exercised by a kind, firm and judicious parent'.

Much as the codes reflect conflicting gestures towards self-discipline alongside demands for obedience, teachers and administrators hold a range of disciplinary philosophies related to school rules. As illustrated in chapter 3, many staff argued that the rules are related to order or safety, and they must therefore be followed with no questions asked. This philosophy was maintained by almost all of the Whitton vice-principals we interviewed, as well as a number of teachers in both Whitton and the Big City. Kupchik (2010) similarly found such a perspective to guide most of the staff approaches in the American high schools he studied. He called this 'teaching to the rules,' which means focusing on obedience rather than listening to students; he argues that such a climate retains adult authority and resonates with a broader culture of security. While an obedience-centred understanding of discipline makes certain rules non-negotiable, a number of teachers and administrators in my own study who focused on order and safety frequently did feel it necessary to explain to students the rationale behind the rules, with the belief that this would increase compliance. Others did not feel such explanation to be necessary, however. As Whitton vice-principal Mike stated, 'These are the school rules. You're gonna follow the rules like everybody else or . . . there's the door!' Barb (Whitton teacher) agreed that sometimes simple obedience is required: 'So [I tell them], "they're the teacher, you're the student and if they ask you to do something, whether it's right or not, sometimes you just have to do it."' Those staff who emphasized the importance of obedience to the rules were frequently those who also believed in the need for future obedience, particularly at work. As Robin (Whitton vice-principal) stated: '[School rules are] preparing kids for the law and order environment that exists out there.'

While most staff had some kind of inclination towards such a custodial approach to discipline, desire for adherence to blind obedience was rarely consistent across individual interviews, perhaps reflecting the wide range of behaviour that school rules address. For example, Barb's comments above are complicated by her later emphasis on the need for student involvement in decision-making. Mike and Iron similarly advocated unquestioning obedience to authority while at the same time stating that they have an 'open-door' policy for students who feel that they have been treated unfairly or who do not agree with some of their school rules. Joe felt that students should learn to follow rules for rules' sake but also engaged his class in making their own rules.

It is also interesting that those staff most likely to discuss the need for student self-discipline or the development of future citizenship were some of the most obedience-oriented teachers. For example, Whitton teachers Patrick and Simon discussed the role of the rules in preparing young people for future citizenship, framed through obedience:

PATRICK: There's also things like character building and citizenship built into our curriculum now. That language is in the documents. I'm not helping a student succeed if I create a situation where they can behave in any way that they want.

SIMON: With no rules we'd have chaos, an open house for destruction. We need a sense of order. We need to make students into good citizens, though not that we want them all to be automatons.

For these participants, young people's future success as citizens is premised on their ability to follow certain rules, a skill that is shaped while they are students. The contrast between this perspective on citizenship and a more democratic one that is premised on citizen voice illustrates how citizenship too is a contested concept.[5]

While most teachers at the secondary level tended to emphasize order and/or obedience, a small minority worked from more humanistic approaches. This position was advocated by staff who were particularly likely to take into account the importance of the personal (and sometimes broader) context of students' infractions, which meant listening to the students' perspectives and sometimes jointly negotiating how to address the situation (see chapter 5). Only two staff members that I interviewed could clearly be identified as having such a humanist, or liberal, approach, although four others had definite inclinations in that direction. Spencer (Big City principal) articulates this position:

> Every school's different. It's a unique puzzle. And my staff brings the pieces of the puzzle, and my kids bring the pieces, and the community – and my job is to provide a framework for that and to really encourage them to bring those pieces of the puzzle, and bring new ideas.

These staff members tended to consider the viewpoint of students, to work with students to address misconduct, to account for the context of rule infractions (including the students' age or background), to provide clear explanations for rules, and to focus on the need for staff self-reflection.

Evaluating Approaches to Discipline

To many, demands for obedience to authority indicate a strong commitment to discipline, an approach often favoured by parents and teachers (Kupchik 2010; Hoy and Weinstein 2006). For vice-principals, who are responsible for the safety and order of the school and are consequently accountable when things go wrong, an emphasis on obedience to authority may be particularly compelling or logical. Yet this overarching approach, evident in most codes of conduct and many of my staff comments, raises concerns. A number of researchers in addition to Goodman (2006a) argue that such an emphasis is counterproductive because it fosters blind obedience (Lewis 1999a). Schimmel (2003) contends that school rules are ineffective when they concentrate on controlling and punishing students in order to teach responsibility and self-control; really what these rules teach is that breaking rules is about not getting caught. Thornberg (2006) agrees that when rules emphasize order they fail to foster self-discipline, critical thinking, and children's democratic skills.

Thornberg is concerned that systems of rules relying on obedience might frequently lead to inconsistent applications and moral dilemmas for students which ultimately undermine the teacher's authority. He provides the example of hushing, based on observations of primary and middle school classes in Sweden and interviews with teachers and students. Frequently when the noise in classrooms rose while students were doing seat work a teacher would respond with a general 'shhhhhh!' This need for silence may be functional or practical, as it allows for an ordered, working environment. It may also reflect inter-personal morality, as noise can undermine others' work. But sometimes when students were talking they were helping each other with their work, unacknowledged by a general hush. In these instances, students confronted a dilemma between obediently completing their own work in silence and helping others. Some students reconciled this dilemma by interpreting the 'hush' as unintended for them and therefore dis-obeyed their teachers in order to behave according to their own moral standard but many did not do this and instead opted for obedience, even if they did not agree with it.

Obedience may seem to be a benign choice, particularly in the above example, but Thornberg counters this position by citing Stanley Milgram's well-known experiments in the 1960s with obedience to author-ity (1963). Milgram's participants frequently obeyed the commands of someone in a position of authority, even when it went against their own moral standards and they believed that they were significantly injuring another person. Thornberg draws on his work in moral education to argue that 'responsibility to authority' (98, italics in original) is a prob-lematic 'basis for moral reasoning, decision-making and acting' (98). He consequently recommends that teachers reflect on the hidden cur-ricula behind rule enforcement, take students' views into account, and talk with students about moral dilemmas.

Olafson and Field (2003) also reflect on school rules as moral code. They studied a school that focused on obedience, with a 'punishment culture' that prevented staff and students from thoughtfully choosing the better path, or the right thing to do. Rules were applied in a for-mulaic manner that often seemed illogical. Olafson and Field contend that this culture fostered student anger, alienation, disrespect, and re-sistance. Agreeing with Thornberg, they advocate that young people should learn morality not through obedience but through moral re-flection and conversation. Indeed, in their review of literature that ad-dresses the effectiveness of disciplinary approaches, Hoy and Weinstein

(2006) find that the 'get tough' approach is problematic in that it often humiliates students, is incongruous with the development of strong and caring relationships with students, and fails with some culturally diverse groups.

Why this gap between authoritarian staff views, which are in turn echoed in school codes of conduct and some broader legislation, and researchers' cautions regarding obedience and punishment? A similar gap is evident between political, 'common sense' rhetoric on getting tough on youth crime and social science research showing the failure of such approaches. Often mandates for school discipline come from higher echelons of government as part of their election platforms rather than from research. The 'get tough' approach has been utilized within various election campaigns in both the United States and Canada, constructing troubled youth as scapegoats during electioneering. Ontario's 'zero tolerance' policy that was introduced under the Conservative government is just one example of this. Futhermore, an emphasis on obedience and punishment is one that may also resonate with some school staff because it reflects their own schooling experiences as young people and then as teachers. Also, secondary teachers are more likely than primary ones to take a more traditional, obedience-focused approach to discipline, perhaps reflecting secondary school culture and beliefs or fears regarding adolescents.[6] Several staff suggested that they first came to secondary teaching with more inclusive, participatory ideals but that the reality of the job, including class sizes and student disinterest in participation, led them towards more authoritarian discipline – this indicates that inclinations towards obedience-oriented discipline have been deeply institutionalized.

Dominant beliefs about teenagers as needing containment, concern with losing order, and fears regarding classroom safety may shape this institutional culture. Porter (1996) reviews arguments provided by some humanist scholars who suggest that teachers tend to espouse authoritarian approaches because it is hard to give up power imbalances such as those based on age. Part of this position is a belief that power is a zero-sum game: either the teacher is in control or the students are. Porter (1996) also suggests that when teachers are in a stressful situation, they may be most likely to resort to authoritarian attempts at control because they feel out of control, have limited training in other approaches, may blame students and therefore feel personally threatened by them, and are themselves positioned in a hierarchical school staffing structure. Hierarchical staffing, in turn, extends beyond the school, as school boards and provinces mandate policy. Significantly, a default to obedience and punishment also reflects a lack of resources. At various points in my interviews with school staff, participants mentioned a need for more counselling staff, hall monitors, or the resources to support in-school suspensions. In the United States, chronic underfunding for school infrastructure, counselling, books, and so forth often exists alongside state and district financial support for security measures such as scanners and police officers (Dickar 2008; Saltman and Gabbard 2003). Faced with limited support, staff people seek quick solutions to disciplinary issues (Hoy and Weinstein 2006); responses such as authoritarianism and automatic suspensions can be easiest in the short term.

In the face of the above concerns with an emphasis on obedience, approaches which instead seek to cultivate student self-discipline through guidance strategies may seem ideal, though challenging goals, yet these have also raised some concerns for scholars (Fendler 2001; Pongratz 2007; Millei 2011). Both Millei and Pongratz draw on governmentality studies to argue that self-discipline may penetrate much deeper into a young person's inner self or soul through the regulation and evaluation of emotions and desires, for instance, than superficial requirements for obedience. Millei is concerned that this depth of governance is insidious, permeating all aspects of young people's lives, well beyond the walls of the school. As Foucault stated, modern governance of a population is efficiently managed when people take responsibility for their own actions (1978a). From this perspective, processes of school governance frame students as actors with freedom, but a freedom that is guided as people come to be regulated through making the right personal choices (Harris 2004) for their own self-sufficient and responsible futures (Hannah-Moffat 2000). For example, when codes of conduct link rights, responsibilities, and consequent self-discipline, students are guided towards a certain kind of self-regulation (Kemshall 2002). It may then be particularly difficult for students to identify the source of their control (Pongratz 2007). I return to these concerns in chapter 9 to consider when and how such self-disciplining processes are more, and less, worrying.

In addition to these contentions that emphasis on self-discipline obfuscates dominating power relations, thinking about discipline in terms of self-regulation can also place too large a burden of responsibility on the individual student. In other words, students who come to be marginalized when they are labelled a 'problem kid,' for example, can be held responsible for their failure to choose to self-discipline. In this way, structural processes of social disadvantage and exclusion from school are presented as resulting solely from the individual student's own choice (Kemshall 2002). Consequently the student who chooses badly is blamed and ultimately subjected to mechanisms of authoritarian control and repression, absolving the principal, the school, or indeed the wider society of responsibility (Levinsky).[7] Kemshall (2002) is rightly concerned that relevant structural processes and inequalities are thus overlooked.

There are many different theories and practices of discipline. In this section I have only reviewed some of them, and with broad brush strokes. Practically speaking, and as I have illustrated above, codes of conduct and staff philosophies draw both on guidance-type approaches to foster self-discipline and quite top-down forms of punishment, as the references above to obedience underscore, reinforced by zero tolerance and other policies resulting in suspension; schools also punish those who fail to self-govern, dividing the 'good' students from the 'bad' (Hannah-Moffat 2000, 528). Furthermore, my review of school rules and staff philosophies suggests little clear adherence to specific, individual theories of discipline – staff beliefs for the most part reflect a grab-bag of positions (Millei and Raby 2010). Relationships between theories and practices of discipline are not always consistent but instead the latter often draw on a variety of theories that may even sometimes contradict each other. Rather than deeply investigating specific theories, I have instead sought to discuss patterns and tensions within my data as they relate to broader disciplinary approaches. Tensions are compounded when we explore discipline in relation to our conceptualizations of young people, which I address below.

Why Students Break or Follow Rules

Philosophies regarding discipline are intertwined with beliefs about why students break or follow school rules. In this section I focus on the beliefs of teachers and administrators about their students' rule-breaking. These beliefs tend to relate to questions of age, adolescence, and human nature. I have organized them into two categories. *Future orientations* are those that address student 'becoming,' particularly in terms of their preparation for future roles, such as employees or citizens, and through aspects of developmentalism. *Present orientations* are those that are more likely to consider young people for who they are in the present through reflection on human nature, adolescence in the moment, age and status hierarchies, and context. I conclude this chapter by discussing how these beliefs, alongside those specifically addressing discipline which I have examined already, are not always consistent, as teachers and administrators draw on quite distinct explanations for student behaviour in different situations. These inconsistencies are made possible by shifting conceptualizations of adolescence, the authority of school staff, the complexity of disciplinary moments, and the diversity of students in the school. They also provide students themselves with insight and critique.

Future Orientations

Despite some recent work which argues that adulthood is currently destabilizing, particularly with the erosion of long-term careers within neoliberal economic systems (Blatterer 2007) and life-long education (Lee 2001), adulthood is commonly framed as a stable endpoint, with childhood and adolescence defined by forward momentum towards this endpoint (Lesko 1996a). As a consequence, we often think about young people less in terms of who they are in the present than what they will become in the future (James 2004). Within my research, school rules were often discussed through such a lens, primarily in terms of how they prepare young people for future employment or citizenship. A future-orientation is also a powerful feature of developmental theory, which dominates theories of discipline and much broader research about young people. I will briefly discuss links between developmentalism and discipline theories, although it should be noted that the school rules and staff comments that make up this project's data rarely addressed development directly except in terms of increasing leniency as students mature and in present conceptualizations of adolescence.

GUIDANCE INTO THE FUTURE
   BLAIR (Whitton vice-principal): I'm trying to have kids think for themselves so that when they leave high school they don't need me or a parent to tell them how to behave, on a job or in a relationship.

One thing that differentiates school rules from laws governing adult behaviour is that they are frequently grounded in the premise that

Table 4.1 Future orientations

Description	Link to beliefs about discipline
Becoming future adults: Young people as becoming certain kinds of people in the future, e.g., citizens or workers.	Approaches to discipline reflect the kinds of adults imagined for the future, e.g., an interest in future obedience of workers may foster an authoritarian approach while an interest in future democratic citizenship may foster a guidance approach.
Developmentalism: Understanding young people as in a developmental process of maturation.	Expectations that students change as they age/mature, with developing maturity, morality, and skills. Allowances are made for young people's age/maturity when determining consequences, although often neglects other explanations for behaviour, such as context, and locates adults as fully developed and knowledgeable about young people.

young people need to be guided or socialized towards certain kinds of futures.[8] In chapter 2 I discussed how codes of conduct themselves referenced the preparation of students for work and/or citizenship. In this chapter we have seen how staff views also reflect these intents behind schooling – preparation for future employment, employment for which they are presumed to need punctuality, neatness, and obedience, and preparation for citizenship, understood as obedience to laws by most, although very occasionally as democratic participation.

Through these future-oriented lenses, young people need guidance to learn the skills and self-discipline necessary to take on future responsibilities. As such, young people need to learn responsibility, respect, acceptable interpersonal behaviour, and self-control, goals reflected in most approaches to discipline (Porter 1996). This emphasis on what students will become is particularly reflected in the belief that certain present rules are for the students' own future good. As Laura (Whitton teacher) suggested:

They may not respect structure or understand the structure. When they're older they'll certainly look back and say 'Thank God.' When they're older and they look back to see where their friends who were allowed such freedoms got nowhere and they themselves have been able to progress, that's when I think they will understand.

While concern about young people's development into future adults is logically a key focus of schools, through this lens, schooling is about prioritizing the children's future possibilities over their present situations (Devine 2002). This approach resonates with a caretaker position on rights, which argues that the prevention of choice for children (e.g., through mandatory school rules, including attendance) will help children make reasoned choices when they become educated adults (Archard 2004). A future focus does not inevitably lead to authoritarian, top-down rules, however. As we will see in chapter 9, many advocates of student participation in school rule development also reference their futures, primarily in terms of democratic citizenship.

STUDENT DEVELOPMENT AND LENIENCY

Developmental theory dominates current research and practice in the areas of childhood and adolescence. Grounded in psychology, developmentalism examines young people through a focus on cognitive, moral, emotional, and other changes that they go through as they move from being infants to adults. Commonly, development is assumed to be incremental, linear, measurable, and embodied in the individual (Burman 2008). Through research, developmental psychologists have identified normative developmental processes, pinpointing potential areas for problems or risk within individuals, and consequent needs for intervention.

Drawing on developmental theory, certain approaches to discipline identify children as passing through stages and the need to design disciplinary programs in accordance with these stages. For example, when Nucci (2001) examines moral education he includes specific discussions about young people of various ages and how their orientation to morality changes over time, with middle school students more likely than older students to interpret rules to the letter and to therefore seek to manoeuver around them through loop-holes, for instance. The preceding emphasis on teaching young people certain skills in preparation for adulthood also rests on a loose application of developmentalism. Jones and Jones (2007) similarly draw on developmental research to argue that adolescents are best met with classroom activities supporting positive peer relations, opportunities to have meaningful participation, and possibilities for self-exploration. They find it problematic that teachers tend to distance themselves from secondary students through creating more structure, for instance, when adolescent students are in particular need of more support and equality at their age.

Given this dominance of development in child and youth studies, I was surprised that, apart from blanket generalizations about teenagers (which I discuss under present orientations), staff rarely referred to age-based differences in behaviour and consequent disciplinary needs among students. A practical application of developmentalism would suggest graduated rules over the course of students' time at school, yet distinctions in rules across grades at the secondary level were rarely raised except for one pattern mentioned by a few staff and students; age was also formalized as a mitigating circumstance in new provincial legislation in 2008.

Several staff suggested that students in the junior grades are more immature and therefore more likely to bully, spill food, talk in class, dress inappropriately, and to simply get in trouble. For this reason and because the rules are also thought to be less familiar to students in the younger grades, some teachers favoured (and others critiqued) a tendency to be stricter with these students. In contrast, older students were considered more mature, more familiar with the rules, and more likely to engage with their schooling, so some teachers were less strict with them. For instance, one participant considered seniors more mature and thus able to competently decide if they needed to skip a class to work on an assignment, suggesting that seniors are better at weighing the educational consequences of rule-breaking than juniors. Several teachers similarly mentioned that they are more flexible with older students because they can 'handle the responsibility.' Bill (Whitton teacher) argued that if his juniors can't 'meet him half way' then he goes to the letter of the rule whereas 'with my seniors, I feel that they're at the point where they can have some more responsibilities for their actions.' Incidentally, some students agreed that older students should have more leeway because of their levels of responsibility.

ANGELINA: When you're 18, they allow you to sign yourself out.
I: Right.
ANGELINA: So I think it, I think maybe as you get older, [attendance] should be . . . become less important.
KIERSTYN: Yeah [. . .] in older grades, 'cause in grade 9, people would just go crazy. You have to be responsible.
JEREMY: Start taking advantage of it.

I: So younger people, yes they should have [an attendance rule]?
ANGELINA: It depends.
KIERSTYN: Yeah, but in grade 12, like if we have it: optional. (Whitton FG 6)

Reflecting a distrust of younger students and a distancing from their younger selves, these students argue that as young people grow up they no longer need direct rules, as self-discipline has been accomplished. Responsibility is learned through obedience and students should be rewarded *after* it has been proven, again through obedience.

Yet leniency with older students also seems incongruous with some of the above, future-oriented logics of student discipline. If one assumes that younger students are less able to understand some of the contextual or contingent nature of rules, as Nucci suggests (2001), and therefore require a more 'black and white' or rigid application of rules in order to learn them, then this age-based, differential treatment makes some sense. But if the rules are as important as some staff suggest they are, and older students are both more mature and more familiar with the rules than younger students, then it would seem logical to be stricter with older students because they should know better. From this position, important allowances should be made for young people based on their developmental location, a pattern which may be reflected in primary school teachers' inclinations towards guidance theories.

A focus on young people as being in the *process* of becoming more rational, able to self-reflect, and able to understand the consequences of their actions importantly bolsters their exemption from certain responsibilities of adulthood. By understanding young people as in the process of maturing, they are provided with accommodation for mistakes and consequent learning. As Glenn (Whitton teacher) noted, 'But sometimes too I think, you know, they're kids and that's part of their maturing process, to make stupid mistakes.' Several staff emphasized that students have a valuable opportunity for guidance and understanding before they turn eighteen, the age of majority, when they will be held fully responsible for their actions. A similar recognition that young people's competencies are developing is embedded in the *United Nations Convention on the Rights of the Child* and is assumed by many to be a key humanitarian advancement in terms of our understanding of young people. From this stance, then, it seems illogical for staff to be less accommodating with students who are younger.[9]

While the potential leniency granted to children on account of their incomplete development has been an important advance for many children's welfare, it should be noted that concerns have also been raised about developmentalism, as it produces normative assumptions that are often based on Western, middle class ideals (Walkerdine 1993), frequently frames difference as problematic (Dannefer 1984), often neglects other influences on behaviour, such as social context (Walkerdine 1993), and reinforces the idea that young people are incomplete versions of adults (Lesko 1996a). I return to some of these concerns when discussing adolescence below.

Present Orientations

Staff philosophies focused on young people through future-orientations were used to mobilize both more rigid and more accommodating approaches to discipline; this is also the case with present-orientations. Many staff focused on students in the present to discuss their beliefs about discipline, rules, and student rule-breaking. A present-focus was evident with references to human nature, adolescent nature, status hierarchies, and recognition of context. These positions were often in tension with future-orientations, and also with each other.

HUMAN NATURE

Some staff focused on inherent human nature to explain why it is that students break rules and to advocate for certain forms of discipline, particularly deterrence. For example, while Lana talked about how young people follow rules to learn consequences and boundaries, she then said, 'Yeah, and well because they can [break rules]. I mean, who wouldn't, you know [. . .] go to work if they didn't have to!' In another example, Big City principal Spencer suggested that it is human nature to try to break rules out of fun or to get away with it:

> I mean, you know, it's like when we park and we put money in the meter and we got enough in there for an hour and we know it's only an hour, we take an hour and a half to get back, and if we don't get a ticket we sort of feel kind of good about that, you know? And the reality is that we should have gone back and put more money in the meter but we didn't. You know, so I think that human nature is that we all like to be a little defiant at times. Some kids more so than others.

Table 4.2 Present orientations

Description	Linked to beliefs in discipline
Human nature: Assuming inherent human traits, such as defiance or rationality.	Rule-breaking reflects inherent behaviours either in all people or in specific groups or individuals and therefore we all need rules and their enforcement. Often reflected in behaviourism and other deterrence theories, although can lead to giving up on certain students assumed to be incorrigible.
Adolescent nature: Traits such as defiance or irrationality are considered inherent to the temporary location of adolescence. Links with developmentalism.	Expectations that students change as they age/ mature, but that they are currently 'trapped' by adolescence. This position leads to disciplinary approaches supporting both guidance and containment. Neglects context except as it may exacerbate inherent traits. Locates adults as knowing young people.
Status hierarchies: Valuing hierarchies based on students' current age and/or status in relation to staff.	Reflected in authoritarian approaches which emphasize hierarchy; although may also be used to support guidance. Locates adults as knowing young people better than they know themselves. Linked to role expectations.
Context: Recognizing students' immediate or past social context.	Reflected in guidance approaches and critical pedagogy. Opens questions of discipline to broader social issues and inequalities. Can become overly deterministic.

JEN (Whitton teacher) '. . . it's a natural, almost human response like, to want [chuckles], to want to not give in to authority or to test authority . . .'[10]

It was quite remarkable how many staff drew on traffic metaphors in their interviews, reinforcing the idea that maintaining order in schools is much like maintaining the order of traffic on roads. From this perspective, rule-breaking is like speeding; many of us do it and hope to get away with it. In making these comparisons, students are understood as being like adults, and school rules are naturalized as top-down and logical, with penalties assumed to deter future infractions. By attributing the same motives to both students who break minor rules and people who fail to follow minor traffic laws (i.e., that rule-breaking is pleasurable or convenient) the context of student infractions is less relevant.

In chapter 2 I explained how many students understood rule-breaking in terms of practical needs. A prominent theme among staff was that students will break rules because they can. Gemini and Jen both suggested that students would rather be doing something else and so they will break rules if they are inconsistently enforced, hard to enforce, or easy to break. For instance, sometimes senior students can skip classes by claiming they are on a 'spare' period, which is difficult for teachers and administrators to track. By reasoning that rules are broken because they can be or because we have an inherent desire to break them, solutions that focus on deterrence become quite logical. Indeed, deterrence of both reoffending and of other students copying an offence was emphasized by many staff, particularly Vice Principal Blair and teachers Joe and Glenn, as a key mechanism to ensure discipline.

Deterrence approaches are to some extent future-oriented as they attempt to influence behaviour in the future, but they also frame young people as rational choice-makers in the present. People are thought to weigh the pros and cons when consciously deciding to break a rule. Can I get away with it? Is it worth it? From this position, the consequences for breaking a rule must be sufficiently swift, sure and significant for an individual to choose no, it's not worth it – hence arguments in favour of zero tolerance. In this context, students follow rules because it is not worth it to break them (Glenn) and they want good relations with staff (Patrick and Glenn).[11] This position assumes that rules are broken or followed based on sober reflection of the pros and cons. As such, it is in some tension with conceptualizations of children or teenagers as irrational or unable to fully think through the consequences of their actions, which I explore in more depth shortly. While we can often hold two contrasting positions such as these, and young people (like adults) can be both rational and irrational, this tension does create challenging contradictions in disciplining teenagers: can they rationally weigh the pros and cons of breaking a rule or not? A focus on assuming human inclinations to defiance also fails to recognize a range of other factors that can impinge on rule-breaking, from classroom context, including teacher assumptions about specific students, to students' personal lives, practical needs and personal traumas.

ADOLESCENCE

In *Beyond Discipline*, Alfie Kohn (1996) is concerned that discipline approaches are often grounded in negative beliefs about young people:

they must be told exactly what to do or there will be chaos, or children are only nice with positive reinforcement, for example. Teenagers often are included in such beliefs about children, but are also defined by beliefs specifically about adolescence. Developmentalists and related stage-based theorists have categorized adolescence as a time of identity development (Erikson 1963) and risk-taking (Steinberg 2007), for example, as young people move away from childhood and towards young adulthood. Adolescents are considered to be in the process of becoming, yet have also been variously described in popular commentary and academic literature as at-risk, peer-focused, irrational, and emotional in the present (Lesko 1996a; Griffin 1993; Raby 2002). Such characterizations are frequently naturalized as hormonal or linked to their developing brains (Payne 2009). It is in part due to such characterizations that school dress and discipline codes involve rules that are directly applied to young people as minors, often covering activities not considered infractions for adults, such as 'horseplay,' throwing snowballs, or public displays of affection.

The staff respondents in this research often used such descriptions to explain why it is that teenagers break rules in the first place: they are forgetful, hormonal, risk-taking, wanting negative attention, weak at decision-making, in the present, wanting to fit in, pushing limits, testing rules, and overly energetic.[12] Six respondents specifically mentioned adolescence as the *primary* reason young people break the rules.

IRON (Whitton teacher): Today they'll follow the rules, tomorrow – I don't know, a hormonal thing – they don't want to follow the rules. The next day, they follow the rules.
I: Yeah? So you think it's just because they're teenagers?
IRON: Yeah! Yeah, I think it's just because they're teenagers.

BARB (Whitton teacher): And that's, that's part of the teenage mind too, that it's here, it's now. Half an hour from now I may be really sorry [chuckles] for what I did. But right now it was really a lot of fun.

LOUIS (Big City principal): Teenagers need to express themselves in a very different way. They need to, uh [pause] yeah, remember, I mean these are, their hormones are raging! [. . .] They're in their teenage years. Their hormones are growing, you know? They're leaving the, they're trying to [pause] the separation from the home. Daddy is no longer the coolest thing, mommy is no longer the coolest thing. Mommy isn't all-knowing, daddy isn't all-knowing anymore. 'I don't want to hold their hands, I don't want to be hanging out with mommy and daddy anymore, I'm cool now!' Rules? Rules are the same thing. 'I know better!'

These comments alternatively suggest that teens fail to follow rules because they are fickle, 'in the moment,' and distinguishing themselves from adult supervision – all naturalized as either due to hormones or their developing minds. Other teachers referenced teen rebellion or deviance, peer pressure, and students testing limits to see what they can get away with. Ironically, adolescence was also referenced as a reason that students *follow* rules, e.g., when Bill (Whitton teacher) suggested that it is because they are attracted to routine and structure.

Such descriptions of adolescence are popular and convincing, yet they also problematically imply an adult opposite that is rational, thoughtful, independent, and conforming which, in turn, legitimizes the need for adults to regulate students, in part through school rules and their enforcement. These processes have a number of potential consequences. First, as I have addressed above, when adolescents are understood as incomplete and immature, they are importantly granted leeway to make mistakes that is not similarly accorded adults and may consequently be less harshly punished. Yet second, understanding adolescence in this way suggests that adults know adolescents better than adolescents understand themselves, consequently undermining the possibility of their legitimate self-representation or grievances. Third, conceptualizations of adolescence are conflated with specific young people. For example, Gottfredson, Gottfredson, and Hybl (1993) suggest that most discipline problems are associated with only a small group of problem youth, an observation that was repeated frequently in my interviews, but staff proceed to explain that 'unsocialized behaviour' is a common feature of adolescence in general. Fourth, institutional processes in turn participate in producing the very forms of adolescence they describe. For instance, through segregating and age-grading, teenagers become more peer-focused (Lesko 2001); and through the imposition of many additional rules and constraints, teenagers are more likely to end up breaking them. Finally, by defining young people through a naturalized adolescence, other contextual contributors to their rule infractions, including any potential staff responsibility, is denied and differential patterns in discipline are left unexplained (Gregory and Mosely 2004). Many of these consequences suggest that adult representations of adolescent angst may not be simply describing a transparent truth but creating understandings of young people that are often, in turn, used to dismiss or contain them.

STATUS HIERARCHIES: THE EXAMPLE OF RESPECT

> BARB (Whitton teacher) [in dealing with a student complaint about a teacher]: I usually end up telling [sigh], telling the students, 'What your teacher did was not right. But [pause] you'll, unfortunately you're not going to win this argument between them. That's [pause] the way of the world, unfortunately.'

Another, related categorization of adolescence as a present orientation references the hierarchical statuses of age, experience, and roles. From this perspective, students are understood as unequal with adults because of their age, lack of experience, and different social roles. This position, resonating with more custodial or traditional beliefs around discipline (Hoy and Weinstein 2006), was rarely overtly stated within codes of conduct I studied, but was occasionally suggested by staff, particularly in arguments against student participation in rule creation. An emphasis on status hierarchy was less directly, though much more frequently evident in how codes of conduct and staff deployed the provocative concept of respect, which I will focus on here.

In many schools mutual respect is the cornerstone of their disciplinary structure. Respect was mentioned in over 90 per cent of the codes of conduct I examined and was also a central concept raised by most staff. Most rules were seen to rest on the underlying premise of respect: respect for staff (e.g., through removing hats, not swearing at teachers), respect for school and surrounding property (e.g., through not littering or vandalizing), respect for others (e.g., through punctuality, respecting differences among students, not making fun of others), and respect for self (e.g., through attendance, dressing appropriately).

Respect can be understood in multiple ways, as explained by David Middleton (2004). 'Rights' or 'human' respect is a kind of respect that everyone is entitled to simply by the very fact of being a person. Calls for students and others in the school to respect each other reflect this position and do not imply status hierarchies. In contrast, 'earned' or 'merit' respect is linked to having *done something* that others respect (Middleton 2004); on this basis, teaching and administrative staff should be granted respect based on their professional roles or based on excelling in these roles. Finally, 'differential' or 'status' respect is based on social custom and can be linked to an ascribed status, such as age, or achieved status; in the latter case, status respect overlaps with earned respect. Each of these forms of respect is evident in school codes of conduct and in staff comments from my interviews. Some school codes of conduct specifically state that everyone is deserving of respect, including the student (rights respect). Many schools also emphasize respect for others when they discuss anti-harassment, anti-bullying, and non-violence policies (rights respect). For many urban schools there is a strong emphasis on respect for diverse cultures; some also address sexual orientation under respect for others. In contrast, frequent emphasis on respect for authority draws on earned or status respect and is framed in terms of social hierarchy, with respect being indicated through obedience. Many school codes of conduct emphasize this respect for authority, e.g., when some schools state that students must be respectful while they are being disciplined.

While respect was a shared concern among staff, they did not all agree on what respect means, nor how it is cultivated. The majority of staff emphasized that students must be respected, with at least five directly stating that young people today require respect in order to be respectful, in part as a form of role-modelling. Four respondents acknowledged that some teachers can be disrespectful towards students and were concerned with this, although one felt that students tend to exaggerate examples of disrespect. Others simply framed the question of respect in terms of inherent values: everyone needs to be treated with respect and dignity. For one Big City principal, Spencer, this was particularly important because of the inherent inequality between adults and students when adults govern the school, a position supported by Thomson and Holland (2002) and Middleton (2004). Spencer was the only participant to talk about the need to specifically define respect. For him, respect was about empathy rather than obedience, and therefore rights respect rather than earned or ascribed respect. This definition foregrounds the key site of division between staff in terms of the concept of respect. Many of the staff mentioned above commented that students need to have respect modelled, through staff following the same rules as the students, for instance. Yet others' views reflected a desire for respect based on status hierarchies. For instance, one participant directly stated that respect is learned through obedience to authority, a position implied by a handful of others – that it is through meaningful rule enforcement and student compliance that students respect the rules and the staff. From this latter perspective, disrespect warrants particularly serious consequences, such as being sent to the office and potential suspension.

Unquestioned respect for authority did not resonate for students, however, and was a source of much frustration for them. When students discussed respect it was most frequently when commenting on the expectation that they respect their teachers no matter what. While most focus groups ultimately chose to put 'respect teachers' into the category of 'good rules' (see Table 2.2, p. 39) this was usually after much debate around the potential unfairness of this rule, opting for a rights respect position over respect premised on professional or ascribed status.

> CARMELLA: I think for that to work the teachers have to respect the students too. Cuz if you have a teacher that's completely biased and rude and talking back, well not talking back, but kinda condescending, it's kind of hard to respect them if they don't respect you.
> WILLY: Yeah, so it depends, I mean you should be respecting teachers, but yeah, the teachers have to respect you. (Big City FG 5)

> JAY: [You shouldn't have to respect teachers] if they don't respect you.
> MATTIAS: Because there are really some teachers who are really un–[pause] worthy of respect.
> CRYSTAL: Yeah, respect should be given as [well as] taken. (Whitton FG 9)

While some participants said that respecting teachers is important because they are older and are educators, most felt that this respect needed to be mutual and were critical of teachers who seemed to disrespect their students.

These student views resonate with those identified by Helen Jones (2002) in her British study of young people's interpretations of respect. Jones found that young people value respect that is shown through listening to their opinions and taking them seriously, recognizing their self-identifications in the present, and accepting that they will change. They value respect that is mutual and developing over time, rather than inherently owed to someone based on their particular position. Following on these findings, Jones suggests that one-way respect for authority is obsolescent and therefore bound to fail because it does not resonate with many young people's (and adults') current cultural values. This position is echoed in research by Thomson and Holland (2002) and Middleton (2004). These findings suggest that obedience based on conventional status hierarchies in the present has little resonance for many students.

Finally, one specific category of respect that arises in school codes of conduct is self-respect, which I would like to develop here, for it also comes to be a present orientation linked to obedience to external rules. About a third of the school codes I studied, and the Ontario *Code of Conduct* introduced in 2001, mentioned self-respect. This part of codes of conduct was mentioned by several staff and a handful of students. The kind of self-respect outlined in these rules is not a form of rights respect, or a recognition of students' own self-worth. Rather, certain rule infractions such as wearing provocative clothing, swearing, or using drugs and alcohol are frequently listed in codes of conduct under concerns with self-respect, yoking self-respect to compliance. It is implied then that students have self-respect and deserve respect from others *unless they behave otherwise.* Thus, self-respect exists through meeting external criteria rather than students' intrinsic worth as people with moral rights or based on their own personal achievements. Furthermore, by emphasizing that self-respect requires certain behaviour, a justification is provided for undermining another rule, 'respect for others,' if the individuals involved are assumed to disrespect themselves. For example, if students who wear provocative dress are considered to lack self-respect, then responsibility for their marginalization is shifted onto themselves rather than sexual harassment or 'slut-bashing' from others (Tanenbaum, 1999). Finally, it is interesting that use of drugs and alcohol is presented as incompatible with self-respect. Arguably, certain sexual practices and alcohol consumption are pitched to Western young people as markers of adulthood. To respect oneself then, a student must do so *as an adolescent* – according to rules specific to adolescence (Raby 2005) and not to adulthood.

Respect is a central concept to many codes of conduct and to stakeholders' beliefs about school rules. It can be, and is, deployed in ways that emphasize students' present equality and rights, but it is also used as a primary device to reinforce present age-based status hierarchies and obedience in that respect can be either earned or lost through following the rules. Furthermore, like other traits such as responsibility, respect is framed as something that students are both expected to demonstrate in the present and as something students are to learn. For some, this learning happens through modelling, for others through obedience to authority. Finally, while calls for respect for others reflect a communitarian spirit, they potentially conflict with emphasis on self-respect that is premised on individualized obedience.

Lastly, in addition to foci on human nature, adolescence, and status hierarchies, a consideration of context reflects a present orientation to school rules. Discussions of student rule-breaking that emphasize human nature or adolescent development tend to concentrate on the individual adolescent rather than the wider social context of students' lives. While overall teachers and administrators were much more likely to explain rule-breaking in terms of such individualizing approaches, context arose briefly in a number of interviews, usually in reference to the limited context of family or peers rather than structural inequality or the organization of the school. At various points staff spoke about 'problem students' lacking good parenting, especially good guidelines and modelling for behaviour, for instance, a common pattern also noted by Cothran et al. (2009), Gregory and Mosely (2004), and Bowditch (1993). Overall, attention to family, community, and even global contexts of students' lives locates them in the present in a way that recognizes that students' actions at school are not solely those of autonomous or developing individuals but people whose actions reflect broader issues.

Six Whitton teachers and one vice-principal mentioned underlying personal issues as contextual factors contributing to rule-breaking. As vice-principal Blair argued, 'I really believe people are basically good people but when a student is acting out against a teacher there's a reason for it.' Blair even raised issues related to socio-economic status and its potential effect on social skills, a concern discussed by only one other respondent, Jim (Big City teacher). For Laura and Glenn, students might be seeking negative attention because they are not getting attention at home. Martha and Iron did not focus on more personal issues such as home life, but observed a link between students' academic difficulty in class and breaking the rules, a pattern that has been heavily theorized by those working in critical pedagogy, and which is pursued further in chapter 6. Finally, Laura alone suggested that young people are currently dealing with stressors related to the broader, global context of warfare and environmental issues. She also felt that many problem students are dealing with biological factors such as fetal alcohol syndrome, arising from their family context.

Half of the Big City participants also made some kind of reference to the broader context of students' lives and the consequent need to attend to this difference when allocating consequences. For Louis (Big City principal), for example, personal life experiences or mental problems, must be considered.

> When you're dealing with some hard [inaudible], school rules is the last thing on their priorities, because maybe they're living alone, or their family life is so awful? Or they're abused, or there are all sorts [pause] a myriad of other things [. . .] That's why I say, you know what, you can have general rules, but you've got to do it the most consistently. But in any rules there's always exceptionalities [. . .] because, if the kid is going through a psychotic episode, do you really think enforcement of [the] uniform is the most important piece there?

Yet this argument came immediately after Louis contended that there can be no discretion in enforcing the rules: 'There is no discretion. If you're going to have a rule, you're gonna have a rule.' While this example is particularly clear, as I discuss in the next chapter, almost all respondents at some point emphasized the need for consistency alongside deference to such contextual issues. Notably, however, almost no one problematized the context of the rules themselves – the school – as potentially contributing to student rule-breaking.

This section has reviewed diverse logics used by staff to understand student rule-breaking. Rule-breaking and enforcement is understood in terms of future orientations around guidance into becoming certain kinds of adults and related student development, beside beliefs about young people in the present in terms of human nature, adolescence, status hierarchies, and their lived context. By examining such a range of staff beliefs, the complexity of staff logics and disciplinary processes is laid bare.

Conflicting Beliefs

> Young people are both 'imprisoned in their time (age) and out of time (abstracted) and thereby denied power over decisions or resources' (Lesko 1996b, 456).

This chapter has examined various approaches to understanding what discipline is or should be, with a particular emphasis on how philosophies of school rules and why students break them reflect diverse understandings of discipline but also of young people – as beings developing into the future and beings in the present, as adolescents and as human beings, as essentialized and as contextualized. These multiple approaches reflect and reproduce tensions, and even contradictions, in how school rules are conceptualized and deployed.

A primary tension arises between desires for immediate obedience alongside aspirations for current and future self-discipline. Immediate obedience is directly supported by school rules and staff comments about them. It is also indirectly evident through limited explanations of the rules within conduct codes, the lack of discussion of positive reinforcements either in codes of conduct or among staff, an ongoing emphasis on automatic consequences for rule infractions (even under the new purview of 'progressive discipline'), the top-down presentation of rules to students, and the absence of students' genuine involvement in shaping school rules. By far the majority of the staff involved in this research can be characterized as having traditional, or custodial, views of school rules in which rules are believed to be about providing structure and authority over young people, and focusing on obedience, order, and safety (Hoy and Weinstein 2006).

Despite this concentration on obedience, many other comments directly and indirectly advocate self-discipline. Some staff emphasized more liberal approaches to discipline and many codes of conduct began with a preamble gesturing towards developing self-discipline. Both staff and codes of conduct also emphasized cultivating present and future responsibility, often through the language of choice-making. These desires to cultivate self-discipline do not replace top-down consequences and emphasis on obedience to authority but become part of an 'embodied logic' in which multiple, shifting, situation-specific beliefs are used to understand and enforce student discipline (Millei and Raby 2010).[13]

This embodied logic includes a wide range of other discourses, as this chapter has outlined. As adolescents, young people are conceptualized as unpredictable, irrational, and out of control but also beyond the irrationality of childhood and developing into adults of the future. As young people, they are considered liable to make mistakes, unequal to adults and in need of deference yet as human beings, they are conceptualized as rational thinkers who are also inclined to push against the rules. As located within specific and broader life situations, they are contextualized. Finally, young people are understood as both unchanging and malleable. They are unchanging because of essential features of what it means to be adolescent, or human, or to have life experiences or health problems (such as fetal alcohol syndrome). They are also malleable because they are in the process of growing up and presumably respond to consequences.

While at times these various discourses can provide leeway for students through guidance, understanding, and recognition of their own context and agency, arguably these diverse discourses are most commonly deployed to increase authority over young people, even when these discourses are contradictory. Thus as irrational beings, young people should obey the rules and defer to authority for their own safety and socialization into acceptable ways of being; similarly as rational beings, young people should make the right, responsible choices and obey the rules. Most schools require that students face immediate consequences for what they do in the present. From talking to staff it became clear that sometimes these immediate consequences are about guidance for the future, sometimes about displaying deference to authority, sometimes about deterrence predicated on a rational weighing of options, and sometimes about retribution or punishment. Codes of conduct, and staff understandings and applications of them, blend assumptions of developing, dependent, un-self-regulated teenagers in need of guidance and protection with consequences that assume their ability to make rational choices, to take responsibility, and to self-regulate (Fallis and Opotow 2003).

What are some effects of these tensions? For the most part they remain unacknowledged as they reflect tensions that persist more broadly within current conceptualizations of adolescence, tensions that allow adults to easily make statements about adolescence that often categorize and dismiss what teenagers do (Raby 2002). These tensions are also facilitated by the unequal position of adolescents in relationship to adults, particularly as almost every understanding of young people and discipline, both overtly controlling and more humanistic, can be deployed to support the overarching ideas of care-taking and concern for students' futures. Demands for obedience are in turn supported by staff responsibilities for student safety and a certain understanding of young people's education premised on order and attentiveness. These flexible beliefs and status hierarchies, alongside culturally normative individualizing, also allow staff to see students' problems as internal,

or linked to their home lives. There is little focus on classroom dynamics or teachers' behaviours as explanation, or on taking apart conflicting beliefs about discipline (Brophy 2006; Cothran, Kulinna, and
Garrahy 2009). Rather, ideas that are often in conflict with each other
are deployed seamlessly, often to legitimize control (Millei and Raby
2010).

Tensions are also eased through dividing students into two categories: the good student and the problem student. The good student is an
appropriate and willing receptacle for guidance towards self-discipline
while the problem student is contained and punished in the present
(Millei and Raby 2010; Hannah-Moffat 2000). Others' research on
teacher beliefs supports this contention, as punishment is considered
more appropriate when students are considered aggressive, disruptive,
and defiant (behaviours which may be seen as more immediately dangerous), while help strategies are considered more appropriate when
students are shy, anxious, rejected, or low-achieving (Brophy 2006).
A potentially destructive consequence of this process, Fallis and Opotow
(2003) argue, is that certain students become morally excluded; understandings of fairness do not apply in the same way to them because
they are considered unworthy of the effort. Fallis and Opotow contend
that through such moral exclusion, students who break the rules are
seen as entirely deserving of the outcomes, (e.g., because it is seen as
their fault), or certain students are seen as inherently 'bad' (or even
a whole school of students is 'bad') rather than being seen as young
people who are marginalized. Thus, Fallis and Optow argue schools
become 'locations of systematic violence' (114) as violence is embedded
in the *status quo*. The effects are felt primarily by the most powerless
who either endure a system which may psychologically deaden them
or who may seek relief through rule-breaking, especially skipping,[14] or
even dropping out. I have already addressed this spectre of the repeat
offender in chapter 3 and we will return to it again in the next few
chapters.

Finally, there are several things missing in the general staff understandings of young people's rule-breaking. First, despite occasional
reference to family context, scholastic achievement, and class backgrounds, staff philosophies did not account for how patterns of student rule-breaking vary by race and gender, with Black and male
students more likely to get into trouble than others. Gregory and
Mosely (2004) found a similar pattern in their qualitative interviews

with nineteen teachers in an American high school. Teachers would explain rule-breaking as rebellion and lack of control due to adolescence, for instance, leading Gregory and Mosely to ask: Why then is there a gendered and racialized pattern to students rebelling and being out of control? Teachers would also individualize problems by arguing that low-achieving students get frustrated and act out or that certain students bring a family or cultural background that did not fit well with the school. Gregory and Mosely conclude that teachers tend to look to both generalized and individualized explanations for student rule-breaking without taking into account intersections such as race, cultural differences, or gender, even though there are very noticeable disparities in rule-breaking related to these criteria. Also in each of these cases, the student and never the school itself is considered the problem.

Second, despite some important gestures towards context in attempts to understand student rule-breaking, there is little room within school and staff philosophies of rules, or broader understandings of adolescents, to recognize that young people can and should have formal avenues to challenge school rules, or that they may have legitimate reasons to do so. A focus on students as future-oriented denies young people's legitimate voices and needs in the present (James 2004). While an understanding of children in the present opens up possibilities to recognize young people's rights, agentic capacities, responsibilities, and abilities to participate in their immediate lives (Such and Walker 2005; France 1998; Devine 2002; Roche 1999), this recognition was quite absent in most of the interviews I conducted with school staff.[15]

For some it might seem easy to simply dismiss students' complaints: students don't know what's good for them, school isn't supposed to entertain, or students are being immature, selfish, or just plain bad. Meanwhile, educational staff are themselves overburdened with limited resources, large classes, difficult students, and unwieldy, top-down curricula. But it is important to remember that students have little choice about being there, little say in how or what they are taught, are understood in ways that undermine possibilities for legitimate grievance, are treated as a homogeneous group, and have little institutionalized power. Yet students can be thoughtful, recognize their own responsibilities, and present legitimate concerns (Fallis and Opotow 2003) – I and others have seen numerous examples of this in various research projects which I will present in chapter 9.

In the meantime, by focusing on obedience both in students' present and in their future, individualizing or naturalizing students' problem behaviours, and disconnecting discipline issues from those of pedagogy, discrimination, and/or structure, schools fail to consider that underlying institutional problems or conflicts ever affect student behaviour.

5 Consistency and Context

I'll suggest that there's not a principal alive probably, principal or vice-principal, who doesn't have concerns about the consistency with which a staff does or does not apply or enforce the rules. (Chicago, Whitton vice-principal)

For the teachers and administrators I interviewed, the primary concern to rise again and again was the consistent enforcement of the rules, with most lamenting a lack of consistency within their schools. This concern with consistency is also raised within many classroom management texts (e.g., see Emmer, Evertson, and Worsham 2003; Porter 1996; Gottfredson, Gottfredson, and Hybl 1993). As this chapter will show, however, consistency quickly becomes a complicated goal, particularly against the backdrop of the diverse understandings of discipline and student rule-breaking outlined in chapter 4. Should expectations for behaviour be consistent across all circumstances? Should the same standards be applied to all students? And should the consequences be the same across misdemeanours? Through a deeper investigation of staff comments, classroom management advice, student voices, and provincial legislation, the balance between consistency and flexibility becomes quite a challenge, suggesting that simply resorting to more rigorous enforcement does not work.

Staff Views: By the Book?

For many teachers and administrators, it is important that rules and their consequences be clear and applied 'by the book' – there is no point in having rules if they are not enforced by *all* staff in response to the infractions of *all* students. There were repeated comments, across most interviews, that greater consistency is needed in this regard, between teaching staff and also in administrative follow-up. Many were very frustrated with colleagues who were seen as not enforcing rules. Why this emphasis on consistency? When did staff feel it was appropriate to take context into account? Of the thirty-one staff members interviewed across the two regions, half (fifteen) were univocal: consistency must always be of foremost importance. Another five shared the ideal of consistency but noted that they have occasionally failed to enforce a particular rule. Others were a little more flexible and eight specifically emphasized the need to address the context of a rule violation, particularly in terms of the specific situation of the student(s) in question.

Consistency Is Vital

For those embracing consistency, it was linked to a number of concerns. Although many administrators suggested that non-compliance in enforcement occurred with only a minority of teachers, just over half of the respondents felt that there is a great deal of difference among staff members in terms of their rule enforcement and many were angry at their colleagues for failing to enforce certain rules. They felt that non-enforcement undermined the rule itself, fostered disobedience and left them to be the 'heavies.'

> MARIA (Whitton teacher): You know? [. . .] Everybody has to be on the same page, that's what I found. Even if you have one teacher not [. . .] following the rules you've set out or the school has set out, it's not going to work. And it just happened so often.

> TEACHER X (Whitton): They have rules, guidelines, but teachers are not enforcing them so those who do are considered mean. Teachers need to enforce them.

> MARTHA (Whitton teacher): But I'll watch teachers walk by this kid and I have to be the hard-ass that says 'take off your [sun]glasses.'

Porter (1996) similarly argues that inconsistency is an issue when teachers fail to detect misdemeanours, either because they cannot see and enforce everything or because they are not invested in specific rules. Certainly frustration with other staff was most evident when three teachers suggested that other staff simply 'don't care.' Several staff members were a little more understanding, suggesting that teachers want to avoid confrontations and may sometimes even be intimidated by students.[1] A lack of others' enforcement, in turn, created a broader spiral of passivity, with rules unenforced by some because they were tired of feeling like the only ones repeating the rules, particularly when they were busy trying to focus on their teaching. A number thus spoke of the need to 'pick their battles.' Finally, six also raised the issue of administrative support for the enforcement of rules, with several suggesting that they are less likely to enforce a rule if they do not expect such support. As Sandy described, 'I know of one teacher who – when she reported [inappropriate dress] to the vice-principal – did not get support [. . .] And, since then, has pretty much turned a blind eye to anything else unless it's been truly, truly indecent. You know, but she thought, "What's the point? I mean, I've tried to do what I think is right, I'm getting old, I'm getting close to retirement. Forget it." '

I have illustrated that staff felt it harder for everyone if certain staff did not enforce the rules. It was also assumed that the rule is only as good as its enforcement.

> PATRICK (Whitton teacher): Whether you're in love with the rule or not, because it exists as a [pause] as an example of students not having to follow a rule if you don't enforce it, which calls into question everything you're trying to do.

> SPENCER (Big City principal): Um, I think that we have rules that we're really not very good at enforcing, which is probably – in my mind – worse than having rules that [pause] worse than not having a rule. Um, because I think there's nothing that destroys our credibility quite as quickly as having a rule and then not enforcing it, as far as kids are concerned.

From this perspective, it is only through consistent enforcement of the school rules that students learn to comply and the rules have any kind of weight. It is for this reason that two strong supporters of consistency also argued that the rules should therefore be kept to a minimum. Consistency is also thought to provide clear structure and guidance for students. It means they know what to expect and that they will see the rules as fair – a position well reflected in classroom management advice (e.g., see Emmer, Evertson, and Worsham 2003; Gottfredson, Gottfredson, and Hybl 1993). Finally, two participants linked consistent enforcement to the retention of staff authority, a position echoed by Dickar (2008), who is concerned that differential enforcement between classrooms teaches students that rules are malleable and school authority is weak.

Attention to Context in Practice

Yet despite such strong feelings in favour of consistency expressed by many of the staff interviewed for this book, and convincing reasons to support such consistency, almost every single respondent cited a rule which they were unlikely to regularly enforce. Many teachers and administrators who argued adamantly in favour of enforcing rules consistently across the school, later, in another part of the interview, suggested that often the specific context of infractions must be taken into consideration. For example, Chicago, whose quote on the importance of consistency opens this chapter, also felt that students are sophisticated enough to recognize that context should not be ignored. Iron (Whitton teacher), who tended to frame himself as quite strict and held the position that 'small' rules should be policed with vigour in order to prevent more serious infractions,[2] later said that first-time offenders should be treated with some flexibility and at another point suggested that there are always grey areas and that 'kids are kids' so they will always make mistakes. Similarly, despite Maria's assertion above that consistency among teachers is vital, particularly when addressing lateness, she supported her own non-enforcement of the dress code and the importance of teachers' autonomy within their classes:

> So, even though everyone has the policy in the school, it just depends on how much you use it. So it works if you use it. And there are probably other rules that I probably don't enforce that other teachers do. Just because you have to decide what's important in your class.

These examples illustrate some of the various ways in which staff who advocated for consistency also selectively attended to context.

One reason for such flexibility was that sometimes student backgrounds were considered relevant. For example, a number of staff argued that repeat offenders should be treated more seriously, a philosophy embedded in the provincial policy of 'progressive discipline,' which I will discuss later in this chapter. Similarly, three respondents mentioned that rules should shift for special education students, a caveat also mentioned in provincial policy. The second reason was based on certain kinds of rule-breaking. For instance, several respondents argued that flexibility was more acceptable when more minor rules were violated. The third reason was in the context of a specific incident. As Chicago explained:

> . . . every student is unique, their circumstances are unique, and the context of every situation is *completely* unique. A fight one way can be completely different from a fight the other way.

The final reason addressed diversity across classroom contexts. While students were far more likely to argue that rules should shift across types of classes (see below), three of the staff who generally supported consistency suggested that certain rules were more important in certain classes (such as no backpacks in chemistry, for safety reasons) than in others (such as listening to music in art class).

Staff comments muddy strict adherence to consistency, suggesting that there are points when consistency is important and others when it is not. Emmer et al. (2003) similarly argue that it is quite appropriate to expect different kinds of behaviour for different tasks, but that it is important to be consistent *within* a certain kind of activity (e.g., during seat work), a point echoed by Sprick (2006). These points indicate why blanket rules that are expected to be applied across all situations equally can be a problem. There are also different kinds of inconsistency. For Emmer et al., while it is sometimes necessary to treat certain students, such as students with special needs, with more leniency, inconsistency becomes problematic when it arises because of unreasonable rules, insufficient monitoring of students, or when teachers just do not care about enforcing a particular rule.

A Philosophy of Context

As I have described, most staff advocated the ideal of consistency but also noted particular contexts which could warrant flexibility. However, about a third argued much more strongly in favour of attending to context by acknowledging factors such as those mentioned above but grounding them in their overall philosophy regarding school rules and their enforcement. Several expanded a focus on classroom context to argue, like Maria above, that teachers should generally have the leeway to determine the rules of their own classes, for example. Others broadened attention to the context of students' lives in determining consequences of rule violations, a point raised in the previous chapter.

> DYLAN (Whitton teacher): . . . sometimes you know a kid can just be having a rotten day and that happens too, you know? Woke up on the wrong side of the bed or whatever, it just seems to me. I don't think it's malicious – like there's no intent behind it to try to tick you off. It's something that happens and then things just snowball and escalate.

> LAUREL (Whitton teacher): . . . but these kids have a lot going [on] outside this building, an awful lot. And teachers don't necessarily get to know that for the kid.

For these staff members, flexibility was vital. Indeed, two specifically argued that there are times when it is more *substantially* consistent to treat students differently based on their situations. As Luraleen explained:

> I think it's a responsibility to explain to those kids that you know, that [pause] the consequences match the behaviour and the individual that did the behaviour. And if I was having a marathon race, and I had a kid over here who was uh [pause] paraplegic and this one who's fully able-bodied, I would certainly not expect the same results from both. And, in order to make it fair, I have to somehow give the other child some help, and the skills and the tools in which to work so that we're looking at a level playing field.

In this instance Luraleen drew on the language of equality of condition over more surface-level equality across individuals and she felt that students understand and accept this logic. For this third of the staff respondents who favoured context over consistency, their approach to consistency was itself contextualized. The position held by these staff members is also reflected in some of the more humanistic approaches to classroom management which specifically advocate that students' individual situations be taken into account and consequences for misconduct be adjusted to best fit their needs (Jones and Jones 2007; Porter

1996). Of course, such attention to context raises the question of who determines when and how such circumstances should be taken into account.

The Ongoing Tensions

Overall, despite divergent philosophies, most respondents at some point suggested that it is important to take students' individual circumstances into account, such as their home situations (i.e., whether they have an abusive home situation) or the circumstances of a specific infraction. Similarly, some teachers spoke about their own occasional bad moods or misunderstandings that led them to overreact. Almost all respondents suggested that there are extenuating circumstances to many rule infractions, but staff differed in the breadth of contexts they would consider and in their underlying philosophical beliefs about context. This tension between consistency and context is clearly linked to the rules themselves. Is it worth it to have such detailed school or school board rules related to dress, hats, and so forth when it is the enforcement of these rules that seems to most challenge teachers? Do disagreements and burnout in the enforcement of minor rules ultimately undermine staff authority when it comes to the bigger ones?

As indicated above, staff spoke of 'picking their battles' in the face of multiple demands on their time and their primary focus on teaching. Further, as Spencer and others noted, a rule is only as good as its enforcement. For this reason, two respondents advocated for simpler rules, a position echoed when staff members tended to prioritize the enforcement of major rules over minor ones, and one advocated codifying 'wiggle' room into the rules themselves: 'Because then you're not seeming like you're going against what's written in black and white' (Gemini, Whitton teacher). Keeping rules to a minimum, keeping them simple, and keeping them flexible thus emerged as possible ways to help bolster consistent enforcement. Finally, central to teachers enforcing the rules was that they must either 'buy into' the rule itself or accept the idea that rules must be enforced even when they disagree with them. For instance, several respondents noted that in their schools, the hat rule was a success because of wholesale staff support for the rule. This final observation in turn supports communication and rule-negotiation with staff members, which many teachers in this study felt was lacking in their schools (see Blase and Blase 1997).

Students' Concerns with Context

Students had a somewhat different view of consistency and context than staff: the context of a rule infraction needs greater attention than a hard adherence to consistency, and differences in rules across schools and teachers is, for most, acceptable. But students also identified limits to such flexibility.

There were various ways in which context was important to the students in this study. First, they were particularly attentive to the context of a transgression. For example, as I already touched on in chapter 3, several groups were quite critical of the 'no fighting' rule in which anyone involved in a fight will be suspended.

I: OK, no fighting.
SADDAM: That's not fair.
MARIAN: How the hell is that not fair?
LALA: You have a right to fight if someone fights with you . . . (Big City FG 4)

MARIO: But if someone hits you, then [the rules say that] you gotta just stand there [said with some exasperation] and not hit them back and if you hit them back, then you get expelled . . . (Big City FG 9)

These students felt that there are different forms of fighting and that fighting in self-defence is different from initiating a fight. This question of context also links back to the discussion of practicality in chapter 2. Students frequently explained rule infractions as resulting from their practical needs, needs which they framed as contextually relevant. Big City students were especially likely to discuss context in this way, arguing that sometimes reasons for lateness and even skipping classes are quite legitimate (e.g., due to late buses in the former and an upcoming exam in the latter). Of course, one of the challenges for staff in such situations is determining what specifically happened in a fight or the legitimacy of a student's excuse.

Second, while administrators frequently discussed the need to treat the school as a homogeneous space sharing the same rules across sections, areas, and times, students understood the school as divided by time and space, where the same rules should not apply all the time and in all places. They felt that the distinct geographic spaces of the school, free time versus class time, and specific class content should influence when certain rules are in force. For instance, some rules made sense to students in the classroom but not the hallway[3] or outside. This was particularly the case when they discussed the use of personal music devices and cell phones (see Domitrek and Raby 2008). While a recent trend has been to ban all cell phones from the school, students vigorously debated the use of cell phones through this question of context, as this lively excerpt illustrates:

> ɪ: No cell phones. Why is that a 'stupid' rule?
> LINDSEY: That's a good rule.
> MARK: [at the same time] No it's not! You're working, what the hell you need a cell phone for?
> AMY: If you're in class turn it off, but if you are in the hallway/
> ɪ: Sorry? [Too many people talking at once] [Everyone laughs]
> LINDSEY: Cell phones don't work in hallways.
> MARK: Well why would you need it anyways, you're working! [Yells] You're doing your work, you're learning!
> AMY: You're learning in a classroom.
> JAMIE: Trust me, I got my cell phone on me when I am at school, still/
> STEVEN: But what about lunch, when you are outside?
> AMY: Yeah you're at lunch and you're outside [but] my teachers say 'turn it off.'
> LINDSEY: No you're allowed to have it outside, they can't say shit!
> AMY: In [school name inaudible] they can.
> JAMES: Cell phones don't work in school anyways.
> ɪ: We have mixed feelings about cell phones in this room
> JAMIE: Yes [others say 'yes'] (Whitton FG 2 – with much talking over each other during this conversation)

Students overwhelmingly considered it inappropriate to have electronic devices on and in use when a teacher was actually teaching a lesson. This was considered rude, but also personally detrimental to students who would be missing out on their education. However, many saw it as perfectly acceptable to be able to listen to music or talk on a cell phone during lunch, which students consider personal time, and in areas that are not teaching areas, such as the halls, the cafeteria, and outdoors. They also saw listening to music as beneficial during certain class times, particularly during seat work or while drawing in art class – a position that they found many teachers accommodated informally.

JASON: I think in any class it should be [al]right [that] you can listen to music, as long as there's not a lesson. All my teachers found that I focus on my work more when I have my CD player. So my math teacher asks me everyday 'where's your CD player?' After her lesson, she tells me I can listen to it. (Whitton FG 9)

BEN: I know some of our art classes and stuff and drama and music, they let you have them. The teachers let you listen to them cuz it's like creative, it helps you be more creative, so . . . (Whitton FG 8)

In these latter cases, music was seen as helping students in their concentration or creativity and they were frustrated when it was disallowed. The importance of recognizing differences between kinds of classes was also acknowledged in terms of swearing (OK in drama or shop) and backpacks (OK in a large classroom but not a small one), in each case prioritizing the intent behind the rule over its universal application.

Third, there were several instances in which students discussed situations where misconduct should be treated differently based on the situation for the particular student. There were a few examples where this was discussed in terms of students with special needs.

I: OK so what about um, do you think the rules get enforced in the same way for all the students?
[. . .]
THE FERG: The ones that have like special needs, because they really can't. . . [explains term 'special needs'] like they can't understand the rules. [The Ferg then describes a particular boy in their school who will start swearing a lot when provoked.] They'll just be like '[student's name], watch your mouth' or 'watch your language.' And he's like 'OK, sorry,' and then he'll like do it again in like, the next classroom. But they don't really say anything because he doesn't/
BACON BOY: He doesn't understand/
THE FERG: he doesn't understand it. (Whitton FG 7)

In another instance, students discussed the unfairness of teachers favouring students who are doing well already when it is other students who need such advantages. As Bibi explained, 'I'm talking about what about those students that are falling through the cracks and that need the extra help and [don't] need you to favour *other* students that are already up there, that are already making their way, right, that are already actually at the performance [level] they need to be.' For the most part, however, students were less likely to discuss occasions when individual students should be treated unequally based on their backgrounds or situations. This may be partly due to their much more frequent focus on discussing instances of favouritism and discrimination.[4]

Favouritism and Discrimination

Despite their accommodation of context, students were quite concerned with what they perceived as instances of favouritism and discrimination, issues that staff were far less likely to acknowledge. About a third of staff felt that the rules are not always applied fairly across students, with Whitton teachers talking about students sometimes being favoured according to extracurricular involvement and Big City teachers suggesting that some discrimination occurs based on grades and on race. For instance, Sandy (Big City teacher) observed that 'some of the kids who are, you know, positively contributing members of the community, or they're doing various kinds of things [pause]. When their dress is a little questionable it's [pause] it's overlooked.' The other two thirds, however, felt that the rules are applied fairly across students, except in cases of repeat offenders. This was particularly the case among Big City staff, most of whom argued that there is little to no discrimination in the application of rules and in the rare event that a staff member did cite discrimination, it was individualized to certain (older!) teachers, or to the fact that people just do not always get along.

Students, on the other hand, routinely perceived favouritism and discrimination in rule enforcement. Students across focus groups, although particularly in Whitton, critically noted that certain students are favoured by some teachers and administrators and others are not. Reflecting the pattern of staff comments, Whitton students tended to note discrimination based on student dress and extracurricular involvements while Big City students primarily discussed disciplinary inequality in terms of grades and race. Gill's concerns about dress reflected those mentioned by other students:

Yeah, people who dress differently, like if you dress like gangster or whatever, like thuggy, they will, like, anything you do wrong, if you like

talk, they will send you down to the office and maybe, like, someone
dressed like me, like, they don't care, I can do anything basically. (Big
City FG 2)

Gill's comment points to the meanings that are placed on student dress
which in turn affect how students are treated. As Gill observed, while
students often felt that the context of a rule infraction should be taken
into account, they were sensitive to the selective enforcement of rules
for particular groups of students. Indeed, to them it was such selective
enforcement that undermined the legitimacy of the rules themselves
and trust in staff to enforce them fairly. In addition to dress, students
commonly observed that 'good' students tended to get away with rule
violations, with 'good' students including those who were popular,
members of students' council, athletes or cheerleaders, high academic
achievers, and friends of teachers/administrators.[5] For the most part
such favouritism was framed as problematic, even when it worked in
their interest:

> PATRICIA: I was on student council for a lot of years and so the teachers
> really like me a lot, like I am one of the favourite students but it's really
> unfair [girls laugh]. No it's extremely unfair cuz I am no better than any
> other student. Like I've broken rules, I've done all the stuff but [. . .] if
> you get on student council you're pretty much good for high school
> [laughs] [girls laugh] because they look at that as something better and
> we get benefits and stuff, like when we have motivational speakers we
> get private meetings with them and we get to go to camps and stuff that
> no one else gets to go to – it's pretty bad, like it's not fair at all. (Whit-
> ton FG 1)

Arguably, just as certain school rules reflect middle class constructions
of value, so do such categories as 'good' and 'bad' student, determined
by involvement in organized school events, comfort with staff, and
good grades, which can reflect access to cultural and social capital. Recall that cultural capital involves familiarity and ease with the dominant values, skills, dispositions, and so forth that are socially rewarded;
social capital involves the institutional and group connections that can
be mobilized as resources and ultimately converted into economic capital (Bourdieu 2001). In Whitton, student council was recognized as an
especially powerful source of favouritism. As observed by Jason in FG
9, 'They get treated like gold.' In Big City, students who were strong

academically seemed to be particularly favoured, quite likely as teachers tend to interpret good grades as compliance with the student role (Rollock 2007).

As the flip-side to favouritism, a number of students observed the over-policing of other students, particularly students who fell into three distinct categories. First, some groups suggested that students who are weaker academically are more likely to be disciplined by staff. Hoy and Weinstein (2006) cite various studies that have similarly found students to be very aware of differential treatment of students based on high and low achievement. Such perceptions are supported by Oakes's classic examination of streaming in high school which argues that such public categorization processes then lead groups of students to be valued unequally (1985), with disproportionate emphasis on discipline among students in the low achievement stream. Others have also argued that students and schools that are considered lower achieving are more likely scrutinized and disciplined, particularly where achievement intersects with race and/or class (Brown 2003; Dickar 2008; Ferguson 2000). Second, students who seemingly belonged to a particular subculture, such as stoners, punks, goths, skaters, or politically active teens, were seen to be disproportionately disciplined, especially in Whitton.

> I: Angelina, you were saying that um, that there are some things like physical appearance, that leads to people getting in trouble more. So what specifically are you thinking of?
> ANGELINA: Um [pause] people that – I don't really wanna label people as like, just saying 'punk' or just saying like . . .
> TETRAD: I know what you mean.
> ANGELINA: . . .'hardcore' or something. (Whitton FG 6)

> BETTY: At my school they have that same [dress-related] rule only they don't enforce it. The only people they enforce it with are people that um, like the principals didn't like. 'You're wearing all black, you're not allowed to wear that.' (Whitton FG 9)

In such instances, students standing out as different in dress or style were thought to suffer the consequences. This pattern may in part arise as such subcultural self-representations are more easily perceived by staff as examples of students bringing their 'street' cultures into the school (Dickar 2008). For example, one Whitton staff member suggested that subcultural styles, specifically punk, can be intimidating to other students and are therefore unacceptable, reinforcing a narrow, 'acceptable' norm. Finally, discrimination on the basis of race and/or culture was raised in almost all Big City groups, as well as the new immigrant group in Whitton, a pattern to be examined in the next chapter.

Beyond these specific patterns many students, especially Big City ones, simply emphasized that teachers play favourites – if they like you then you can get away with breaking rules, and if they don't like you, you can't. Students were concerned about these examples, partly because they felt that students who are negatively labelled find it hard to escape their categorization, but mostly because such practices were simply unfair. Students felt that administrators should be attentive to the specific context of rule-breaking, yet this attention clearly needs to be carefully weighed against fostering perceptions of favouritism or discrimination (a concern also expressed by staff). Students saw teachers who surrendered to their prejudices as being hypocritical when schools put so much emphasis on tolerance and inclusiveness – ultimately students' observations of such hypocrisy seemed to undermine their overall confidence in the rules and their fair enforcement.

Difficult Rules such as Bullying

Students also expressed concern over certain rules that they felt are important but difficult to enforce, and therefore insufficiently and inconsistently applied. At the top of this list were interpersonal or relational rules around rumours and bullying, some of the few rules that students saw as *for* them rather than *against* them. While respondents tended to relay experiences with bullying that occurred during elementary school, most students noted that bullying did not cease in high school, but rather it became more covert and psychological than physical (except as described by the street youth in Whitton FG 2 and by several groups in Big City which were more likely to be involved in fighting). But students' previous experiences with bullying and the lack of teacher intervention made a lasting impact on students and they saw this as a very important area where adults need to exercise *more* authority. For Nicole, this issue was central:

> I remember in elementary school somebody was, like, bullying me and I'd be crying and I'd go to a teacher and say, you know, 'so and so did this'

and they'd be like 'deal with it yourself' or something. And it's just like, you know, you're the teacher, you're the authority figure. You have this job [and] part of your job description is to help protect us and make our school environment a safe place. [pause] And I also think in high school it gets – like, when you're on the playground you see people like physically fighting and that and it's obvious. But I think in high school, anyways our high school, like for sure it has a kinda, like there's more like psychological. There's some teachers who will do something but there are just so many who will brush it off and say, 'You're in high school now you can deal with it.' And it's like 'no, you can't.' Like, like how many kids do you, [you] hear all these stories like Columbine, kids who have been teased and come in with a gun? (Whitton FG 4)

Inaction around bullying was also noted within Big City focus groups. For example, as Lily (Big City FG 8) stated:

That's not like, they always say it, but they don't ever take action to it, I mean they're like 'OK guys, no bullying when you're walking the hallways when you see kids, help them out, blah blah' but when actually something comes to it, they don't take as much action as they did when they said the rule itself so that should be like, what's the word I'm looking for? It should be more enforced, there we go.

Bullying is not an easy thing for staff to address, of course, as it is often covert, but once again students' concerns in this area underscore the value they place on certain rules over others. As with the staff, the students felt that greater consistency is needed when considering more important rules, and they included bullying in this category. That said, as will become evident in the discussion of sexual harassment in chapter 7, while it may be easy to say 'no bullying,' a determination of exactly what kind of behaviour is problematic can be difficult.

Teachers' Own Rules

DYLAN (Whitton teacher): You know what, pencils! Drives me crazy too! Certain people [say] 'OK you're not prepared for class, you don't have a pencil. Go and find one and don't come back until you get it.' OK, well if I forgot something at home, would I not borrow it from another teacher? Would I not say 'you know, I forgot my clipboard or I forgot my lesson plan. Do you have something I can do for math or whatever?' But that's a biggie with me, *like kids are being treated differently than what we would expect ourselves to be treated.*

A final concern that students raised in relation to the question of consistency was in the area of teachers' rules. Students generally felt that adults did not have to abide by the same rules as students, that they could break rules without consequence and that students were more closely and rigidly regulated than the staff – all of which they felt to be unfair.[6] Students were frustrated that teachers could attend to their own circumstances and moods in ways that were not available to students themselves because of rules:

ALLISON: I mean we had this one case where our one teacher's like, father was in the hospital. And he's the biggest nutcase about having cell-phones. He sees you with a cell-phone, he freaks. And his father's in the hospital, and he's like 'my cell-phone might go off at anytime!' And we're just like 'jerk.' Here he is yelling at us if you have any electronic and he has his cell-phone on waiting for a phone call. (Whitton FG 9)

VEE: I had a teacher who has a coffee maker and like in class she'll be eating a granola bar or she'll be like eating her salad or whatever or her pasta whatever and she's like 'OK class um, so next question' [pause] and I'm like 'Miss, why can't I eat my lunch here?' And she's like 'Well it's the rules.' (Big City FG 8)

LILY: It gets cold outside, like that's why I had a problem with [pause] if it's really, really cold if it's freezing, even if the teacher has a coat on she says for us not to have our [jackets] on, or not even like sweaters, that's a bad thing . . . (Big City FG 8)

Some students relayed worrying stories. In one instance, for example, a teacher was making inappropriate comments to girls and yet he continued teaching even after the principal was told. Another student discussed a teacher who was consistently drunk for class, but even after her complaints to the administration, no disciplinary actions were taken.

Students' beliefs that the adults in their schools should follow the same rules as the students are supported by Mary Williams (1993) in her work on moral education. She argues that respect is best taught through modelling such respect, rather than teaching about it in classes in morality. Students in her study indicated that ideal teachers were sincere, worked hard, listened to students, and had high expectations. They also followed the same rules that the students had to.

Thornberg (2008a) similarly argues that teachers' failure to abide by the same rules conveys a problematic, hidden curriculum regarding the use of power: people in power can make rules but do not have to follow them. To some extent Weist (1999) concurs, but draws on fifty-eight surveys of teachers in middle schools and thirty-eight middle and high school principals in Indiana to suggest that sometimes the different positionality of teachers means that they need to follow different rules. While 86 per cent of teachers and 87 per cent of principals agreed that teachers should follow the same rules that students follow, often they do not in practice. The remaining teachers argued that their professional role and difference in status meant that the rules should not be the same for them. Weist draws on the latter to argue that it is appropriate to have different criteria for staff and students when it is practical, but not when it is simply preferred. For example, in a class where no beverages are allowed it is acceptable for a teacher to drink water if she or he is talking a long time and getting a dry throat, but it is not acceptable for her or him to sip coffee. The key here is to recognize professional responsibilities over status hierarchies.

Overall, students were much more inclined than staff to favour discretion in the application and enforcement of rules in terms of both specific incidents and distinct contexts, but not in ways that reproduced inequality. This makes sense because students see circumstantial reasons that rules might be broken and would like an opportunity to explain themselves. Yet while they felt quite strongly about the need for flexibility and its justifiability, they took issue with patterns of discrimination or favouritism in rule enforcement – specifically when features of students' social background, dress, school involvement, or grades were taken into account. When considering students as members of groups, they wanted to see greater consistency. There were also other instances wherein students wished for greater consistency, specifically in terms of addressing bullying. Finally, they took issue with what they felt to be teachers' selective flexibility around rules when applying them to themselves.[7] They did not feel that teachers as a group should have special privileges, provisions the students did not see themselves getting. The student comments come together to suggest that they are concerned with fairness and able to discuss and distinguish between what they consider acceptable and what they do not. For educators, these comments create some challenges: how to distinguish attention to the specifics of context from what might be considered discrimination or favoritism; how to address bullying when it is hard to identify; and how to clearly distinguish rule exceptions for teachers that are related to doing their jobs from rule exceptions that are simply based on preference.

School Strategies

Concerns over consistency and fairness are addressed not only through the actions and philosophies of specific teachers and administrators but also through policy at the school, school board, and provincial levels. At the local level, interviewees discussed various school strategies to try to monitor student infractions with the goal of consistency. The most prominent strategies involve codifying, educating, and monitoring. In the first instance, schools and school boards develop the codes of conduct discussed in chapter 2 in order to outline standard rules and, in many, standard consequences. In the second, it is hoped that by repeatedly educating staff and students about infractions and their set consequences that consistency will prevail. Finally, schools also develop specific monitoring strategies. Jack (Whitton vice-principal) describes his school's card system, for example:

> . . . like we have a tracking system here, every kid has their own card [. . .] I think the way we made a big change in the culture of this school for example, is that then kids would come in with the uniform undone, the hat on, this kind of thing. Like, teachers were saying, 'Take your hat off, do up your uniform,' right? But then it's forgotten, right? Cuz then the kid goes round the corner, does it again and another teacher might say it but there's no consistency in tracking it. So the minute we went to [the cards] – all of a sudden I had the teachers at the different entranceways when they come in [inaudible] on our property, 'Oh, you know, you forgot to do up your uniform.' 'Oh sorry about that.' 'What was your name?' So now they're thinking, 'Oh, they're recording that they warned me!' Right? So nothing has changed, there's no consequence. But at the same time, when they get sent to the office and I pull up their card, 'You know, you were warned four times in the same day. About the same thing. We've got a problem.'

Similar attempts at monitoring were mentioned by several other teachers, yet more critically. For example, Sandy and Jim (Big City teachers) flagged the degree of bureaucratic paperwork that can be involved in such monitoring systems. As Jim explained with exasperation when discussing his school's strategy to address lates:

> I don't want a green piece of paper, a white piece of paper, a computer generated piece of paper. I think if a student, and I talk to students too, but if a student is chronically absent and truant and late, and I can't convince them that that's not a good idea, um, you know, the vice-principal needs to [. . .] intervene as to whatever is going on.

These kinds of tracking systems become particularly important within a context of 'escalating consequences' and 'progressive discipline,' as I will examine below, developing a paper trail of surveillance. Such strategies are also thwarted due to staff turnover, however. Administrators are often expected to change schools every three to five years, for instance, bringing with them different approaches to discipline and specific rules. Whitton students and staff, in particular, commonly mentioned adjustments to new principals or vice-principals and their systems of governance.

Beyond the school and school board, strategies are implemented at the provincial level. As discussed in chapter 1, the most well-known and controversial strategy that has been implemented in Ontario and elsewhere in North America, in part to deal with issues of consistency, is a form of zero tolerance. I will first discuss zero tolerance and then its current replacement in Ontario, progressive discipline.

Zero Tolerance

Zero tolerance policies became particularly popular in the 1990s in the United States, beginning with the federal Gun Free Schools Act in 1994 and then expanding at the state, district, and school levels to cover many forms of infractions, including possession of drugs or alcohol, fighting, verbal abuse, repeated lateness, *etc.* (Sughrue 2003; Stinchcomb and Bazemore 2006). It also expanded into Ontario. Zero tolerance is based on the idea that certain consequences will be mandatory for certain infractions, with the underlying philosophy that swift, sure consequences deter future problems and send a clear, consistent message that schools are concerned with safety and discipline. Some zero tolerance policies also emphasize that even minor infractions will be seriously punished (Skiba and Rausch 2006). In Ontario, the discourse of zero tolerance was mobilized by the provincial Conservative government from 2002 to 2006, when the *Safe Schools Act* was introduced, with automatic consequences for some rule infractions such as possession of a weapon, alcohol or drugs, physical or sexual assault, being under the influence of alcohol or drugs, swearing at a teacher, committing an act of gross vandalism, or uttering threats. However, Ontario's policy also made allowance for mitigating factors such as a student's inability to control his or her actions, his or her inability to fully understand the likely consequences, or the lack of threat a student poses to other students, leading some to contend that it was not truly zero tolerance (Daniel and Bondy 2008). Nonetheless, the original *Safe Schools Act* was commonly presented and discussed using the language of zero tolerance.

Daniel and Bondy's (2008) research of school staff members at the time found that many appreciated the mandatory consequences outlined in Ontario's *Safe Schools Act*, as it supported their interest in the consistent application of consequences to rule violations, and a clear outline of mandatory consequences was assumed to provide a nice deterrent function for the student body as a whole. Within a climate of zero tolerance it is assumed that students will not transgress rules because as rational actors who weigh the consequences of an action they know they will not get away with it (Daniel and Bondy 2008). Such policies also reflect a broader 'war on crime' philosophy in which tough, consistent consequences are assumed to indicate that a government is taking issues of discipline seriously.

Yet despite the popularity of zero tolerance type approaches, much of the research on the effectiveness of zero tolerance strategies have found them to be unsuccessful (Harvard Civil Rights Project 2000; Sughrue 2003). Skiba and Rausch (2006) can see the appeal of zero tolerance policies in terms of safety but argue that overall they are unsupported, ineffective, and unfair because the personal and social contexts within which rules are broken are disregarded, those who are most likely to break rules are simply punished, and despite its links to consistency, certain groups of students are more likely to receive 'zero tolerance.' For example, participants in Daniel and Bondy's research noted that most of the students getting into trouble under the *Safe Schools Act* had various socio-economic, psychological, and behavioural problems that prevented them from doing well in school and could affect their ability to rationally weigh consequences. Zero tolerance policies have thus also been seen to significantly reproduce social inequalities along the lines of race and class discrimination.

Zero tolerance has come under critique for blurring the line between misbehaviour and violence, being rooted in retribution, and for ignoring children's ability to understand that fair treatment requires attention to the context and severity of violations (Sughrue 2003). In response to zero tolerance, children in turn feel less a part of the school and more disconnected from staff, particularly among those in need of support (Sughrue 2003). Sughrue also examines various occasions when zero tolerance expulsions were taken to court in Virginia. Based on the outcomes of these legal decisions that tend to favour the school, Sughrue is concerned that the courts and schools are neglecting students' rights. Finally, despite being hailed for their consistency, Dunbar and Villarruel (2002) conducted interviews with forty-two principals in Michigan on their zero tolerance policy and found great disparity between principals in terms of how they understood and enacted the policy. For example, some principals they surveyed were unsure about the exact details of zero tolerance, and some used zero tolerance to discipline all misdemeanours while others used it only in instances when safety was an issue. Other relevant intervening factors that principals raised as influencing their decisions were age, grade of student, first timer or repeat offender, and whether a parent was there to provide home support.

In terms of my own data, non-urban codes of conduct did not mention the *Safe Schools Act* or zero tolerance; urban codes were more likely to make such references but even here the references were only occasional. Whitton staff (who were interviewed while the *Safe Schools Act* was in place) were generally aware of the *Safe Schools Act* and that it was under review, though several felt that the legislation was unnecessary because the principle of mandatory consequences had already been present prior to the *Safe Schools Act*.

CHICAGO (vice-principal): . . . it's hard for me to comment on that because, maybe it's because, from the schools I've been at in Whitton and things like that [. . .] I found the whole thing kind of odd. Because when you looked at some of the language of it and it's suggesting that you know, drugs and threatening language and weapons and fighting and this kind of thing; yeah, that's unacceptable no matter what, always has been [. . .] and so I never understood the whole fanfare about it to begin with just because we already had rules in place to deal with all those situations.

A number of Whitton staff stood behind such mandatory consequences and the language of zero tolerance, because it was felt to clearly indicate when something is unacceptable and to suggest consistency in addressing it. Most also agreed that for certain kinds of issues, zero tolerance made sense, specifically in response to students bringing a weapon to school, instigating violence, fighting, bullying, being racist or homophobic, or using marijuana and other drugs. A few simply said that they liked the idea of zero tolerance and one argued that the original *Safe Schools Act* had not adversely affected any students that she knew of. In contrast, among that minority of teachers who favoured attention to context in most cases, the *Safe Schools Act* was considered overly rigid and tying the hands of staff.

Comments among Big City staff were similar. Three staff members were in favour of a zero tolerance approach because they felt it ensured real consequences, although Lana felt that even when zero tolerance was the goal, there was still pressure not to suspend or expel students. Of the remaining interviewees, two were supportive of the change to progressive discipline (discussed below), but without much comment on it. The remaining four felt rather strongly that zero tolerance did not work because, as Sarah explained, 'Every kid is different and every circumstance is different.' Tim also argued that zero tolerance is overly punitive, and Monster said that zero tolerance simply does not work.

Meanwhile, while zero tolerance was supposed to work as a deterrent, many students I talked to were unaware of it while it was part of Ontario policy.[8] Whitton students (and even some staff) had little awareness of the *Safe Schools Act* or the zero tolerance component that was present when they were participating in this study. Whitton students were aware of some mandatory consequences but not all, did not know that these were provincially mandated, and did not know that there had been concerns with how they were implemented within schools, although they were interested to learn about the *Safe Schools Act* once it had been mentioned by the facilitator. Big City students were much more familiar with the *Safe Schools Act*. This regional difference between participants quite likely results from different school board approaches to publicizing the *Act* and their related regional, demographic differences, suggesting the relevance of context and consistency between school boards themselves.[9] Another reason for the different student knowledge of zero tolerance between regions was due to the politicization of zero tolerance in the Big City. One of the main concerns with zero tolerance was that it was disproportionately applied to minority ethnic and racialized students as well as students with learning disabilities (Bhattacharjee 2003). It was primarily students, parents, and activists in the Big City who were concerned with this, leading to much press coverage there. Indeed, for Big City FG 3, part of their involvement in their youth leadership program involved reviewing the zero tolerance policy and its critiques. Meanwhile, for some of the more marginalized students in the Big City focus groups, their awareness of the *Safe Schools Act* was from having received suspensions themselves.

Once the concept of zero tolerance had been explained to the Whitton students, some of them were concerned with its lack of attention to context.

> NICOLE: Well like the law [stammers] how do you, you know 'give out'? You like distribute the law according to the situation and you distribute/
> Tina: Like [pause] yeah/
> NICOLE: . . . consequences according to the situation. You can't just, like you know this fight has this penalty, and this is this penalty. Like somebody might've like just been out, who knows, even camping that weekend and had their Swiss Army knife with them and forgot to take it out of their pocket, um cuz, you know, they threw it in the laundry pile. (Whitton FG 4)

Students pointed to extreme examples that they had heard about from elsewhere when students had been suspended for things such as bringing a butter knife to school. They were also concerned about the educational consequences to students when they were suspended or expelled. Very few argued in support of zero tolerance because they associated it with inflexibility and overreaction.

Big City students had mixed feelings about zero tolerance, perhaps reflecting the debate about it that they had seen in the press and also the high stakes in their school district where issues of violence and racism were considered particularly salient. Yet again, like the Whitton students, Big City students felt that people and their circumstances are diverse and that this diversity, and the context of infractions, needs to be taken into account.

> JULIE: No, I think people should consider the individual before punishing them. Zero tolerance, I hate zero tolerance, unless it's like a really bad subject like, assault like with a weapon, or like racism, but if I think it's like

> fighting or something I think zero tolerance should not be there because everyone is different and every situation is different and maybe it's not a just punishment for, yeah. (Big City FG 2)

Students suggested that the zero tolerance approach seemed extreme, with harsh consequences that do not give students the chance to make a mistake. Students in the youth leadership group were particularly damning of zero tolerance, suggesting that it isolates students, stigmatizes them and is insufficiently backed up by supportive programs to help students get back on their feet. Most significantly, they argued that zero tolerance has been used to target students of colour. Overall they saw the *Safe Schools Act* as linked to students either dropping out or being 'pushed out' by teachers who did not want them there. That said, there were a number of students who echoed Julie's comments above, suggesting that there are times when zero tolerance is needed. Specifically, various students felt that zero tolerance is appropriate for repeat offending, bringing weapons to school, racism, bullying, and any other serious or major issue.

Progressive Discipline

'Progressive discipline' is the formal discipline strategy that was embraced by Ontario's Liberal government in 2008 after a review of the previous government's *Safe Schools Act*, a review prompted largely because of the criticisms and concerns regarding its 'zero tolerance' component. Ontario's Ministry of Education explains that progressive discipline is a whole-school approach to student misbehaviour that aims to encourage positive behaviour through drawing on a range of interventions, supports, and consequences. This approach was intended to shift the focus from a punitive to a corrective one through various intervention strategies intended to develop a positive school climate and to help students to concentrate on improving their behaviour (Roher 2008). The consequent new *Safe Schools Act*, 'Safe, Caring and Restorative Schools' maintained a list of offences that should lead to suspension or expulsion, including offences determined by school boards and individual principals (potentially leading to very broad possibilities for suspension and expulsion).[10] Yet it expanded the mitigating circumstances to include things such as the student's age, family situation, and special needs as well as the nature of the specific infraction. Also, beyond suspensions and expulsions, the new

Act recommended that schools consider a much wider range of preventative and progressive alternatives, including peer mediation and anti-bullying initiatives. It was supported by the Ontario Teachers' Federation, with the proviso that safety issues would still be appropriately addressed.

This shift towards progressive discipline suggests an increasing attention to context, particularly with the widening of mitigating circumstances. It also includes an emphasis on escalating consequences, primarily to address issues such as lateness, dress code violations, or the use of cell phones. As introduced in chapter 3, this approach expects that the response to a repeated misdemeanour will escalate with its repetition, for example from a warning to detention, contacting parents, and ultimately suspension or even expulsion. It is a way to more formally and gradually link repeated minor rule violations to gradually more significant consequences. This kind of approach was embraced by many of the staff I interviewed both during the reign of zero tolerance and after the introduction of progressive discipline.[11] It also raises some concerns, however, with regard to consistency versus context. While generally staff felt it to be logical that an offence should be treated differently when it is repeated over and over again, some Big City staff members were critical of progressive discipline for being overly vague and thus undermining consistency.[12] They also felt that progressive discipline was being used in some schools as an excuse not to do anything in response to a situation.[13] Others noted that it is difficult to track. The idea of escalating consequences requires some kind of monitoring system, much like those I have described within individual schools at the beginning of this section and which some staff find frustrating. Paper trails are difficult to maintain in this need to govern a population 'in its depths and its details' (Foucault 1978a, 102). Such attempts to ensure fairer consistency can thus deepen processes of surveillance and categorization (Foucault 1977). Teachers' concerns with their colleagues' consistent enforcement expands to include frustration with their colleagues' failure to adequately keep track of misdemeanours, and consequently escalates a surveillance of each other.

In a circular process, escalating consequences and consequent record-keeping in turn contribute to creating the 'repeat offenders' whose differential treatment then becomes justified.

CHICAGO (vice-principal): Um, there are a handful of kids who are so difficult, who are so, um, behaviourally challenged, maybe emotionally, uh, maybe unbalanced, maybe a whole series of things [pause] that [resolu-tion in the classroom is] going to be very hard to do and then we need to put in place much stricter, much more formal, much more aggressive constraints on their behaviour and say, 'Hey Billy, cross the line a little bit and you're gone.'

LOUIS (principal): If a kid is chronically not following the rules and chroni-cally not respecting our policies, then that kid is going to get hammered. OK, I'll change my word. That kid is going to get consequenced, the full discipline.

These comments prioritize the punishment of chronic repeat offenders: once a student is categorized as a chronic problem, the rigidity of en-forcement escalates towards more direct and severe displays of admin-istrative domination – a strategy embedded in progressive discipline but reminiscent of zero tolerance. In this way, progressive discipline in-stitutionalizes a way to up the *ante* when students fail to self-discipline, including redefining offences as 'opposition to authority.' As Gemini (Whitton teacher) explains in terms of lates: 'If it becomes beyond five or six lates, then [. . .] they're in opposition to authority, or to rules, and they might get suspended.' As discussed in chapter 3, conventional rule violations are thus codified into moral ones.

While progressive discipline is intended to shift the focus from un-equivocally consistent enforcement to attention to context, such effects of escalating consequences suggest that ironically it may be in instances when consideration of context is most vital that consistent and harsher consequences are applied. Those who repeatedly break minor rules may be most in need of other kinds of intervention and support due to their marginalization, family problems, learning difficulties, and/ or the structure of their schooling. Indeed, as we will see in the next chapter, certain students, often minority, working class, or otherwise marginalized young people, are more likely than others to 'become' repeat offenders as their actions are more likely to be interpreted as infractions, their infractions more likely to be noticed, and their infrac-tions more likely to be remembered or recorded (Bhattacharjee 2003; Ferguson 2000; Morris 2005; Skiba and Rausch 2006). To most staff par-ticipants, such escalating consequences were logical and fair, however, only undermined by inconsistency of surveillance, record-keeping, and enforcement.

Contextualizing Consistency

This chapter has illustrated some of the complexity embedded in what may at first seem like a simple goal of consistent enforcement of school (and classroom) rules. Through drawing on staff and student comments in addition to other research reflected in classroom management, I have emphasized that questions of consistency versus context must be considered across transgressions, time and place, and specific students' lives. This chapter has also illustrated another significant gap between the views of staff and students, with staff, following provincial and school board direction, much more likely to idealize and attempt to enact a consistency of rule enforcement across the entire geography and student population of a school and students much more likely to recognize and value the need for flexibility across contexts. At the same time, students seem much more likely than staff to point out instances of favouritism and/or discrimination in rule enforcement. Staff and students also have very different understandings about which rules are important to enforce across all contexts and which can and should be addressed more flexibly. The centrality of this tension between consistency and context is evident in provincial legislation that has tried to provide guidance on this issue. Yet clearly, these legislative interventions do not entirely resolve the tension, partly because the question of consistency versus context becomes so complicated on the ground.

Teachers and administrators are in a difficult position when faced with the question of consistency, as the discussion above has indicated. There are many good reasons to aim for a certain kind of consistent enforcement of rules, a feeling that is undoubtedly particularly acute for a teacher faced with a student who is vociferously demanding leeway that has been granted to her or him in other classes. Staff must also guard against possibilities of favouritism and discrimination, which attempts at blanket consistency often hope to address. Further, as many staff suggested, a rule only holds weight if it is enforced (which suggests the value of keeping the number of rules to enforce to a minimum). However, as this chapter and other chapters of this book have pointed out, sometimes it is actually inconsistency that more fairly recognizes the different, unequal circumstances of students' lives and that lies behind students' rule violations.

6 The Contexts of Class, Ethnicity, and Racism

Edward Morris (2005), who conducted an in-depth, ethnographic examination of disciplinary processes within an American school, argues that the differential application of 'petty discipline,' particularly through regulation of dress code details, is based on intersections of race, gender, and class. Staff can be well meaning in their attempts to teach students how to better self-present, but Morris found that the end result is serious inequality in rule enforcement, with consequent student alienation, disengagement, and resistance. As an example, Morris discusses how Black, female, African American students were more likely than other female students to be described as 'unladylike' and therefore in need of reform in dress and mannerisms.[1] As I will develop below, Morris draws on the concept of cultural capital to explain how clashes of class, culture, racialized assumptions, and gendered norms come together within distinct school contexts to perpetuate unequal disciplinary processes and consequent student marginalization.

This chapter considers class but focuses primarily on race and ethnicity. How is it that schools, institutions commonly hoped to fulfill the dream of ending discrimination, produce unequal effects through disciplinary strategies, frequently without school staff noticing or able to identify how? Significant research has already addressed class- and race-based inequalities embedded within school discipline processes; consequently, I will draw largely on this research here as well as considering the perceptions of the students and teachers I talked to. I will follow in the footsteps of those who draw on critical pedagogy and the concept of cultural capital to further pursue points I began to address in chapter 2 when examining how the rules themselves can reproduce certain values. I reflect on how their enforcement also does so, with negative consequences for certain groups of students within particular racialized or cultural categories. This chapter therefore builds on chapter 5 as it re-examines the question of consistency versus context through the question of differential treatment.

Questions of Class-Based Inequalities in Schools

Within critical pedagogy and critical race literatures, various researchers have contended that school discipline is differentially applied to students according to the shifting categories of class and race. The contexts within which such studies take place are quite diverse and it is important to remember that how class, race, gender, and other such identifications intersect can vary greatly between countries, regions, urban/rural distinctions, the class or race complement of specific schools, what schools prioritize in terms of extracurricular activities, and how they are organized in terms of pedagogy and discipline (e.g., see Frosh, Phoenix, and Pattman 2002). Research focused primarily on class-based inequalities was particularly prominent in the 1970s and 1980s, reflected in the work of social reproduction theorists such as Bowles and Gintis (1976), Oakes (1985), Bourdieu (1977), and Apple (1990) and resistance theorists such as Willis (1977), McRobbie (1978), Giroux (1983), and McLaren (1986). More recently, North American scholars have drawn on this earlier work in a shift towards a stronger emphasis on racialized inequalities and their intersections with class as we see in the work of researchers such as Ferguson (2000), Morris (2005), Dickar (2008), and Skiba and Rausch (2006). While class inequalities remain deeply relevant to processes of schooling, discipline, and student contestation of rules, it is perhaps due to the pervasive myth of classlessness that my interview and focus group data touched far less frequently on class than on race. Class was raised on occasion, however, in two specific ways.

The first, and most common, was to focus on the levels of disposable income available to individual students, particularly in discussion of school uniforms. Despite some recognition that uniforms are a cost to parents, teachers often suggested that uniforms equalize financial inequalities between students and prevent class-based bullying. A similar argument was made within four focus groups, although other students countered this position, arguing that uniforms are expensive and therefore difficult for students from poorer families to afford. Several student groups also argued that rules against ripped or torn clothing are unfair to poorer students. Finally, a group that was clearly familiar with poverty was concerned that their school had been known to call Children's Services based on what the students were wearing. These comments were almost invariably sympathetic to students without sufficient funds, although they also individualized problems of class inequality to specific students and narrowed the discussion of class to what students wear.

The second way that my participants addressed class shifted observations towards more structural concerns through generalized comments about students from low socio-economic backgrounds and patterns within schools reflecting such a demographic. Apart from a few negative student comments about certain schools' reputations, these comments were sympathetic to specific issues that might be encountered by students from lower socio-economic backgrounds. This pattern was more likely among the teachers than the students. Staff from both districts suggested that students from lower socio-economic backgrounds frequently have more challenges succeeding in school. One teacher observed that working class students were at times unconvinced of the need for education, especially for boys if their fathers were successful in the trades, although most suggested that generally parents from across socio-economic backgrounds want their children to succeed in school. As Liz, one of the more economically marginalized students pointed out in arguing for the need to go to class, 'Do you want to work at McDonald's for the rest of your life? "Hey you want fries with that order?"' (Whitton FG 7).

The general socio-economic status of a school was also seen to have ramifications. One teacher observed, for example, that the financial background of the student body influenced her school's ability to successfully fundraise and to thus provide extracurricular opportunities such as field trips. Schools located in lower socio-economic status areas were also seen to have more safety issues and drugs and alcohol problems to deal with. Linked to these perceptions, one focus group observed that poorer schools tend to have more cameras in them, a pattern of unequal surveillance that has been documented in American schools (Saltman and Gabbard 2003). Tim (Big City teacher) similarly argued that privileged schools are more flexible with their rules than those with poor and minority students. Finally, one of the most politically aware student groups, Whitton FG 3, argued that processes of social reproduction are taking place among schools, with private school children being taught to think, while '[letting] the rest of us just slop around.'

Despite these important references to financial inequities and class-based patterns of school engagement and organization, class was not a predominant focus in my interviews or focus groups. They were much more likely to discuss culture and race, a pattern that is also evident in more recent research on differential applications of rules. Class is a challenging concept to measure and arguably one that is less identifiable in the present individualized, consumer-oriented culture. Patterns of ethno-cultural and racialized differences, while often overlapping with class, are frequently much easier to see.

Questions of Race-Based Inequalities in Schools

Racialized inequalities in school discipline are well-documented by many scholars in North America, Britain, and beyond. In Ontario, the provincial government's report, *Roots of Youth Violence* (McMurtry and Curling 2008), which drew on meetings with 143 students across the province, over 500 responses to an online questionnaire, and an in-depth literature review, argues that racism remains pernicious in Ontario, particularly against Black and Native[2] students. Other supporting research is provided by Ruck and Wortley in their quantitative examination of racial and ethnic minority students' perceptions of school discipline processes in Alberta (2002), by Ferguson, Tilleczek, Boydell, and Rummens in their assessment of early school leavers in Ontario (2005) and by Dei (1996) and Codjoe (2001) in their work on Black students' classroom experiences. Research addressing zero tolerance initiatives has also addressed this issue. It is ironic that one key criticism of zero tolerance policies – policies intended to introduce consistency in the enforcement of rules – is that they have been used subjectively in ways that have discriminated against young people of colour. In Ontario, for instance, the Ontario Human Rights Commission's report *The Ontario Safe Schools Act*: School Discipline and Discrimination (Bhattacharjee 2003) argued that the *Safe Schools Act* disproportionately affected students of colour and students with learning disabilities, as these students were treated more harshly than others.

While the above research focuses on Canada, much more looks at the American context, citing the commonly disproportionate and often normalized levels of suspension and expulsion of Black students compared to others and students' frequent perceptions of racism (e.g., see Kupchik 2010; Gregory, Nygreen, and Moran 2006; Raffaele Mendez and Knoff 2003). Racialized consequences have also been specifically cited in reference to American zero tolerance policies. Skiba and Rausch (2006) found that students of colour in the United States are consistently overrepresented in suspensions and expulsions, partly due to an overlap between Black students and students with low socio-economic status, but also when researchers control for class background. Additionally, they found that student self-report studies indicate no difference in behaviour between Black and White students, but that Black students receive more severe punishments for less severe behaviour. White students are sent to the office for more concrete 'objective' incidents such as vandalism or smoking while Black students are sent for more subjective ones, like disrespect.

Such inequalities are not only about zero tolerance, however, and have persisted over time in the United States. In 1987 McCarthy and Hoge found that Black adolescents were much more likely to get into trouble at school, even though they reported similar levels of offending to White students. McCarthy and Hoge argue that the greater rates of punishment for Blacks occurred as a consequence of teachers' perceptions of the students' behaviour, their knowledge of students' race, academic performance, and their knowledge of students' past records of being sanctioned. Much more recently, in a large, national quantitative study, American scholars Kupchik and Ellis (2008) examined students' perceptions of fairness. They found that while African American students generally felt the rules to be clearly communicated, they perceived them as less fairly applied to Black than either Latino or White students. A comprehensive study of these patterns is reported by Wallace, Goodkind, Wallace, and Bachman (2008) who conducted a longitudinal, national, self-report study of students in grade ten over three five-year intervals from 1991 to 2005. They found that a small percentage of Hispanic, Black, and Native American students were more likely to have had drugs/alcohol or a gun at school, but that this difference was insufficient to account for the significant disparities in school discipline. These students were between two and five times more likely to be suspended and expelled than White or Asian American students. Boys of all groups (except Asian American) were more likely to be disciplined, although Black girls were more likely to be suspended or expelled than White boys and overall Black girls were 5.4 times more likely to be suspended or expelled than White girls. For the most part, they found these to be ongoing patterns, except for an increase in suspension and expulsion rates of Black students over time. This research counters arguments that non-White students simply do more wrong or that these patterns are only a by-product of socio-economic status. Despite such findings, as we saw in chapter 4 and as Gregory and Moseley (2004) found in their research, most teachers fail to reflect on the racialized patterns in school discipline and are more likely to attribute problems with discipline to adolescence, low achievement, class size, inconsistent rule enforcement, and individual teachers' disciplinary and pedagogical practices. Some do point to culture and community, but commonly to attribute problems solely to the context young people face outside of school.

American scholars have also identified unequal cultures of discipline among schools themselves based on the class and racial complements of their student populations, with schools that have more working class and minority students most likely to draw on authoritarian disciplinary approaches and extensive forms of surveillance. For example, in Amy Best's examination of high school proms, she found that the working-middle class school was far more authoritarian in its approach than the middle-upper class art school she also studied (2000). Brown (2003) similarly compared two very different American schools in terms of pedagogy, discipline structure and the role of the military, finding that the school serving wealthy White students was better funded, more tolerant of minor rule infractions, and offered a wide range of courses while the school serving poor and exclusively Black students was in decay, deployed a wide range of student surveillance techniques (including metal detectors and guards), and prioritized links with the Junior Reserve Office Training Corp in order to recruit students into the military. Brown's observations are in turn supported by Verdugo's quantitative study (2002) which found zero tolerance policies to be most prominent in large urban schools, schools with a larger percentage of students on a subsidized lunch program, and schools with more minority students.[3] Zero tolerance policies also tend to overlap with the use of uniforms, drugs sweeps, metal detector checks, and controlled access to school, all of which also overlap with minority and poor communities.

Based on these patterns, Henry Giroux (2003) and Lawrence Grossberg (2001) have both proposed the provocative argument that within global, neoliberal economics, marginal youth are no longer considered a worthwhile investment for the future but simply problems to be dealt with now. As a consequence we have seen both a disinvestment in marginal young people through underfunding of housing, education, health care, etc. alongside their concomitant criminalization through zero tolerance policies in schools and courts, as well as their regulation on the streets and in malls. This argument is supported by Katz's ethnographic work on Latino students' experiences in a Californian high school. In this school, the administration maintains its reputation as a high achieving school by overtly investing only in students who will do well on standardized testing and encouraging the weaker students, who tend to be Latino or African American, in special education or ESL, and from impoverished neighbourhoods, to stay home (an example of being 'pushed out' that was also discussed in the previous chapter). Skiba and Rausch draw on Ferguson (2000) to contend that fear, emerging from stereotyping, may also increase the likelihood that Black students will be referred to the office as teachers are more likely to respond to their minor threats to authority. Others have similarly pointed at such discrimination (Alladin 1996; Ferguson 2000). Finally, cultural differences have been considered important contributors to the marginalization and disproportionate disciplining of students of colour (Sheets and Gay 1996; Weinstein, Tomlinson-Clarke, and Curran 2004; Wallace et al. 2008; Delpit 1995, 2006), a point I return to later in this chapter. As a whole these patterns ultimately illustrate deep inequality, particularly as many students are in turn disenfranchised from the education system, often through disciplinary strategies.

Student Views on Racism in Schools

While the previous chapter considered student and staff comments on favouritism and discrimination more generally, specific, unequal treatment based on race, language, and cultural background needs particular attention. Among the students I talked to, such unequal treatment was referred to as racism, a term that is appropriate, although emotionally charged and often ill-defined. The students used the term 'racism' to refer to any kind of discrimination they identified that seemed to be based on students' racialized identities or ethnicities. Usually they focused on individual examples of racist behaviour, e.g., of specific students or teachers, although there was also some consideration of institutional racism, or 'those established laws, customs, and practices that systematically reflect and produce racial inequalities, regardless of whether the individuals maintaining those practices have racist intentions' (Alladin 1996, 12), e.g., in discussions of zero tolerance.

Whitton and Big City are very distinct from one another in terms of the general ethnic and racial composition of their schools, with Big City far more diverse than Whitton. Big City focus groups were similarly more ethnically and racially diverse (see Appendix B). Discussion of issues related to race and racism emerged in almost every single focus group with Big City students, and their comments resonated with much of the research cited above. Students shared a consensus that racism is unacceptable and they were vehement about this, reflecting urban codes of conduct that tend to specifically denounce racialized bullying. For example, in Big City FG 6, offensive writing on clothing was seen by some as acceptable *except* if it is racist.

JIMMY: It's just clothes
I: Just clothes
ASHLEY: Well the racism, and the other things.
JIMMY: What, there's racism on it?
I: Yeah.
JIMMY: Ohh, sorry.
ASHLEY: The racism part, like nobody should wear anything about racism because if you peel somebody like a banana, we're all the same. So, like racism, nobody should wear something about racism.

Racism was a serious offence. In fact, Julie (Big City FG 2) put it right on a par with using a weapon: 'Zero tolerance, I hate zero tolerance, unless it's like [for] a really bad subject like, assault like with a weapon, or like racism.' Not surprisingly, then, many were critical when they described teachers and administrators acting in ways they considered racist. On seven different occasions students talked about specific teachers they thought were racist, although sometimes this also led to debate that reflects how racism can sometimes be difficult to identify.

I: OK. So you guys feel like the Black kids, the darker kids get singled out more?
MALE PARTICIPANT: Yeah, the White guys always get away.
[Laughter]. (Big City FG 1)

JANE: . . . [our school's] racist, that's what I think/
MACK: No/
SHELINA: No no, they're not racist, they have favourites, like, at that school/

JANE: Some teachers are racist, very racist/
JILL: Yeah. (Big City FG 7)

Students talked about teachers discriminating against students of co-lour, and of favouring students of their own race. The students in Big City FG 3 also expressed frustration arising from an incident in which they tried to address the actions of a racist teacher and were told that nothing could be done as 'it's just the way she is.'

Students also addressed racism beyond specific teachers or incidents, however. When asked about the *Safe School's Act*, for example, several groups referenced recently publicized research to voice concerns that such zero tolerance policies unfairly target students of colour. Zero tol-erance therefore raised concerns about the institutional reproduction of racism.

> BIBI: Oh that's because like I'm the [cites her role in this student organiza-tion], right? So I pretty much look at the no tolerance policy, the zero toler-ance policy a lot lately and it's just I don't like it, I hate it, I/
> ANNA-HOLLY: It's [an] excuse to students to get rid of students they don't like . . .
> BIBI: . . . Ya, it's an absolute excuse for teachers to get rid of students that they do not like and it's very, it's racially/
> ANNA-HOLLY: Motivated. (Big City FG 3)

This criticism echoes the aforementioned reports and commentary on zero tolerance in Ontario and beyond which have suggested that zero tolerance policies disproportionately affect students of colour, with the deleterious consequences of suspension and even expulsion (e.g., CBC 29 August 2003; Bhattacharjee 2003; Skiba and Rausch 2006). In a related example, native students in Big City FG 9 talked about rules being enforced differently based on stereotypes of indigenous people. As Greg explained, 'They wouldn't, like, put no races or whatever, like all that stereotypical shit, and whatever [on White kids].'

Overall, among many of the Big City students the perception was strong that racism and racial discrimination were present in their schools. These concerns are not new to Big City, for issues of racial-ized marginalization and inequality had been discussed frequently in the press and in response to zero tolerance initiatives in the schools. The general attitude was that racism is problematic and should be addressed.

Racism was also discussed among some Whitton students, but far, far less. While a few groups commented on clothing with racist comments being unacceptable, it was almost exclusively those in FG 8, the new immigrant group, who discussed discrimination in Whitton schools based on race, cultural background, and also language. It was in this group, for example, that students were concerned with an administrator's assumption that a congregation of new immigrant students made up a gang:

LATINO HEAT: I'm hanging out with people – like I'm hanging out with all Spanish kids. They don't like that. Or all the Black people are hanging out with Black people and they don't like that.
I: Ahh, so what do they do?
LATINO HEAT: They just tell you to go somewhere else. Like 'don't hang out around in one place.'
MOE: Yeah. Yeah.
//
LATINO HEAT: At my school, my uh [pause] vice principal? Right, cuz we're always talking in Spanish/
I: Right
LATINO HEAT: So he goes, 'Oh no, you always try to speak in English.' And one day I was speaking Spanish with my friend and he came to me and he told me not to speak in Spanish. He speaks in Spanish.
I: He was speaking to you in Spanish?
LATINO HEAT: Yeah. And he told me he was taking Spanish lessons because they thought we were like, forming a gang and all that.[4]

Within this group students also talked about student divisions along the lines of race or culture, with students segregating themselves within sections of the school. During this discussion the students debated among themselves – some felt that there was logic in students hanging out with friends from similar backgrounds while others felt that such segregation increases racism towards the group. Both sides were concerned that other students would not walk down the halls where the ESL students sit. Clearly, for these new immigrant students, issues related to race, culture, and racism were quite relevant.

This discussion of discrimination on the basis of race and culture was unique among the Whitton focus groups although a few other students recognized issues of ethnocentrism and religious/cultural diversity.

MATTHEW: Yeah there's no reason that taking your hat off is respectful or whatever (Tracy laughs) but all religions have these rules and I know if you go to Israel, right, I know in all the schools you have to wear hats inside, you know, Jews have to wear hats, Christians can't wear hats, what do Muslims wear? (Whitton FG 1)

TINA: I just think though it's impossible because offensive language is different for everyone. Like someone might be offended if you like called them like – there's different words that have like different connotations to different people. So it's impossible to really judge entirely.
CARRIE: All depends on like your religion or your race and/
TINA: Yeah exactly. (Whitton FG 4)

These observations pointed to the structurally normative assumptions behind certain school rules, assumptions which, in turn, link to religion, culture, and race.

Despite the Big City students' acute awareness about the evils of racism and problematic discrimination within their schools, this did not make them immune from being racist themselves: stereotyping Asian students and mocking an African Canadian vice-principal's accent, for instance. Within a few Whitton groups, students similarly made fun of boys wearing baggy pants hanging low on their hips, a 'ghetto' style particularly prominent among Black students. In two Whitton groups and one Big City group, students talked about how they should be able to draw on racist terms in playful banter with their own friends. These comments reflect students' narrow understandings of racism as only overt, blatant, and individualized (Raby 2004).

Staff Commentary on Racial Discrimination

In Whitton staff interviews, the topic of race tended to arise when the interviewer asked about why local codes of conduct did not include a rule specifically against racialized harassment, a common rule in more urban school codes. As many Whitton staff members noted, Whitton is quite racially homogeneous, particularly when compared to Big City – most students and staff are White. Staff suggested that this was probably a key reason why school codes of conduct are unlikely to specifically state that racism, racist discrimination, or race-based bullying is unacceptable.

A number of staff, nonetheless, emphasized the importance of teaching acceptance by addressing racist comments in class and talking about anti-racist language. Barb noted the need to teach about different religions in order to help students learn acceptance and Jenn lamented that anti-discrimination education is not required. Others wished to see specific rules against racism and were critical of 'zero tolerance' for reasons of discrimination. Yet there were also Whitton staff who did not see anti-racism as a high priority because of the area's homogeneity:

MARTHA: We have an anti-bullying policy and we address it in the code of conduct [pause] so yeah. We talk about – I wouldn't say racism, we don't talk about that. It's not even an issue [. . .] Um, mostly because we're completely, almost a completely homogenous community, we have very few other races. Some. But it's not even an issue so much. [. . .] We have like this blanket statement about respecting everybody.

JENN: And I think, what I've noticed here is that either, you know students have not grown up with many people of colour or, the few that there are in the school [pause] what am I trying to say? It's a White [school] board, there's not a lot of discussion of it going on in most schools so therefore I don't see how it would become a priority for the higher levels to make it an issue.

In sum, six respondents suggested that racism is not really considered an issue in Whitton because there are few non-White students. This pattern resonates with the work of Mélanie Knight (2008) who found that Canadian teachers tend to suggest that diversity only needs to be addressed in schools if ethnocultural diversity is present and if there is a conflict. This in itself is an interesting commentary on race, positioning Whiteness as outside of diversity and race (Dyer 2000; Roman 1993) and problematically implying that issues of racism emerge only when people of colour are present and voice discontent. But as Knight argues, equality and social justice must still be goals even in the absence of overt, visible, racialized conflict. The above teachers' observations also provide a notable contrast with those from several other participants: one teacher suggested that it is exposure to diversity which teaches tolerance and, within a Big City focus group, there was talk about how students would never wear racist comments on their shirts *because* their school is a multicultural space. These divergent comments raise the question of where racism occurs and why, because they suggest that

homogeneity and diversity in turn decrease the possibility of racism –
on the one hand, racism is absent in a White, homogeneous setting and
on the other hand, racism is absent in a diverse setting (see also Raby
2004). And yet, based on research, including the student comments
above, racism and perceptions of racism are evident across a diversity
of schools in Canada.

Finally, there were a few respondents who suggested that there
may be valuable reasons for not mentioning racism in codes of conduct at all.

JACK: . . . we talked about all those different types of bullying situations
with maybe anti-racist, anti-homophobic, that kind of stuff. I mean I don't
know – I find there's some schools in [. . .] larger urban centres that can be
a little bit more bold maybe with things they write in there. And I don't
wanna say that we're [a] more conservative um [pause] school board [. . .]
But again, it's something that if you put it in the code of conduct, you've
got to understand how parents and people might react to that kind of
thing, you know what I mean? Positive or negative. Like you might have
a lot of parents that, that look at that 'well I disagree with that' because
they're racist themselves! Or they're homophobic themselves, right? And
you kind of have to look at the culture of who you're dealing with.[5]

LURALEEN: You know, do you want to go and have a big [pause] anti
[pause] anti-racism lesson, whatever, a big week-long 'let's not use this
kind of language' if it's not being used in that school? [. . .] Because research proves that the minute you start talking about an issue, bringing it
to the forefront, that issue becomes bigger before it dies down. You make
things worse before they get better. Do I want to take that risk?

In these cases, addressing racism was thought to potentially stir up
conflict rather than address diversity in a proactive way. Overall Whitton staff wanted to see cultural and racial acceptance but for the most
part did not feel that it was much of an issue in most of the region –
quite contrary to the concerns expressed above by the new immigrant
focus group.

Reflecting the significant diversity in student populations in Big City,
Big City teachers and administrators talked about issues of culture, race,
and racism very differently from the Whitton staff and, like the Big City
students, far more often. As stated in many of the more urban codes of
conduct I studied, Big City staff tended to mention more frequently that

racism is not allowed in their schools. To this end, some schools had certain programs in place to address issues related to race and cross-cultural understanding. One school held workshops on cross-cultural conflict resolution, for instance, and another had an intervention program to support Black youth. Several respondents also commented on their schools' embrace of diversity through celebrating various cultural events and providing space for prayer groups.

There were also very mixed views on whether discrimination exists in Big City schools or not, however, with many downplaying that possibility: some staff members commented that the programs above indicate the tolerance within their schools. These staff members suggested that while Black students might more likely be suspended, this is not due to discrimination on the part of their staff. As Tim explained:

> It's, if you look at our statistics, it's consistent that students who happen to be Black are more often suspended. And that's [pause] we are, um, a little bit better than most of our neighbouring schools but worse than the [school board] when it comes to ethnicity rates of suspensions [. . .] and so that could be seen as [pause] discrimination from the outside? However, from the inside, our administration and our teachers are very – say – in-discriminate when it comes to um, say misbehaviours and breaking of the rules. It doesn't matter who you are. And nobody's getting a free ride.

Another teacher suggested that while there may still be some racist attitudes, it is not intentional and these are decreasing as new staff members, trained in anti-racist education, enter the school. Finally, students who argue that they are picked on for race, culture, or other issues might feel there is discrimination, one respondent argued, but they are ignoring the escalating process in place that treats students fairly as they move from counselling to consequences. For these staff members, racism tended to be individualized – evident when certain students are treated more harshly than others, directly based on their skin colour. Institutional processes based on consistency and fairness, in contrast, were set up to counter any possible discrimination.

Finally, several Big City staff talked about cultural differences outside of questions of discrimination, but in regards to behaviour. For example, one respondent argued that Asian students and their parents are more likely than other students to take suspensions very seriously and another that Asian students would prefer uniforms. These comments, in addition to the observation that drugs are less of an issue in schools with high Muslim populations, suggest possible movement towards culturally responsive teaching (see below) but they also problematically homogenize and stereotype cultural groups and embed issues related to discipline in the student, her family, and her culture rather than the cultural context of the rules or the school itself.[6] In contrast, Spencer (Big City principal) emphasized cultural differences in terms of a *gap* between school assumptions and what students hear:

> And I think the other thing is, certainly in large urban centres, is that we have to quit assuming that kids know what we mean when we tell them they have to behave better. I mean, how often do we as adults say to kids, 'Your behaviour is not very appropriate'? And the kid says, 'Oh, OK' and walks away and you know when the kid walks away they're saying, 'What did he say? I have no idea what they're talking about!' And there are differences culturally in behaviour, so we feel that through our programs like the conflict-resolution and stuff like that, that we create a situation where everybody has the same skills. And therefore we have the same expectation . . .

Spencer's position begins to move away from solely recognizing culture as embedded in the individual to identifying the complicity of the school.

Those staff members who expanded their understandings of race and racism to include contextual and institutional processes of discrimination were more likely to identify these patterns in their schools. For example, Jim, the Big City teacher with by far the most critical analysis of race, supported observations that schools with higher numbers of immigrant and working class students focused more on enforcement than those with primarily White and middle class populations. This respondent, along with another, also talked about how the wearing of hats is a cultural issue, so that when schools regulate hats they are instituting a values education from a specific perspective. This latter observation was echoed by several other Big City respondents from a particularly community-focused school who argued more broadly that with a diverse student population it is difficult to have arbitrary rules without community consultation. As Spencer (principal) further explains, 'And so, unless we reach out and we bring that community in and we actively engage that community, um, we're asking them to follow a whole bunch of rules that probably have not a whole lot of

meaning to them. You know?' These respondents also addressed parent
and student mistrust of authority figures due to the experiences they
have brought from their home countries.

Overall then, some staff identified patterns of inequality in the application of school discipline, but many did not. Students were much
more likely than teachers to comment on instances of all types of discrimination. In part this might be explained by the likelihood that students will notice individual instances of inequality and then generalize
them beyond those individual contexts when asked if the rules are applied fairly or not. Also, there is the possibility that students might turn
to examples of inequality in order to absolve themselves of responsibility. Certainly, one Big City principal contended that this is sometimes
the case.

> LOUIS: The kids are always saying, 'We're being picked on because I'm
> Black, because I'm Chinese, because I'm Brown, because I'm White, be-
> cause I'm fat, because I'm short, because my hair's long.' You know, it's
> fifty different things. But they don't see the background work that has
> been done already.

Students' comments on racialized discrimination are bolstered in a
number of ways, however. First, in terms of racism, my study found
significant repetition of student concerns across focus groups that included any students of colour – in FG 8 in Whitton and in almost all of
the focus groups in Big City. Second, students narrated quite specific
incidents of racism to support their positions. Finally, student experiences of inequality are well supported through significant external literature which suggests these students are not alone.

Why, then, were most staff members less likely to comment on, or
even see, such inequalities, particularly as those arguing that they did
not see examples of discrimination were quite convinced of their positions? Staff were invested in fairness: they sought to be fair in how
they treated the students and they wanted their schools to be fair. It
is also quite probable that some schools are less likely to perpetuate
racialized inequality in the application of rules than others. As I will
explain below, however, we are not always aware of how we participate in reproducing inequalities, especially within the context of our
own organization. It is hard to stand back and to see structural or institutional patterns of inequality; for instance, both staff and students
were far more likely to point to examples of individual people who

discriminate against certain students. In contrast, an expanded use of the concept of cultural capital provides one lens through which to understand how more systematic inequalities can be perpetuated even when individuals and institutions are committed to fairness, and it has been increasingly common to see this class-based concept applied to examining racialized inequalities.

Understanding Inequalities: The Lens of Cultural Capital

As introduced in chapter 1, scholars working in the area of critical pedagogy contend that in addition to (and related to) social control and socialization, schools have had the ongoing function of sorting students into future occupations through dividing mental and manual labour and favouring the former, streaming, and rewarding cultural capital. It is the concept of cultural capital that I wish to examine in more detail here, first through reviewing its link to the reproduction of class inequalities and then through examining how it has been applied to an examination of race and ethnicity in relation to questions of school rules and classroom management.

Pierre Bourdieu's work suggests that the school is not neutral territory but rather rewards dominant 'cultural capital.'[7] Cultural capital was just one form of capital discussed by Bourdieu. In 'Forms of capital' (2001), Bourdieu explains social capital (the advantages of group membership and how these reinforce the position of dominant groups), economic capital (financial assets), and cultural capital, all of which ensure that social success is based less on chance or equal opportunity than on the reproduction of social structure. Before discussing cultural capital in more detail, however, it is necessary to describe Bourdieu's related concept, habitus.

Bourdieu argued that each of us grows up within a particular habitus, or class-based environment which includes family and community and which fosters our specific ways of being, comforts, dispositions, tastes, values, and so forth. As such, embodiment is central to this concept – the body is located within the social world but the social world is also located within the body (Reay 1995). Some have understood this concept to be overly deterministic, suggesting that we are inevitably trapped in our dispositions, yet Bourdieu also linked habitus to agency. While one's habitus ensures a certain predisposition and inscribed choice, there is also a 'wide repertoire of possible actions, simultaneously enabling the individual to draw on transformative and constraining courses of action' (Reay 1995, 355). Habitus must also be understood as both a combination of individual history and the collective history of one's family and class, and a combination of past and present, as one's habitus is constantly modified by what happens in the present (Reay 1995). Cultural capital, in turn, reflects the habitus of the dominant group, or the values, beliefs, norms, attitudes, and skills deemed valuable by dominant members of society and in need of cultivation (Bourdieu 1984), recognizing that what is considered dominant can shift by context. Such dominant members tend to make up the policy, curricula, administration, and teaching staff of schools, creating a setting which both imparts and rewards cultural capital.

Based on students' backgrounds then, some will be more familiar and comfortable with the dominant values and dispositions that are embedded in the (middle class) school, including the rules and how to negotiate them (Nelson 1996). A nice example of this was illustrated by Dylan (Whitton teacher) when asked if certain students were more likely to get into trouble than others for the same infraction:

> [sighs] [3 second pause] Yes, I think it tends to be the ones who don't know how to advocate on their own behalf, a lot of the times too. [For instance] a student council kid is walking down the hall with his hat on. 'OK, your hat's on.' 'Oh sure, sir, sorry I didn't mean to' [then he] might take it off and keep going. Another one of my guys upstairs: 'Bobby, hat.' 'I just fucking had the thing on you just find me . . .' [angrily]. I think it's because they don't have the skills – again stereotyping – but that a lot of your, student council-y type kids will have. Like they're the ones who can say things appropriately and know how to get themselves out of situations in a more, what we as teachers would see, as more appropriate ways?

Dylan talks about how the student councillor has the cultural capital to negotiate his hat wearing; he has the recognized, accepted, and valued verbal skills of the school whereas the second student, who does not (or does not wish to use them in this instance), may find the encounter escalates into accusations of defiance of authority when he more sullenly removes his hat. As Archer, Hollingworth, and Halsall (2005) explain in their examination of British youth style, the life-worlds of those in the middle classes are advantaged because they are more in sync with dominant institutions and thus more easily 'understand and play the "game"' (220). While certain students benefit, more marginal students do not as their more comfortable ways of being, and which may be valued *outside* the school, are dismissed or punished within the school.

Michael Apple (1995) links the production of cultural capital to student sorting and, ultimately, to questions of deviance and discipline. He suggests that schools produce and naturalize a division between mental and manual labour that favours mental labour. He then links the development of mental labour to cultural capital by arguing that because dominant values and language are used in teaching, children from poor and minority families often end up performing less successfully in school and therefore end up in manual labour. Those students who are 'sorted to the bottom' are then more likely to disrupt classes out of frustration and alienation, and to consequently be targeted as repeat offenders such that their exclusion becomes self-fulfilling as they face escalating sanctions (Noguera 2003). When schools in turn define whole groups of students as deviant, and even seek to 'diagnose' or 'treat' them through remedial help, the school may seem like it is trying to help increase students' mobility, but is actually defusing critique of the sorting role of schools by defining the deviance as in the child (or child's culture) and not due to larger social inequalities and patterns, including the school's own reproduction of cultural capital at marginalized students' expense (Morris 2005).

Students can respond by rejecting the system. For example, in Willis's oft-referenced ethnography of lad culture in Britain, he perceives their challenges to the rules as resistance to these unequal structures, even though it is not consciously thought out by the students in question. McRobbie's (1978) research on working class girls similarly argues that girls embrace traditional femininity as an alternative to elusive school success by focusing on dating and preparing to have a family. Yet through their anti-school self-presentations and behaviour, both the boys and the girls ultimately reproduce their own futures, a pattern more recently observed by Archer, Hollingworth, and Halsall (2005) in their examination of youth styles of dress. Archer et al. argue that in response to their marginalized status in schools, youth performances of style provide strategies for marginalized youth to foster identity worth. But this style frequently ends up reproducing their marginality as lower class styles are not valued by dominant groups. They argue that the styles of marginalized youth add to their educational marginalization through conflict over uniform/dress code, especially in terms of 'bling' culture and girls' sexualized dress. The regulation of boys' dress seems to most commonly police racial and ethnic identities through attempts to regulate gangwear (Garot and Katz 2003), low-slung pants, and heavy jewellery (Dickar 2008).[8]

Cultural Capital, Ethnicity, and Race

As the example above suggests, while Bourdieu concentrated on class habitus, the concept has been considered increasingly relevant to other forms of culture, including ethnicity, and related racialized inequalities that in turn intersect with class. For example, both Ferguson (2000) and Dickar (2008) draw on in-depth ethnographic research to argue that school success is premised on 'acting White,' reflecting a dominant, middle class and Anglo set of values, even though for many young people this means giving up community and family culture. The cultural capital of the school, in such an analysis, is not just middle class but also Anglo and, commonly, White. An application of cultural capital to racialized or cultural differences in schools thus provides a lens through which to consider the differential application of school rules in a much more structured way than by simply focusing on how certain teaching staff might, or might not, be racist.

In her analysis, Ferguson (2000) draws on cultural capital as well as Bourdieu's concept of 'symbolic violence' in which practices embedded in the hidden curriculum, such as assumptions about proper behaviour, reproduce social hierarchy. She argues that while the school she studied functioned as if racism did not exist and located student misbehaviour in students' individual choices, culture and race were powerful forces shaping these young people's conflict with certain values and processes within the school. Suggesting a clash between the Black students' habitus and the school, Ferguson provides a powerful exploration of how certain interpersonal styles within African American communities are interpreted by White, middle class professionals as disrespect. She provides some compelling, descriptive material of how such injustices may unfold.

In one example Ferguson illustrates how a small action, a grade four girl talking excitedly with her friends as they are walking up the school stairs, escalates into her being sent to the office because her response to a reprimand is interpreted as oppositional: when she goes back up the stairs as requested she does so quietly, but with a tiny hint of parody which suggests she is not sincere, and when she is being lectured she shifts a bit from foot to foot. Ferguson argues that adult policing of student behaviour is framed behind the 'reasonable' façade of a school rule which calls for courtesy, cooperation, and respect but that it is adult staff who interpret what kinds of displays of emotion are acceptable and what kinds are punishable. Here African American cultural patterns such as 'stylized sulking' or a 'humph' while holding your head up are interpreted as 'bad attitude,' which in turn affects teachers' interpretations of students' intentions and also academic potential. Vavrus and Cole (2002) similarly argue that students whose backgrounds do not reflect the same values as school staff will find themselves censured. For example, European teachers may be uncomfortable with a more active and boisterous style of African American males, reflecting the argument that habitus shapes our values, tastes, and mannerisms. They thus contend that suspension often results from violations of a normalized classroom code which is more familiar to Anglo-American students than African-American or Latina students. In interviews with staff at a secondary school in Britain, Rollock (2007) similarly finds that staff conceptualize school success as antithetical to boys' 'Black street culture.'

Ferguson specifically argues that Black males do not get the same dispensations as others because school staff tend to interpret Black boys' naughtiness as insubordination and viciousness. She cites other research to suggest that Black boys are also more likely to be portrayed as adult-like, responsible, and willful and are consequently more inclined to be watched for fear that their reputations might in turn endanger other Black boys. Ferguson argues that as a consequence of such institutional processes, Black boys will disidentify, or distance themselves from school. While the school is not a source of self-esteem then, hegemonic masculinity, popular knowledge, and Blackness are, so these are embraced (Dickar 2008; Ferguson 2000). The boys in Ferguson's study illustrated their masculinity through heterosexual posturing, class disruption, and fighting, all of which lead to trouble but also to a reputation as successfully masculine.

Similarly, in the British context, Youdell (2003) draws on institutional racism and post-structuralism to talk about this dynamic in terms of Black male students' identity traps. Within student subcultures, she argues, performances of a certain kind of subcultural Blackness garner a high degree of status among peers but these kinds of performances are not valued in the school as they are seen as antithetical to the ideal student learner role. One might assume that the answer then is for Black boys to change their style, but she argues that this is rarely a wise choice for the students because frequently their Blackness in itself leads them to be considered undesirable learners within the structures of the school. Boys end up choosing between the unlikely position of being successful in school through a pro-school identity and an incompatible, high status position in Black subculture, the latter of which helps their self-esteem; thus to have the protection of Black subcultural identity, these students cannot also be pro-school.

Carter (2003) examines this pattern through an expanded discussion of the concept of cultural capital by suggesting that there are dominant and non-dominant forms of cultural capital. She categorizes familiarity with Black cultural style as non-dominant cultural capital, which brings valuable community status. In interviews with forty-four low-income, African American students, she found that some students quite consciously and smoothly negotiated dominant and non-dominant cultural capital. Students do not all seek to achieve this balance, however, and instead foster non-dominant capital, in part due to their negative experiences within classrooms. Carter explains, for example, that 'students frequently refused to fully seek the acquisition of dominant cultural capital at school, especially during those moments when they perceived that school officials demeaned their own cultural resources' (147). Such students were still invested in high educational and career goals, but did not want to compromise their own community culture when faced with teachers' negative assumptions, especially based on ideas about 'appropriate' dress and demeanour.

Both Ferguson and Dickar use the concept of cultural capital to argue that school success is premised on 'acting White' and thus many young people are being asked to give up or devalue their own community and family culture to succeed in school. Some researchers have identified 'community forces' as in part creating this dynamic through historical, collective distrust of the school (Ogbu 2003), and yet Ferguson and Dickar contend that young people do not enter school with such an oppositional approach but rather learn it in response to the institution's normalization of Whiteness and devaluing of Black culture. Dickar illustrates this by describing the scanning processes students underwent at the inner school she studied. As part of the scanning process students had to remove any signs of Black culture such as do-rags and beads. Valenzuela (2009) makes a similar argument in relation to Latino students in Texas who face 'de-Mexicanization' through the school's institutional processes. Yet school staff continue to interpret student behaviour as individualized, based on bad families, or on inherent criminality rather than seeing school processes as anything but neutral (Gregory, Nygreen, and Moran 2006).

An offshoot of classroom management literature has begun to address this pattern of cultural clash over ideas of appropriate behaviour in the school (Weinstein, Tomlinson-Clarke, and Curran 2004; Delpit 1995, 2006). Weinstein et al. (2004) review a number of studies illustrating differences between the assumed cultural norms of largely English-speaking, middle class teachers and the cultural patterns of many of the students they teach. For example, they review Cynthia Ballenger's work with Haitian children in which she found that all the disciplinary practices she normally used with students were not working, and so, rather than simply dismiss the students as incorrigible, she consulted and observed her Haitian colleagues. She found that her inclination to refer to the children's internal states and to stress consequences when chastising them was quite different from the Haitian focus on group membership and less immediate consequences such as bringing shame on one's family. For the students, the latter approach was interpreted as caring, so when Ballenger adapted her style, students reacted positively. Weinstein et al. also cite clashes between Anglo, middle class expectations that students will listen quietly and respond individually, and African American 'call-response' style which is more active and engaging but considered rude by many teachers. Delpit describes a number of similar cultural clashes (2006).

In order to better address cultural clashes like these, Weinstein et al. present an argument in favour of culturally responsive classroom management (CRCM), which is intended to build more equitable classrooms. CRCM stresses that teachers must first recognize their own ethnocentrism. White, middle class teachers in particular tend to consider their own cultural norms as universal as they make up the dominant centre that is reflected back to them in the largely White, middle class institutions around them. The concept of cultural capital reminds us that in such classes, both 'sides' are not equal. Geneva Gay suggests that teachers are not necessarily racists but that they are 'cultural hegemonists' in that they expect students to follow their school's cultural norms (Weinstein et al. 2000). As such, a component of CRCM is for teachers to learn more about the cultural backgrounds of those they teach, a recommendation also made by Delpit (2006), but with a very important caution against stereotyping groups and homogenizing individuals within them. CRCM also encourages teacher awareness of the wider, unequal social, economic, and political context. This element of CRCM resonates with the notion of cultural capital as it encourages acknowledgment of dominant institutionalized prejudices. It also goes beyond cultural capital to consider more direct, blatant examples of institutional and individual discrimination in schools and beyond.

At this point some readers may be thinking that while teachers should be sensitive to cultural differences, it is also their responsibility to teach students the normative skills and values reflected in cultural capital so that their students will thrive in their ongoing engagements with dominant institutions in society. This is a significant concern to Delpit who is angry that Native and Black students are often denied education in the 'culture of power' that will allow them to succeed within that culture (2006). This is certainly another caution that Weinstein et al. discuss. They suggest that educators need to open themselves to really think about how students are treated unequally and then to consider what is fair. The concept of mutual accommodation recognizes that staff members must value and accept where students are coming from, but that there is also the need to guide them through the institutional culture they are in. How can the teachers balance between these two goals? How much should students be expected to alter themselves for the school and how much should the school try to alter to meet them? According to Weinstein et al. and Delpit, teachers need to openly discuss and affirm students' beliefs, assumptions, traditions, and language, recognizing how these may differ from the skills and values taught in the school and valued within dominant institutions, and helping students to consciously 'code switch' in order to negotiate the 'culture of power.' While they fall somewhat short of advocating peer based conflict-resolution or increased student participation in decision-making within the school, these are ways to foster dialogue and to ensure that the school better engages with the community it serves. For some readers, this balance may need to preserve dominant values that reflect the cultural traditions of their nation. Others may seek broader accommodation of diverse values in order to ensure greater equality.

A final component of CRCM is to commit to building caring classrooms. As Valenzuela puts it, 'Teachers expect students to care about school in a technical fashion before they care for them, while students expect teachers to care for them before they care about school' (2009, 336, italics in the original). As Weinstein et al. (2004) observe, frequently students of colour feel that teachers do not care about, or accept, them. It is for this reason that Weinstein et al. argue that teachers need to learn about their students' backgrounds, reflect on their own cultural assumptions, hold high expectations of their students, and genuinely care about them. They also acknowledge that caring can be particularly difficult within the institution of the school that is governed by certain rules, systems of tracking, large numbers of students, and so forth. In one particularly powerful example, Susan Katz (1999) details how, in an inner-city high school in California, caring means going against the grain of the school because the school administrators are only interested in high test scores. The explicit message to teachers is to invest only in the students who are successful and to encourage weaker students not to bother to even show up.

The Challenge of Structural Inequality

The above analysis has focused primarily on scholarship from American schools, although Canadian research suggests similar patterns (e.g., Codjoe 2001; Dei 1996; Alladin 1996). It has also concentrated primarily on a Black-White divide, a binary that is complicated by diversity in student backgrounds and racialized categorizing in different ways across North American contexts, suggesting the value of expanding analyses of cultural and racialized diversity and its link to differential histories of inequality and immigration. Nonetheless, such studies which focus on cultural clashes, institutional patterns, and the ongoing reward of cultural capital in schools provide an explanation for why many teachers do not see patterns of race or class bias in their everyday actions and decisions around the creation and enforcement of rules, even while practices and outcomes may be unfair.

Students are evaluated within a broad, structural framework of rules which are assumed to be common sense and yet already have bias built into them. Furthermore, in the immediate instance of discipline, misconduct tends to be individualized within a cultural climate that normalizes and favours certain ways of being over others. Similarly, common understandings of racism tend to focus on problematic, individualized attitudes towards certain people identified with a specific 'race' or culture. Yet as illustrated here and elsewhere, structural, institutional processes can have discriminatory effects that amount to a much more insidious form of discrimination which is particularly difficult to identify and to address, especially for those within the more dominant group. Of course, more individual manifestations of racist stereotyping, categorizing, marginalizing, and bullying are also important to address.[9] but Apple (1995) and Noguera (2003) both conclude that the wider problem is not individual people's views but the structural frameworks of schooling that reproduce inequality. Sometimes it is difficult when you are on the 'ground' to see such processes. Perhaps it is for this reason that subtler, more institutional forms of racism and other forms of discrimination seemed difficult for many staff with whom I talked to identify. By drawing on the concept of cultural capital and how it has been extended to focus on cultural differences somewhat distinct from class, I have tried to illustrate how it is that school rules and their application reproduce discrimination in ways that are not always visible. The classroom management approach CRCM is valuable as it attempts to address such discriminatory patterns through fostering cultural awareness that challenges inadvertent discriminatory practices. While such practical tools are necessary for teachers, however, it is also important to attend to the much more daunting, structural patterns of inequality that operate in broader school systems and beyond.

7 Regulating Sexualized and Gendered Bodies

In addition to producing understandings of what it means to be a successful student that reflect class and culture, school rules and their enforcement are also related to the production and management of gender and sexuality. This chapter focuses on four key areas of such production and management: gendered discipline, dress codes, rules against sexual and homophobic harassment, and regulation of personal displays of affection. This chapter in particular focuses on how school rules and their application can be understood as a process of moral regulation, as discussed in chapter 2. Moral regulation defines what is considered right or proper, encourages certain behaviour over other forms of behaviour, and then rewards or punishes behaviour (Brock 2003). When certain dress is defined as too revealing or certain behaviour as too affectionate, for instance, we can see such processes of moralization at work, creating ideas of what is normal or natural even though they are based on assumptions unique to a time, place or more dominant group of people (Corrigan and Sayer 1985).[1] These processes reflect morality as they are judgments about what kind of behaviour is expected and they are frequently framed in terms of moral language. Such moral regulation also constructs us as subjects, forming our identities and our construction of others' identities in ways that naturalize social relations (Hunt 1999). That said, such regulation is neither uniform nor uncontested. Codes of conduct regarding dress, for example, are both embraced and challenged by students, as will be explored below. I also demonstrate how these areas of regulation prove to be challenging for students and teachers alike as definitions of acceptable behaviour are murky, gendered, and located in the already charged area of sexuality.

Gendered Discipline

This chapter focuses primarily on rules regarding student sexuality, as this is what emerged through my data collection. But, of course, gender and sexuality are inseparable concepts that shape what students do and say in school and also how teachers engage with students, as will be evident when discussing dress codes. Gender also affects rule-breaking and staff response to that rule-breaking. Studies have repeatedly shown that boys tend to be more disruptive in class than girls (Davies 1994; Lewis 2001), for instance, particularly in secondary school. Boys are more likely than girls to engage in aggressive behaviour and to get into trouble (Gilbert and Gilbert 1998) and students perceive that boys get yelled at more by teachers and generally receive more negative attention (Myhill and Jones 2006). Similarly, while in my interviews with staff explanations for student rule-breaking did not touch on gender,[2] it was more likely that a hypothetical rule-breaker would be referred to as a male, particularly if an incident involved violence. When girls were talked about as rule-breakers, staff were more likely to refer to them smoking marijuana, being mean to other girls, wearing provocative clothing, or skipping school.

Overall, boys are more likely to be in trouble with teachers. More essentialist explanations concentrate on boys' need for quick gratification, independence, and inclination towards aggression (Gurian 2002). Some such commentators consequently argue that 'boys will be boys' – they will engage in tasks in a more energetic, exuberant way than girls – and that schools need to better accommodate such natural inclinations in order to help boys thrive and to prevent them from getting into trouble as much as they do (Kindlon and Thompson 2002). A related position that draws on both biological and more social factors contends that because elementary teachers tend to be female, boys come to experience school as a feminine space that is incompatible with their masculinity (Kindlon and Thompson 2002), a worry that goes back to American psychologist G. Stanley Hall's concern at the beginning of the 1900s that female teachers were emasculating young men (Sadker and Sadker 2002). Those taking this stance tend to advocate for more male teachers and for single-sex schooling. Others make similar arguments but ground them in socialization: boys are more likely to break rules and to get in trouble because they are socialized to enjoy more freedom than girls. For example, in Davies' (1989) quantitative study of boys' disruption in, and disconnection from, school, he looks to control theory for explanation, arguing that boys are raised with less restriction and control.

In contrast are those who see gender as constructed through interaction and performance. Through learning, but also performing gendered competencies on an ongoing basis, many boys and some girls aspire to a hegemonic form of masculinity that is likely to become confrontational, physical, and disruptive when more established avenues to masculine power are blocked (Davies 1989; Pascoe 2007; Renold 2001). While hegemonic masculinity can resonate with some structures of competitive schooling and athletics (Connell 1996), the pursuit of a culture of hegemonic masculinity can also lead students into trouble, both inside and outside the classroom, as rule-breaking is admired for challenging authority, pushing boundaries and showing independence (Gilbert and Gilbert 1998). This is a position also outlined by Kimmel (2004) and Ferguson (2000). If successful masculinity is thus marked by action, aggression, and independence, then there is a logical clash when boys aspiring to hegemonic masculinity are in classrooms that reward silence, passivity, and conformity (Sadker and Sadker 2002). Davies (1989) suggests that when boys become frustrated with their academic performance they are likely to retreat to traditional forms of masculinity for recognition. This can create a circular cycle wherein boys are more likely to dominate school time and processes of disciplinary intervention, leading them to become weaker academically (Meyenn and Parker 2001); when weaker academically they then more fully embrace hegemonic masculinity. Meyenn and Parker thus argue that instead of reinforcing gender difference through essentialized programs such as same-sex schools, staff members need to problematize such behaviour, interrupt taken-for-granted assumptions, and provide space for the interrogation of hegemonic masculinity (2001). Robinson (2005) adds that by challenging gender binaries, hegemonic masculinity loses its salience.

Much like patterns of discipline related to culture, race, and class, gender is thus salient, and yet often not well-discussed when considering theories of discipline or techniques of classroom management. Yet hegemonic masculinity creates a significant challenge for schools as it celebrates rule-breaking and exaggerates aggression (see Robinson 2005; Gilbert and Gilbert 1998). Furthermore, as long as rules are also constructed, presented, and policed in a way that is about the assertion of staff authority over students, a climate of power and conflict is generated that potentially fosters masculine posturing.

The culture of gender also shapes how staff respond to boys' and girls' behaviour. Myhill and Jones (2006) argue that teachers' gendered assumptions lead them to discipline boys far more than girls and treat them more severely for the same offence, in turn participating in the production of gendered behaviour. At the same time, when girls are disruptive they can be treated more harshly if they are seen to be challenging traditional femininity (Robinson 1992), a pattern noted in literature on the criminal justice system (Pasko 2006). Such issues came up briefly in my data collection when I asked students and staff whether the rules were applied equally to all. Three groups of students argued that teachers are generally more lenient with the girls, while a participant in another group argued that teachers sometimes do not address boys' behaviour 'because they know they're guys doing their thing – unless it gets out of hand' (Lily, Big City FG 8). Meyenn and Parker (2001) are concerned that teachers often accommodate, essentialize, or recognize boys' disruptive behaviour in ways that allow boys to dominate class and teacher time although Myhill and Jones (2006) add that differential discipline disadvantages boys academically. Two focus groups also argued that due to heterosexual attraction, female teachers favour the boys and male teachers are nicer to girls. Whitton FG 6 cited a male principal who favoured cheerleaders so much that they could get away with almost anything:

> KIERSTYN: They [could] do anything they wanted. If they came in and were like, 'Oh I don't wanna go to school today,' he'd say 'alright.'
> ANGELINA: They're untouchable.

Students were particularly aware of the sexualized nature of some male teachers' favouritism towards girls.[3]

Few staff mentioned gender as a relevant feature of their own rule enforcement, however. Only two teachers commented on gendered favouritism. One Whitton teacher, Jen, recognized a gendered pattern to her rule enforcement, saying that while she is trying not to do this anymore, she used to be more lenient with the boys because they were less mature; girls' greater maturity led her to have higher expectations for them – drawing on a gendered developmentalism to guide her disciplinary practices. A Whitton vice-principal, Brian, also stated that staff needed to be careful to 'make sure there's not a gendered situation, a sexual preference situation' that would emerge from specific codes of conduct.

Thus only several students and staff directly touched on gendered differential treatment of students by male or female staff. This omission is noteworthy in light of the research suggesting that gender plays such a significant role in school discipline processes. Boys get in trouble more frequently, although girls' disruptive behaviour can be more heavily punished. It has also been suggested that male teachers tend to be more inclined to draw on traditional, authoritarian approaches to discipline in their own performance of masculinity than women, who are more inclined to favour humanistic approaches (Oplatka and Atias 2007, Myhill and Jones 2006, Lewis 1999c). Despite a lack of discussion of gender when my participants talked about the rules and their enforcement more generally, gender did arise in specific discussions of dress.

Dress

> Halter-tops, tube-tops, one shoulder tops . . . muscle shirts, see-through or mesh tops (unless underneath a shirt) aren't to be worn. Blouses, shirts or tops that reveal bare backs, midriffs, undergarments, or that have spaghetti straps or revealing necklines are not to be worn in Trent's classes, hallways, class activities, or on field trips. (Trent Secondary)

> Under the guise of social order, a twenty-first century dress code emerged that continued to place the burden of self-control, public decency, and sexual morality in the school on girls' shoulders (Pomerantz 2008, 8).

Almost all schools have a dress code. Sometimes the codes are somewhat vague, with reference to broad, undefined categories such as 'no gangwear' or 'no revealing dress,' implying a shared understanding of what these categories include. Other times, dress code details are very specific, much like Trent's list of dress code regulations quoted above. Like most other rules, dress codes are frequently presented without explanation although their common listing under the category 'respect for self' frames them within the context of morality and individual responsibility in that how students dress is believed to reflect what they think of themselves. If a student wears torn or ripped clothing, for instance, or provocative clothing, they are constructed as lacking self-respect, while the values embedded in the rules themselves are left unquestioned and students' discipline, or marginalization from others, becomes their own responsibility (Raby 2005).

Students who break dress codes face a variety of potential conse-quences. Most are first given a chance to 'cover up' or change their clothes, but if they refuse, or repeatedly violate the dress code, they can be sent to the office and even suspended. There are many reasons why schools institute such dress codes, usually related to concerns about school image and professionalism (e.g., through regulating messages on T-shirts) and also to safety (e.g., through attempts to ban various indicators of gang membership). The dress codes are also gendered through the lens of heterosexuality. While school rules only occasion-ally directly refer to girls' dress, some codes name items of girls' dress or refer directly to cleavage or midriffs, and student and staff discus-sion of them suggest that what girls wear is frequently the primary, underlying concern of dress codes.[4] The gendered nature of dress codes and their enforcement in turn reflects much broader cultural preoccu-pation with girls' dress (Levy 2005; Page 2002; Pomerantz 2007).

Staff Engagements with Gendered Dress Codes

Some staff raised concerns with boys' dress, concerns which tended to fall into one of two categories. Like girls, boys sometimes wear 're-vealing' dress, specifically muscle shirts. Five staff members referred to muscle shirts, one suggesting that boys felt discrimination against them because girls could wear one-inch straps on their tank tops while boys could not wear muscle shirts at all, even though they have wider straps. Another suggested that the issue is not so much that boys are wearing revealing tops but that muscle shirts are also called 'wife beat-ers,' which is sexist and thus comes under rules against sexual harass-ment. In a similar vein, the issue of boys' shirts relaying problematic statements, including statements referencing drug use and derogatory comments about women, was another common staff concern as they seemed far more likely than girls to wear such T-shirts. Consequently, boys would be asked to cover up, or to wear their shirts inside-out.

Despite these observations, girls' dress was three times more likely to be discussed as a problem. As Glenn (Whitton teacher) pointed out, 'Uh, girls especially would have to be covered.' While some specifically mentioned items of girls' dress such as tank tops, halter tops, and short skirts, many others made broader references to girls' revealing dress in general. Even in cases of school uniforms, some girls were found to be overly revealing, by rolling up their skirts, for example. Critical com-mentary on girls' dress also occasionally extended to commentary on other teachers' dress, with three observing that female staff members need to dress 'more professionally,' and even on some female parents' dress.

Usually such concerns with revealing dress were presented as self-evident. Occasionally, however, a staff member would provide a brief explanation for why it is problematic for girls to wear revealing clothes. While one raised the concern that girls' dress is distracting to boys, an explanation that is also occasionally raised in the codes themselves, the most common explanation was that the school context is similar to a work environment and not 'the beach.'

> ROBIN (Whitton vice-principal): The bottom line is that if it's a string halter or something, it's not appropriate for school. It's not appropriate for business and as a result you're not wearing it alone. You'll have to wear something over it.

Only Laura (Whitton teacher) articulated any sympathy for girls' choices, suggesting that in her experience with her own daughter it is difficult to shop for jeans that are not low-cut or for tank tops that have wide straps. Jim (Big City teacher) also uniquely expanded the issue away from specific girls and pointed towards the broader topics of body image and media, feeling that a more appropriate way to address girls' dress than dress codes would involve students in critical analyses of popular representations of girls.

Enforcement of dress codes was considered a particularly challenging task for staff, especially in regards to girls' dress, due to the subjective nature of determining 'appropriate dress' and the difficulty of constantly keeping an eye out for dress violations.

> MARIA (Whitton teacher): Like I'm not sure if it was other teachers or if it was administration but it just seemed like I was the only one or there's like a handful of teachers that actually cared about [girls' dress]. And uh, when I had a student come in with a tank top and you know, well 'Mrs. So-and-so just said it was OK and I just saw the vice-principal on my way in and she thought my top was cute.' And I said, 'Well I'm not arguing that your top is cute or not. You're not allowed to wear it to class.'

Such subjectivity of interpretation made it clear that the problem of revealing dress is not quite as self-evident as some codes of conduct and staff seemed to suggest, challenging the goal of consistency in enforcement discussed in chapter 5. One staff member talked about the need to rely on his own professional judgment in such cases, and another stated that dress codes are straightforward but also vague, capturing this contradiction:

> CHICAGO (Whitton vice-principal): Um, our dress code is fairly straightforward. It has to be presentable, it has to be reasonable. And of course that determination is left up to us. Uh, and is somewhat vague.

One teacher also narrated a story in which a colleague of hers felt unsupported by administration on the subjective assessment of acceptability – her interpretation of inappropriate dress was dismissed because of her non-Canadian background.

The challenge here is trying to solidify and regulate what is a constantly shifting realm of meanings and interpretations that reflect various dimensions of culture: age, fashion, class, ethnicity, religion, and, of course, the intersection of all of these with beliefs about gender and sexuality. As Garot and Katz (2003) discuss in reference to the work of Fred Davis, ambiguity is central to dress, and dress signifies a range of social tensions, including those between youth and age, masculinity and femininity, work and play, and conformity and rebellion. Varied meanings of dress were examined in the previous chapter where we saw that dress can represent cultural and racialized solidarities, for instance, and how dress can also be stereotypically interpreted by staff. Similarly, Robinson (1992) argued that Australian teachers' views of acceptable behaviour for young women were grounded in middle class values that did not resonate with the working class backgrounds of some girls. As we will see below when I discuss student comments on dress, despite a fairly rigid, moralizing language about dress in school codes of conduct, determinations of acceptability were no less clear to the students.

Interpretations of dress are subjective and yet by identifying certain kinds of dress as sexually problematic, staff members find themselves in a difficult situation wherein they must enact an intimate relation to student bodies for 'each act of appearance enforcement reveals the direction and detail of the enforcer's attentions' (Garot and Katz 2003, 431). Garot and Katz argue that this discomfort is partly managed through the use of humour to address dress infractions but within my interviews with teachers, some refused to address girls' clothing infractions at all. Three men and five women specifically raised the difficulty some male staff experience in addressing girls' dress code infractions. Men felt uncomfortable approaching female students and would frequently ask a female staff member to do so instead.

> BILL (Whitton teacher): I have an issue as a teacher, especially a male teacher, you know, in trying to say to a female student, you know, what do I think is appropriate or not appropriate versus what my colleague may think is appropriate or not appropriate.

> BRENDA (Big City guidance): And usually I'll get male teachers coming to me and saying 'Can you please talk to so-and-so um [pause] her [pause] she's got a really tiny top on that's [pause] not appropriate.'

Such concerns were similarly raised by one lesbian teacher.

> It's a difficult thing. Because, you know, I am an out, gay teacher and I am definitely not going to approach a young lady who's buxom and say, 'That T-shirt is not OK, you can't wear that.' I am not gonna do it [. . .] And I would suggest to [a] man not to do it. Do not do it. Is it worth it? Nuh-uh. You know she's wearing a short skirt and she's wearing this top where everything's hanging out [pause] I'm not telling her! Somebody else can do it! Sorry, not worth my job.

In this last comment, the participant spoke not just of discomfort in addressing girls' dress but of worry about preserving her job with a vehemence that was not evident in comments from the men, reminding us of ongoing homophobia in the schools, a point to which I will return at the end of this chapter.

Student Engagements with Gendered Dress Codes

Both boys and girls in the focus groups talked about dress. Such conversations included debates about the relative merits of uniforms, the concern addressed earlier with rules against hats, codes related to gang-wear, and provocative writing or images on t-shirts. There was also significant discussion, particularly in the Whitton focus groups, of girls' revealing dress. While boys were involved in some of these discussions and even the silent ones may well have influenced girls' comments, it was usually the girls who focused most on these dress codes. I argue elsewhere that how these young women engage with dress codes illustrates how they actively, critically, and reproductively engage with moral strictures regarding gender and sexuality (Raby 2010b), a position I will briefly summarize here.

On the one hand, the girls would contest the dress codes for being overly particular about their clothing and for ignoring their practical needs. Rules about tank-tops, for example, drew commentary that sometimes included feelings that these should be acceptable on hot days.[5] They would also criticize teachers for applying these codes in ways that seemed to discriminate against girls and against certain girls in particular.

> CATHERINE: That's like, the spaghetti strap rule is like kind of unfortunate because it's like, for boys it's not a problem, and it's just like, 'Sorry I am a female like and it's hot and I would like to wear a spaghetti strap tank top,' but it's like, 'No, no you must not expose skin' which is kind of ridiculous 'cause/
> JANICE: You are not even showing anything; just your arm [laughs].
> CATHERINE: Yeah you're really not, it is just your body, it's like, 'Oh no, the human body!' (Whitton FG 1)

> BARBARA: [. . .] There is some favouritism.
> LANA: [. . .] with dress code stuff cuz [pause] um, who was it? A couple of days ago she had a – she just had a tank top on and because she had like, bigger, breasts [pause and chuckling] she got told to put a shirt on. But someone else who has like, you know, smaller and everything, they just didn't care. (Whitton FG 4)[6]

> BIBI: What is respectable clothing? Like, does that mean you have to like wear like jeans and like long pants and like long T-shirts throughout the rest of your life? (Big City FG 3)

Also, on a few occasions, the dress codes were criticized based on self-expression, although interestingly it was more likely boys than girls with this stance. Of the girls, Nicole framed this position most directly, yet even when defending freedom of expression she disparaged other girls' dress:

> With dress code rules, just – I understand like you can't wear like racist comments or whatever, like rude comments on your shirts and that. But if a girl wants to dress like a sleaze then she should be allowed to, cuz

that is part of Canada and part of our Charter of Rights and Freedoms. (Whitton FG 3)

The girls also criticized the fashion industry for emphasizing revealing clothing and boys for seeming to prefer girls who wear this clothing. Occasionally the girls spoke of wearing short skirts or bandanas in critical defiance and hoping that the principal would not see them, of speaking out against differential treatment of girls, and of defending their own clothing choices with administration. For example, Nicole (Whitton FG 3) unsuccessfully challenged her administration when she was asked to change her home-made, 'shredded' outfit on the basis that it was not revealing, while Sammie (Whitton FG 7) successfully fought back on religious grounds when her principal asked her to remove her headscarf.[7]

These challenges rarely questioned the underlying logic of the deeply normalized, predominant concern with girls' revealing dress, however, and the girls frequently embraced dress codes as a way to regulate other girls' dress. In fact, girls' critiques of the codes and their inconsistent enforcement were set starkly against hostility towards other girls' 'revealing dress': certain clothing was described as whorish, slutty, disgusting, disturbing, and wrong, with the wearers similarly evaluated.[8] Such 'sleaziness' was explained as resulting primarily from girls' desires to get boyfriends, but also from their attempts to be cool and trendy, and their fashion incompetence. In this way we can see how processes of moral regulation are not only 'top-down' and institutional, but initiated by everyday people in their interactions, though often in the service of middle class values (Brock 2003).

Drawing on similar arguments to those we see embedded in the rules themselves and in staff comments, these girls referred to appropriate dress for an educational environment and to prepare for future work. One group also suggested that formal dress codes are needed to help young women avoid either sexual or peer harassment – they keep girls safe by instructing them on acceptable dress. However, the key concern, particularly in Whitton, seemed to be the need to keep other girls in line so that everyone else wouldn't have to 'see that.'

JANICE: But if you are walking around with a tank top that just covers your boobs then, you know you should probably put a [sweater] on. [everyone laughs] I would kind of be disgusted if I saw you [Marc says 'yeah'] and probably make fun of you behind your back. (Whitton FG 1)

MARJORY: I like the dress code ones a lot cuz I don't appreciate the girls wearing like [group agreeing] the midriff and the thong. I don't like seeing that. (Whitton FG 4)

LANA: I don't feel like staring at someone's butt. (Whitton FG 4)

GREG: . . . No coming to school with bikini top on and like
ASH: [laughter]
SALLY: [laughter] Yeah that's a good rule, like, nobody else wants to see that, like [I wouldn't]. (Big City FG 9)

When students position themselves as dressing 'normally,' or other girls as being 'skanky,' they reflect and reproduce certain moral values about what is attractive or acceptable, judgments which are embedded in school rules and in teachers' comments, and which are in turn linked to unequal identity locations related to race, class, style, and popularity. Pomerantz presents an example of this in Girls, Style and School Identities: Dressing the Part (2008) in which the provocative dress of the popular White and Asian girls is rarely questioned while similar dress among the working class girls in the school's aesthetics program is the frequent target of critique by other students.

It is evident from these patterns that these young women participated, sometimes quite wholeheartedly, in regulating other girls' dress. Yet this pattern is not simply about girls passively reproducing a patriarchal, middle class framework but also about *creating themselves* as appropriate girls within institutional structures and inequalities (Raby 2010b). Teenage girls are embedded in discourses that require self-monitoring and evaluation, comparing themselves to others and to dominant forms of femininity (Driscoll 2002). Driscoll adopts the view that it is through interaction that the gendered self is produced. From this position, these girls were not only regulating each other and potentially jockeying for power, but trying to position themselves on the 'safe side' of the fine line between attractive and unacceptable. They showed their skill in using gendered discourses to locate themselves. Nicole (FG 3) provides a nice example of this because she was at first very critical of school dress codes for how they regulate girls' dress but then made it clear that she is not saying that 'anything goes': 'Oh man, on dress codes I just totally thought of this example. I actually think I have to agree now there should be some sort of dress code.' She proceeded to provide examples of a girl exposing a thong, and another wearing extremely low-riding pants. In this way, Nicole illustrates her own social, gender, and fashion competence, even if it at the same time reproduces gendered moralizing that she had previously argued against. Finally, the girls' focus on how they should not have to look at revealing dress suggests that bodily displays are meant for someone else, specifically boys (who are consequently distracted), locating the speaker as straight, invested in the regulation of displays of femininity and the female body, and focused on other things, including school (or being a 'proper' student). Again, this response can be interpreted as an illustration of gender performance and self-constitution, as well as the perpetuation of gender and class inequality through evaluating and condemning other girls' dress and consequently regulating girls' sexuality (Hey 1997; Brown 2003).

Ongoing Double Standards

> VEE: But it sucks you know that you have to like, a girl has to like be like, 'Oh my gosh, what do I wear today like, is it going to attract somebody, or something?' But also, like, you should have a sense of what is not modest . . . (Big City FG 8)

As I have presented, concerns about girls' revealing dress were reproduced by female (as well as male) students and almost never problematized by school staff, who felt that revealing dress is inimical to the professionalism of school or of students' future work. Preoccupations with girls' dress have been prominent in the media, and reproduced by researchers as well. Ariel Levy (2005), in particular, has argued that currently young women embrace celebrated, sexualized, and sexist identities in a false belief that this is a sign of liberation. In contrast, Shalit (2007) argues that young women who manage to reject raunch culture are 'moral heroines.' Others counter that when we talk about girls being 'sluts,' we are participating in a gendered, sexual double-standard which stigmatizes certain girls. As Tanenbaum (1999) and White (2002) explain, this stigma is one that is difficult to expunge, with sometimes devastating consequences. The moral language of acceptable female dress constitutes the 'slut' category – a 'hot potato' category that no girl wants to have attached to her, particularly as it can have such difficult consequences for her through serious peer ostracization (Tanenbaum 1999). Some codes of conduct state that provocative dress indicates a lack of self-respect, a worrisome characterization as it then suggests that if a student is harassed for her dress, or is bullied for being a 'slut,' then the responsibility of her harassment is her own, rather than located in the social control of female sexuality and bullying from others.

Young people, particularly girls, participate in such regulation as they negotiate their own and other girls' sexuality through discourses that compete and contradict: between sexual empowerment, attractiveness, fashion, growing up, and going 'too far,' all complicated by class, race, culture, and religion.[9] They invest in, play with, and critique dominant representations of femininity (Russel and Tyler 2002; Bettis and Adams 2003); they also use them to jockey for power. In doing so, these girls negotiate a 'fine line' between what is acceptable, expected, and attractive, and what is too much, even though this line is constantly in flux. In all of these cases, and in much of the staff and student commentary in my study, *girls'* dress is the focus of commentary, evaluation, and regulation (Duits and van Zoonen 2006), and individual girls themselves are the ones held responsible. For school rule committees sitting down to decide dress codes, these observations create a complicated situation. It is difficult in the context of a school to address the much broader media and commercial culture that impinges on gendered dress and so what seems like the most straightforward solution is to monitor individual girls' dress. Yet regulation of girls' dress is difficult to do without moralizing girls' choices. It also creates various enforcement challenges.

Through such dress codes and their enforcement the consequent hidden curriculum in turn gets taken up by students to bully and ostracize certain girls. A sexual double-standard clearly remains and girls risk their reputations with each other, with boys, and even with school staff, when they err (either accidentally or intentionally) on the side of being too revealing. Meanwhile, for the most part boys' (hetero)sexuality was only relevant in relation to student dress when student and staff commentators were concerned that boys were distracted by girls' provocative clothing, a position holding girls responsible for boys' sexual desires (Duits and van Zoonen 2006). This does not mean that concerns with boys' sexuality were absent, however, as illustrated by concerns with sexual harassment.

Sexual Harassment and Homophobia

Sexual harassment has been increasingly recognized as a problem in schools and the wider society. It can include gender harassment, inappropriate sexual comments and/or touch, including sexual assault, and the threat of rewards or punishments in exchange for sexual favours. It has been found to negatively affect recipients, creating discomfort at school and affecting academic outcomes, especially for girls (Hand and Sanchez 2000). Loredo, Reid, and Deaux (1995) argue that sexual harassment at the high school level is particularly detrimental because it may be difficult for students to remove themselves from the presence of a harasser, because gender role socialization is especially intense at high school and because there are clear hierarchical power systems in schools that can be abused. Within Ontario, concerns with sexual harassment in schools led to a report, 'Shaping a Culture of Respect in Our Schools: Promoting Safe and Healthy Relationships' (Sandals et al. 2008). This report drew substantially on data from the Canadian Association for Mental Health which found significant rates of sexual harassment in Ontario schools, with 36 per cent of boys and 46 per cent of girls in grade 9 reporting experiencing unwanted sexual comments, gestures, jokes, or looks. By grade 11 this rate had declined significantly for boys, but remained consistent at 46 per cent for girls, and was especially high for girls with disabilities. Robinson (2005) suggests that this gendered pattern in sexual harassment persists because it expresses and confirms hegemonic masculinity.

Concerns with sexual harassment have, in turn, led to the emphasis on school rules against it, rules that were strongly supported by the students in my study, with every single focus group supporting 'no sexual harassment.' One student was supported by her group in specifically framing this rule in terms of girls needing to feel safe at school:

ASHLEY: Somebody comes to school to learn, they don't want to come to school and have somebody come up behind them and feel them up. Especially girls, girls need to be safe in their school too. Like they would like their boyfriends or something to hold their hands, but if people they don't know come up behind them and touch them, it's not safe for girls like that; also guys cuz guys don't like being touched either. (Big City FG 6)

Another group argued that rules against sexual harassment help in cases where girls 'lack the self-respect' to challenge the harassment directly.

At first then, students' overwhelming support suggests that the issue of sexual harassment is far less complicated than other issues such as dress. It is a 'big' rule that students support. But defining sexual harassment in practice quickly becomes a challenge. Through surveys with eighty students within one American high school, Loredo, Reid, and Deaux (1995) found that females were more likely to see certain behaviour as harassment than male students were; some students limited their examples of sexual harassment to instances of physical force, while others defined it more broadly; and some behaviour was seen to be more playful or joking and therefore acceptable when between friends. The intent of the harasser, the reaction of the recipient, and the repetition of instances were all considered by students in their study to be relevant to defining behaviour as sexual harassment. Also, if the target of the harassment was considered to have a choice, in leaving the situation for instance, it was less likely to be seen as harassment. Finally, male harassers were more likely to be exempted from blame based on young men being 'stupid' or 'hormonal.' The authors argue that the students' explanations indicate that they have a difficult time figuring out what is reasonable behaviour to expect from other students. They noted that students have particular difficulty seeing the broader effects of harassing behaviour. Such murkiness was similarly illustrated within some of my focus group discussions.

My first example addresses 'pantsing,' a topic which arose exclusively in Big City FG 2. Julie explained 'pantsing' after the group's agreement that 'no sexual harassment' is a good rule:

JULIE: OK, there's single 'pantsing' where someone just like pulls down [someone's outer pants]/
LIZ: There's like this pantsing craze going on [. . .] when you pull someone's pants like, yeah, and it's really embarrassing and it's really funny for everyone to watch it, but anyways. [laughs]

The students in this focus group then narrated a story of how one of the girls in the group, along with her friend, was disciplined for 'revenge pantsing' a boy who then reported the incident. The girls were threatened with suspension on the grounds that pantsing was sexual assault. In telling this story, all three participants in this group felt the administration's response to be unfair because the girl was pantsing in revenge for the boy pantsing her, because 'everyone' was doing it and because it was a trivial issue:

LIZ: [. . .] we were like, 'OK, well we weren't the only ones who were doing it first, and second/

OWEN: Who cares/
JULIE: Who cares.

I then asked them to clarify their views on pantsing and whether it should be considered sexual harassment.

JULIE: It is sexual harassment, but like [. . . it's not] really bad and whereas we're doing it to friends who don't really care/
OWEN: [I don't think it's] considered assault, but like it's just petty, it's not like you are really touching them.
I: So you think its OK to do that to people?
OWEN: Well, no/
JULIE: I don't think you should be like sentenced to [two years imprisonment].
I: And that's what happens?
JULIE: No, but you know, I'm exaggerating.
LIZ: I know I wasn't like, we weren't like, 'Oh, I want to see your bum,' like we weren't pulling his pants down for that reason, we were simply retaliating.

A series of explanations are given here for why this case of pantsing was considered relatively unproblematic. First, it was between friends and was therefore seen as more playful than harassing, an argument reflected in the research by Loredo et al. (1995).[10] The students' categorization of this as a case of revenge also reinforced their perception that it was part of a game. Second, Owen argues that the pantsing did not involve touching, implying that real sexual harassment is physical, reflecting Loredo's findings, and also the research by Deborah Land in her examination of how students distinguish between teasing, bullying, and sexual harassment (2003). Finally, the students considered the intention of the initiators as non-sexual. They felt that the practice was taken too seriously by staff, despite the fact that a student had complained about it.

Another site of contention in the definition of sexual harassment arose in a discussion of boys wearing T-shirts with sexist comments on them. Whitton FG 6 agreed that it is problematic to wear a shirt advocating violence against women, but also pointed out that a shirt being worn by a boy in the group on the day of the focus group was not problematic, to illustrate that the category of sexual harassment is a difficult one. Their debate around sexual harassment that arose while trying to figure out where to place the 'no sexual harassment' cue card shows how these students distinguished between what is sexist and what is not:

> ANGELINA: ['No sexual harassment'] should go in the middle because that is not like, it depends on that, it could go from Tetrad's shirt, which you/
> KIERSTYN: It's just like a design thing, it doesn't really mean anything/
> ANGELINA: Yeah, to like an extreme.
> [Interviewer asks Tetrad to describe his shirt]
> TETRAD: It says 'Spanky's Lounge and Pool Hall. Come for a nice rack,' and the silhouette of a woman. 'Keep your balls in the pocket' it says. [group laughing] I don't think – oh and a couple of martini's on it. But it's not like implying anything. (Whitton FG 6)

Even though Tetrad's shirt *does* imply something – that the pool hall is a place to see sexy women – it is not considered harassment because it is playful and framed as primarily about design. Yet the group acknowledges that the shirt is potentially controversial because of its gendered and sexual overtones by bringing it up for discussion under the topic of sexual harassment in the first place.

Finally, another group to engage in a long discussion of sexual harassment was Big City FG 8, a group of girls from a Catholic school. This group shared a strong sense of what sexual harassment is, and were frustrated with other girls in their school who wouldn't report harassment or seem to take it seriously:

> LILY: Um, for me in my school, I think girls need to get a click in their heads, like guys are like sexually harassing them but when teachers come around they're like, 'Oh no, we're just playing around'/
> VEE: Or they'll see it as attention like, 'Oh, he likes me' but I'm like, 'No, you don't wanna be noticed like that.'

They felt that other girls did not fully understand what sexual harassment is or how to deal with it and ultimately felt that the girls themselves are responsible for their harassment, drawing on discourses of self-respect and girls' provocative dress to hold these other girls responsible. For example, in talking about some guys in her school who call girls 'bitch,' Lily said, 'I'm like, like personally I don't dress like that, so I wouldn't be put in that situation,' and proceeded to talk about how other girls arrange their uniforms in a sexual way. She added that while

some girls will appropriately tell the boys to 'jerk off, you,' others, who
need to 'get a life,' will like it and just say something ambiguous like
'hey.' Lily felt that these and other girls do not sufficiently stand up for
themselves:

> LILY: I mean like OK, because like some guys they like go to their girl-
> friends and they're like touching them in the wrong way and they're like
> 'Stop it, stop it' [said in a giggly way] and I'm like, you need to stand your
> ground if you're a girl, I mean like 'Stop it, come on,' right? If they're sexu-
> ally harassing you and you know it [but] they take it in a fun way, they'll
> be like, 'Oh just stop it' and they think they're getting serious, that they're
> getting into a better relationship and then when they go home, they'll call
> their friends and be like oh my god, he did this to me. I'm like [. . .] girls
> need to get a sense of what's what. I mean a guy that really likes you won't
> use you, you know what I mean?

The girls emphasized boys' problematic behaviour and drew on a
broad understanding of harassment that addressed a widespread pattern of boys' behaviour, regardless of whether certain girls may have
enjoyed the attention. Yet ultimately they held the girls, not the boys, as
responsible for this harassment because they potentially invited it and
failed to properly address it. Much like the discussion on dress outlined above, there is a line between acceptable attentions and unacceptable ones. These girls positioned themselves on the 'right side' through
comparing themselves to other girls and again, boys' performances of
gender and sexuality received less comment.

Finally, the murky territory of sexual harassment was addressed by
several teachers. For example, Dylan (Whitton teacher) related one incident in which a male student smacked a girl on the butt on a dare. He
received a three day suspension; as Dylan noted, 'Technically that's an
assault.' But the students themselves did not think it was serious. 'The
girls thought it was funny and they told him to "fuck off" or something
like that, you know?'

These examples of debates around interpretations of sexual harassment resonate with the literature currently available on student perceptions of what harassment is. Despite overwhelming agreement that
sexual harassment is wrong, in practice differential definitions of what
sexual harassment is are deeply relevant. Research also finds that these
differential definitions are gendered, with boys less likely to see behaviours as harassing and more likely to be excused as boys being 'stupid'

or 'hormonal' (Loredo, Reid, and Deax 1995; Hand and Sanchez 2000). In her interviews with boys, Robinson found them likely to trivialize harassment as a joke, normal, deserved (e.g., certain girls 'ask for it'), and necessary for building up male status. Boys challenging this harassment would, in turn, face homophobic comments.

As I will discuss shortly, some schools respond to murky definitions of sexual harassment with a rule banning all physical touch. Yet such a blanket response reinforces a problematically narrow definition of harassment based on physical interactions and fails to engage students in vital debates about what sexual harassment is and what kinds of inequalities it perpetuates (Levinson 2009), debates that will inform their lives beyond the walls of the school. In contrast, 'Shaping a Culture of Respect in Our Schools: Promoting Safe and Healthy Relationships' (Sandals et al. 2008) argues that the problem is best addressed through education: early and comprehensive sex education that includes discussion of these issues; education about gender-based violence, sexual harassment and homophobia across curricula; education in critical media literacy; and immediate staff response to sexual, gender, and homophobic harassment.

Homophobic Harassment

While rules against sexual harassment were common across the codes of conduct I studied, a distinct contrast between the semi-rural school codes and the urban codes was around whether they made any specific mention of homophobia, despite the high levels of homophobia in Ontario schools and its significantly negative effects on its recipients (Egale 2008; Sandals et al. 2008). In their survey of 1200 participants from across Canada on homophobia in Canadian schools, Egale found that two thirds of lesbian, gay, bisexual, transgendered, and queer/questioning (LGBTQ) youth felt unsafe in school (compared to 20 per cent of straight participants), over half reported verbal harassment, 41 per cent sexual harassment, and 25 per cent physical harassment.[11] In examining homophobic comments and other harassment in Ontario schools, the Canadian Association for Mental Health similarly found that more boys than girls both receive and make homophobic comments, with 34 per cent of grade 9 boys and 30 per cent of grade 11 boys being victims of such insults, while 38 per cent of grade 9 boys and 33 per cent of grade 11 boys reported being perpetrators. In grade 9, 22 per cent of girls reported being victims and 26 percent perpetrators;

while in grade 11, 12 per cent of girls reported being victims and 16 per cent perpetrators (Sandals et al. 2008).

A stipulation against homophobic harassment was frequently mentioned in the urban codes of conduct I examined but not once in the semi-rural codes.[12] For this reason, I asked the Whitton staff, who were from a more rural area, why they thought it might be that the semi-rural codes I examined did not mention homophobia. In response, a number of teachers emphasized their own intolerance of homophobia and the need for rules against it. Several teachers mentioned that they address any homophobic talk immediately. Two emphasized the need to address homophobia more openly and to ensure an environment without harassment so that students can try to figure out their sexuality within an atmosphere of tolerance.[13]

Staff members were more circumspect about the success of instituting a policy that specifically names homophobic harassment, however, citing a range of concerns: lack of attention to the issue from the school board, other teachers' own homophobia and/or discomfort with the topic, others' denial of the possibility that there may even be gay kids in non-urban schools, and the perception that homosexuality is a more individual issue that should be covered through individual counselling. One vice-principal, Jack, also suggested that parents may react badly if there is a mention of anti-homophobia in the code of conduct as 'it's something that if you put it in the code of conduct, you've got to understand how parents and people might react to that kind of thing, you know what I mean? Positive or negative.' In addition to these more direct discussions of homophobia and homosexuality, there were a number of moments in interviews with staff members when students' heterosexuality was assumed. Staff talk about girls' dress being distracting to boys is just one example; another is when a vice-principal talked of telling students who are misbehaving that they have a lot to lose, 'including their girlfriend.' In her ethnography of an American high school Pascoe (2007) observed that the overall culture of the school is overwhelmingly one of compulsory heterosexuality with teachers commonly invoking heterosexual romance as a tactic to engage their classes. In the meantime, short of one student saying that it was inappropriate to use the word 'fag' at her school, students in my study did not discuss homophobia. This silence may in part have been because they were not asked to directly comment on school rules against homophobia. For the most part they assumed students to be heterosexual, with the rare occasion when they suggested that individual students were (problematically) gay – one because he dressed in tight clothing!

As illustrated in the discussion of racism in chapter 6, Whitton staff felt that the social climate of their geographical location was less diverse and more conservative than in large urban centres. They were therefore less apt to proactively address homophobia in their schools and recognized why school rules might not be explicit about addressing homophobia in non-urban areas. Ironically, however, it is in such contexts that attention to issues such as homophobia is particularly important to students on the receiving end of homophobic bullying or who are trying to come to terms with their sexuality within settings with limited external resources to support them. In Egale's study of homophobia harassment in Canadian schools, respondents indicated that those schools with anti-homophobia policies were experienced as more supportive, allowing students to feel more comfortable talking to a counsellor, more likely to report homophobia, and more attached to the school overall. These schools were experienced as less homophobic too, with fewer homophobic comments coming from other students (Egale 2008).[14] It is also important to remember that homophobic harassment is not only a problem for students who identify as LGBTQ, or those who are questioning their own sexuality, but that it also affects young people who are not following conventional gender norms. Indeed, homophobia is a powerful tool used to regulate gender, creating a hostile climate for any individual who in any way challenges traditional gender roles, particularly boys (Chambers, Tincknell, and van Loon 2004; Frosh, Phoenix, and Pattman 2002; Renold 2001, 2005; Pascoe 2007).

Public Displays of Affection

Some schools have attempted to deal with concerns about sexual harassment in particularly sweeping ways through introducing rules against 'public displays of affection' (PDAs). As one school outlines in its rules: 'Embracing, kissing and hugging are not appropriate for school,' and another, '. . . no public displays of affection are permitted.' Within my review of codes of conduct, I found that such stipulations were generally found in the semi-rural rather than the urban schools although they are widespread across North America. Some of these policies even ban 'high-fives' and hugs between friends, much to the frustration of students who have challenged these policies (Gray 2007). Albright (2009) describes how such 'no touch' policies have been sweeping the United States, particularly at the middle school level, and have also begun to emerge in the United Kingdom. Allen (2009) similarly cites a rule found in some schools in New Zealand that requires students to remain at least five centimeters apart. As Albright quotes, one American school's policy even goes so far as to state that hugging is 'in poor taste, reflects poor judgment, and brings discredit to the school and to the persons involved.'

Rules against such displays of affection and their enforcement reflect several interrelated concerns. Most centrally, the rules against displays of affection are connected to broader 'no touch' policies that have been introduced within the last few decades as schools attempt to address horseplay and sexual harassment (Gray 2007; Levinson 2009). Rather than distinguish between good touch and bad, schools are opting to introduce blanket bans and as students have begun to have long and intimate hugs, schools have included them in the bans. Concerns about the intimacy of hugs and other public displays of affection also point to other issues at stake, however. Such rules are again related to a desire to create a certain kind of school environment that is rational, self-disciplined, professional, and consequently separate from the body (Allen 2009). This attempt to define a certain kind of school environment can be framed as yet another attempt to divide school culture from street culture (McLaren 1993), or the 'business of school' from young people's cultural and private spaces. Staff attempt to construct the school as a professional space distinct from youth culture but also as distinct from certain manifestations of romance and sexuality, evident in particular concern with hugs being 'overly intimate' (Levinson 2009).

In my own research, while unfortunately the topic of PDAs was not discussed during staff interviews, it came up in all of the fifteen focus groups that participated in the exercise in which they sorted the rules into categories of good, bad, and controversial. Reflecting the debate and students' own discomfort with aspects of such a rule, twelve groups categorized this rule as controversial and three as simply a bad rule. The reason 'no PDAs' garnered so much contention was that while students had their own concerns about some student 'groping,' they experienced this rule as one which was used to prevent hand-holding, kissing, and indeed all affectionate contact, which they thus felt to be extreme and heavy-handed:

I: 'No public displays of affection'

MARJORY: Well, like holding hands is alright.
BARBARA: I think in the middle.
BETTY: I think a little kissing is OK, as long as you're not like making out in the hallway. [Various 'yeahs' from group]
SUZY: As long as you're not like eating each others' faces and stuff. [Various 'yeahs from group] (Whitton FG 5)

AMY: Like even if you were with your boyfriend walking down like the hallway/
LINDSEY: Holding hands.
AMY: Yeah holding his hand, you get yelled at for it.
LINDSEY: You get like detention.
I: And why is that stupid?
LINDSEY: It's retarded [sic], cuz why couldn't I – I can understand [inaudible]/
MALE VOICE [inaudible]: Why can't I hold my girlfriend's hand?
AMY: [continues from Lindsey's comment] kissing and being all over each other in the hallway/
LINDSEY: Like I understand about kissing, making out and groping and stuff like that but you should be able to hold his hand [everyone talking]/
JAMES: Or give someone a hug if you haven't seen someone in a long time or something. (Whitton FG 2)

CARMELLA: I don't know if that's fair, cuz if you're holding hands or something, or something minor, I mean if you're being kind of completely insensitive and rude in front of other people, then I can understand why they would be making it a rule, but I think most people know where to draw the line, so I don't know why the rule is really necessary (Big City FG 5).

Students distinguished between what they felt to be acceptable and unacceptable affection between other students in the school setting, seeing heavy 'making out' or 'having sex' in the hall as examples of excess. This was also one of those rules that led to debate about the spatiality of the school, as very well illustrated in Big City FG 1:

MICHAEL: Baaaaaad rule.
I: Bad rule?
OTHERS: Yeah.
SAMMY: Fair.
TIFFANY: Fair.

I: So why is it, why, Michael, why do you think it's bad?
MICHAEL: Bad. It's just a bad rule.
I: Hmm, it's just bad. Why's it fair?
[. . .]
SAMMY: If, if you're in the hall, so, you can do whatever you'd like, any-where. I can understand [this rule for] a classroom, [inaudible] not really appropriate in class, but a hall OK.
I: Oh OK, so you should be able to do whatever you want in the hall?
SAMMY: Oh yeah, and in the classroom you shouldn't . . .
[. . .]
JJ: But both of them are on on school property.
SAMMY: But the hallway's different than the class.
JJ: How is it different?
MALE VOICE: Depends what kind of [inaudible]
MALE VOICE: Cuz we're being teached.

Again we see how the students would pay attention to context, by differentiating between kinds of activity, for instance, and between settings. Overall, however, the students felt that such a rule against PDAs went too far.

School concerns with such problems as sexual harassment are legitimate, as I have discussed above. But clearly not all forms of touch are harassment. Indeed, Levinson (2009) counters that rather than banning touch, schools need to engage students in discussions about defining sexual harassment and distinguishing acceptable from non-acceptable touch. Such vital distinctions are lost in blanket bans. The attempt to define the school environment as business-like and separate from young people's peer relationships permeates various aspects of school rules and staff enforcement of them, as discussed in chapter 2. Yet for students the school is also an important social space (Dickar 2008; Tupper et al. 2008). The school is their living space for a significant portion of the day and for many, their access to private space in general is severely limited (Amit-Talai 1995). It is in such a context that PDAs may be quite important for some young people and over-zealous interpretation of such rules a significant intrusion. Further, Albright cites a number of studies that find touch to be vital to young people's health and well-being while being 'touch deprived' can lead to aggression, reinforcing the illogic of policies against hugging at school. Finally, as part of a regulation of young people's culture, such rules can be considered an attempt to control, contain, or suppress their sexuality, reflecting problematic, Americanized discourses of teens as consumed by their sexualities and therefore potentially out of control (Tait 2000; Schalet 2004; Allen 2009). The implication of rules against PDAs is that any display of affection threatens to open up a slippery slope to uncontrollable excess. Yet students themselves did not see it this way; they were quite able to discuss and debate acceptable levels of affection.

My sense in our focus groups was that student support for what they felt to be acceptable public displays of affection was framed again in terms of students' everyday, lived relationships. As one boy states above: 'Why can't I hold my girlfriend's hand?' Students thus engage critically with schools' attempts to control their bodies and interactions, raising the question of how much the school should attempt to suppress affectionate peer relations, particularly when school and staff practices themselves often draw on students' sexuality, in school events and classroom examples (Pascoe 2007). Meanwhile, however, the rules are welcome in that they address affection that students feel 'goes too far,' a similar approach to their discussion of girls' revealing dress.

The Tricky Terrain of Gender and Sexuality

While some school staff members might wish educational environments to be distinct from issues related to gender and sexuality, this is clearly not possible, for students and staff are embedded in gendered cultural patterns, and are also sexual and sexualized beings. Gender, especially hegemonic masculinity, is of central importance to understanding issues of school discipline and yet remains remarkably underexamined in theory and advice on school discipline. Meanwhile certain rules quite directly pertain to questions of gender and sexuality. These, and their enforcement, reflect and reproduce gendered patterns while trying to contain and manage sexuality. Such containment is made more challenging when such personal issues as dress and intimacy are cultural, and constantly shifting. What is considered acceptable varies across class backgrounds, gender, culture and community standards, student age groupings, religious backgrounds, fashion trends, and student subcultures. Within this shifting, moral realm, school staff and safety committees face significant challenges as they attempt to define and regulate what is considered acceptable and not acceptable.

In my research the consequent challenges were discussed in reference to revealing dress, defining sexual harassment and personal displays of affection as distinctions emerged between what student and staff participants believe rules should cover in the first place and when or where such rules should be enforced. These areas are particularly difficult for staff to deal with because they are in the fraught terrain of student sexuality, peer culture, and institutional goals that include dividing peer culture from the school. The further challenge is that while students may define some of this terrain more loosely than staff, they also want dimensions of each of these rules to be upheld. The students I talked to valued school rules addressing girls' appropriate dress, for instance, but they had broader definitions of what is appropriate and were very concerned with this rule being applied inconsistently across students. Similarly, students did not want to see other students involved in heavy 'make-out' sessions in front of their lockers, but they also did not want all expressions of affection to be censored. Finally, students were particularly supportive of rules against sexual harassment, but also tended to assume a fairly narrow definition of what constitutes sexual harassment. For staff this latter issue raises a particularly difficult challenge in ensuring that rules are experienced as fair but also enforced so that students feel safe.

In light of these challenges, school rules need some reconsideration in terms of the rationales behind them in the first place. How is it that some schools come to a point when they are defining hugging as reflecting 'poor judgment,' for example (Albright 2009)? Whose sense of morality is embedded in such rules and their regulation? What is being normalized or naturalized in terms of gender and morality when staff draw on terms like 'common sense' in reference to appropriate dress? It needs to be recognized that these are attempts to regulate what is not nearly as 'matter-of-fact' as some staff people contend. As moral regulation scholars remind us, such regulation is an area of contestation and struggle over meanings of what is appropriate and what is not.

This latter concern can lead to a conundrum: various more humanistic classroom management texts advocate simple, straightforward rules such as 'respect others' or 'dress appropriately for school' but such rules assume shared values and leave room for significant interpretation. Perhaps it is fairer to students to have clear lists of expectations then, e.g., outlining exactly what is considered appropriate dress and what is not, a strategy that can also be useful in the case of litigation. Such clarity guides students but creates a more formulistic engagement with the rules in which students are incited to look for loopholes. Furthermore, it creates a bombardment of rules from above and reduces possibilities for student participation in discussions of what respect or appropriate dress might mean in their school. Institutional imperatives thus come to transcend discussion, negotiation, and compromise, possibilities shut down when a school simply bans any affectionate touch, for instance.

'Shaping a Culture of Respect in Our Schools' (Sandals et al. 2008) recommends that young people at least have the opportunity to talk about gender-based violence, sexual harassment and homophobia across curricula. Talking about the moral dimension of school rules is something that those working in moral education have advocated (Nucci 2001) as it opens up the possibility for students to explore and to more fully understand why certain kinds of touch might be problematic, for instance. Student comments from my focus groups suggest that they are already thinking about such distinctions. Teachers also need guidance, skill-training, and support in these areas (Sandals et al. 2008), in part to recognize their own investments in certain understandings of what is acceptable or not. The next chapter will investigate such possibilities for contestation, or even resistance, in much more depth.

8 Acceptance and Challenge

NICOLE (Whitton FG 4): Oh I follow the [pause] the no – well like the basic ones like 'no fighting,' 'no bullying,' like the 'must have' rules. I follow all of those. Like I've skipped class a couple of times but then that's cuz if a friend's been like you know heaving sobs and it's like they need someone to talk to. Like, I'll do that for my friends. But it's like – a rule that I think is good and should be, like, more enforced in our school is not using the elevator if you don't have to.

PATRICIA: (Whitton FG 1) … there are some of us who are, like, these rules are ridiculous. I am not following them.

How do students engage with the rules? As we saw in chapters 2 and 3, students frequently accept the rules but they also break them and sometimes they overtly challenge them. Various approaches consider why it is that students accept the rules, and I will touch on some of them here. While there may often be practical reasons for following rules, these approaches tend to focus on young people's socialization or, from a more post-structuralist perspective, on how young people become subjects. The bulk of this chapter, however, will examine students' challenges to the rules. Are all such challenges about defiance and students simply reacting to teachers' authority? Do these challenges reflect a more politicized resistance, e.g., of the working class student towards the middle class school or the containing, ordering function of rules in general? Are student grievances ever legitimate?[1] Various scholars have argued that rule-breaking can be legitimate and important. I will reflect on three such areas of scholarship, informed by critical theory and post-structuralism. This chapter concludes by discussing ways that students challenged the rules through negotiation and organized protest, rather than rule-breaking and how such challenge can be both informed and undermined by an emphasis on young people's rights.

Acceptance

As discussed in chapters 2 and 3, students generally accepted a wide range of rules, particularly those that can be categorized as 'major,' such as those against violence. Rules against bullying and harassment were particularly valued, despite varying interpretations of what these things mean. Students rarely even introduced these rules into discussion. Support for rules was frequently instrumental, with students most likely to support rules that were seen to provide safety and/or to assist in their education. As illustrated in the previous chapter, even certain rules related to personal deportment were sometimes well supported as they served to regulate other students' undesirable behaviour and dress. In many cases students saw it within their interests to accept and perpetuate the rules; others simply accepted that schools have certain kinds of rules and that students are expected to follow them, reflecting their many years within a school system based on such rules.

One way to think about students' acceptance of the rules is through the lens of socialization theory. From this perspective, it is valuable and necessary for young people to learn the rules, norms, values, and routines of the wider society as part of growing up and learning their culture (Caputo 1995). This approach reflects concerns of much earlier theorists such as John Stuart Mill and Sigmund Freud, both of whom argued that it is necessary to guide and constrain children in order to civilize them and society. Agents of socialization, including the school, are therefore responsible for guiding students towards civility, and students' acceptance of the rules indicates their appropriate and necessary socialization. Students' failure to abide by the rules can be thought to reflect individual failing or deviance but also a failure of the socialization process in itself – something which should then be addressed through better classroom management techniques, for example (Jones and Jones 2007). Yet socialization theories have also been criticized for assuming cultural homogeneity and for being too 'top-down,' with young people conceptualized as empty vessels to be filled with culture, including social rules, rather than as actively engaged cultural participants (Caputo 1995; James and Prout 1990).

Sociologist William Cosaro has drawn on symbolic interactionism to counter the top-down nature of socialization theories through the concept of 'interpretive reproduction,' a theoretical approach that considers how children contribute to cultural production as they incorporate cultural content from the adult world into their own peer cultural projects, yet also change that broader cultural content in the process (1997). Cosaro's work provides extensive ethnographic detail on how, through children's play especially, young people learn about, practice, engage with, and also at times challenge adult culture. Much of children's culture is about learning, exploring, and replicating adult cultural norms. Yet children also investigate them through challenge. For example, Cosaro references Goffman's concept of secondary adjustments through which the members of an organization behave in unauthorized ways in order to get around the rule or norms of the organization that set out what a member should do or be. Cosaro suggests that a peer cultural 'underlife' develops even in preschools, often drawing on legitimate resources in order to challenge the rules that thwart children's autonomy. In one instance, children develop ways to stall and therefore avoid helping to clean up. Cosaro argues that such secondary adjustments reinforce students' collectivity as a group but that they also ultimately reinforce the values being challenged as children become embedded in broader culture.

The post-structural position advocated by Davies (1989) and Laws and Davies (2000) extends such a form of analysis that recognizes students as participants in creating and reproducing the social world by examining how students position themselves as good subjects as a way to display their cultural competence. From this approach, students' acceptance of the rules and the consequences for their infraction is one of the ways in which they show their skill in negotiating the school. My own research has illustrated students' weighing and selective acceptance of the rules, their attention to negotiating contexts in which rules are to be followed, and their own involvement in shaping what rules are enforced in the classroom and the hallways. A post-structural feminist approach thus provides a lens through which to address the dual nature of subjection: the acceptance of subjugation, e.g., through acceptance of the rules, but also engagement and challenge as people move beyond the conditions of their own emergence (Laws and Davies 2000).

From this perspective, Laws and Davies suggest that as students are embedded within coercive school practices they tend to take up or embrace the role of the 'good student' as they are invested in classroom order, the idea of choice, and illustration of competence through obedience. Students can also adopt pleasure and pride at their mastery of skills through self-discipline (Parkes 2010). Even those who break rules play a role in their own subjection when they comply with their punishment. Such embrace is reinforced by the discourses of individual, responsible choice-making and acceptance of consequences that are circulated by school authorities. Laws and Davies's position illustrates how post-structuralist theorizing is compatible with an understanding of agency as young people participate in reproducing social practices and can be deeply invested in school structures. As Laws and Davies also argue, however, the role of 'good student' is not always straightforward; as this book is illustrating, it is complicated by practical needs, peer relations, context (e.g., across classes and school spaces), gender, family background, culture, race, class, and previous categorizations such as 'behaviourally disturbed' or 'problem student' (as discussed in chapter 4). Such intersections provide contexts within which students may also use, negotiate, and reject dominant discourses about them, as I will further examine shortly.

Finally, acceptance can be conceptualized through the similar framework of governmentality studies, which has also taken up discourses of freedom and choice to understand how current processes of governance mobilize people's own autonomy and choice by guiding their freedom (Rose 1999) rather than resorting to direct social control. This 'conduct of conduct' (Gordon 1991, 2) facilitates a variety of ways of being, including healthy, virtuous, or self-disciplined (Rose 1999), yet suggests that relations of domination are embedded in our choices as these choices are indirectly guided or shaped. Through this lens we can see how codes of conduct and the spoken language of school discipline attempt to guide young people towards making the right choices, or adopting the rules, through the language of responsibility for instance (Raby 2005, 2010c). Millei draws on governmentality studies in her review of more humanistic approaches to classroom management, such as interactionalist and non-interventionist approaches, arguing that despite trying to decentre the power and control of the teacher in the classroom they actually make it more insidious (2010, 2011). She argues that the interactionalist concentration on fulfilling students' needs for love, power, freedom, and fun, for instance, and the non-interventionist approach that fosters student participation and student self-regulation both suggest that the self-regulated, autonomous person is more free of control and power. But by drawing on governmentality, and also linking it to the traditionally pastoral role of the schools in which teachers are expected to guide and be responsible for students, Millei argues that schools cannot realize such democratic politics. Instead, these inclinations towards fostering student autonomy involve *more* regulation as teachers seek to develop students' internal capacities towards self-reflexivity, self-regulation, and self-control, all in keeping with the development of neoliberal subjects. In sum, humanistic approaches to classroom management can be reinterpreted to suggest that significant forces are at work to foster student acceptance of school structure and discipline, even if they are not entirely transparent. Students' acceptance, in turn, can be understood as their successful governmentalization. This position overtly acknowledges power relations and regulation in governmental processes, in contrast to socialization theory, which tends to frame student inculcation as a benign, functional process. I return to this argument at the end of chapter 9, which concentrates on examining the potential of student participation in schools.

This section has considered several different theoretical approaches to understanding student acceptance of the rules. From a socialization perspective, a significant value is placed on how students are shaped, or participate in being shaped, into what is presumed to be a fairly homogeneous culture: acceptance of rules, in this context, is about the success of teaching to train young people to fit into the wider society of which they are members. Those working from a more Foucauldian or poststructural perspective complicate this process in important ways. The above discussion of governmentality, particularly as it is taken up by Millei (2010, 2011), starkly reminds us that student acceptance of rules and structures may be evidence of deep, insidious incursions of disciplinary and governmental power. Similarly, Laws and Davies (2000) contend that young people are active participants in the process of their own subjection. To Laws and Davies, students are commonly invested in discourses of good choice-making and social competency, even those students who may be getting into trouble. But Laws and Davies also frame such concepts as 'good choices,' 'good student,' or even 'good rules' as discursive, complicated by context and open to challenge or contestation. This latter position raises important questions about the presumed goodness of the rules, student guidance, and student compliance itself. What is being produced through these processes and in whose interests? What are the possibilities for young people to challenge these processes and how do we conceptualize such challenges?

Rule-Breaking

While students are frequently in support of the rules, there are also many points where they disagree with and/or challenge them. Through talking to staff, a number of reasons were raised as to why students might break rules. As I discussed in chapter 4, how staff understood student rule-breaking was linked to their broader philosophies of disciplinary processes (e.g., the value of deterrence), maturity, human nature, and sometimes context. Staff frequently commented that school rules were broken because students needed to defy them or to push against the limits and structures around them as part of the process of growing up, reflecting common, familiar ways of understanding youthful rule-breaking. From this perspective, rule-breaking is interpreted by school authorities through the lens of power and control, with students who break rules conceptualized as choosing not to follow the rules in order to wrest power from school staff, a position resonating with discussions of hegemonic masculinity in the previous chapter. Obedience to rules, meanwhile, is assumed to indicate students' respect for authority (Laws and Davies 2000; Millei and Raby 2010). Staff members were much less likely to suggest that rule-breaking might arise from legitimate needs, contestation, or politicized challenge.

In earlier chapters I have presented various concerns students had with either specific aspects of the rules, or the process of rule enforcement. When faced with rules or consequences for infractions that students disagreed with, they responded in a variety of ways, ranging from breaking rules, to negotiating with teachers or administrators, and even taking collective action. The remainder of this chapter will reflect upon this breaking, and strategic negotiation, of rules.

The most dominant way students talked about their own rule-breaking evoked students' practical needs and specific situations that were considered irreconcilable with certain rules. As Tina explains,

> I think that a lot of the petty rules, like people break them not – like when I, like dumb rules like eating in the hall, I don't break that cuz I wanna rebel, I break it just cuz it doesn't make sense to me and it's like impractical. (Whitton FG 4)

In the face of such practical issues, six students specifically discussed breaking specific rules because they were 'outrageous' or 'ridiculous.' As Patricia said, 'There are some of us who are, like, "these rules are ridiculous. I am not following them"' (Whitton FG 1). More personal needs were also sometimes an issue, like personal crises or supporting a friend in crisis. Such practical and personal examples suggest a conflict between student life and school life (Dickar 2008), with students using what tools they can in order to escape the rigid boundaries of the institution. From this perspective, students have their own business to attend to, business which school authorities often consider incompatible with education or staff responsibilities but which students themselves frequently consider very important. Dress is a significant example of where such conflict can occur. Laws and Davies (2000) cite an example, for instance, in which a student, Shane, refused to remove his hat in an assembly and was subsequently asked to leave. Staff authorities interpreted his action as disrespect and insolence while for Shane the issue was one of pride, for he had recently had a haircut that he did not want to expose to peer ridicule. If we then assume Shane's concerns are unimportant, however, we in turn trivialize and even denigrate his experience and interpretation of the situation, even if Shane and many others may interpret the rule against hats as itself trivial.

Drawing on the work of theorists such as Maslow, Dreikurs, and Glasser, some approaches to classroom management similarly focus on how student misconduct results from students' basic unmet needs for things such as safety, belonging, power, and fun: from this perspective these students are not 'bad' but trying to meet their needs in ways that are not necessarily in their own, or others', best interests (Jones and Jones 2007). As I have already noted, rule-breaking is also framed within classroom management as arising from skill-deficits, suggesting that once students are better taught how to behave, rule-breaking will be less of a problem. These orientations to rule-breaking shift the focus away from power struggles or from framing the student as an inherent problem, suggesting that the classroom context needs to better address student needs or to foster student skills. Yet these approaches also continue to individually problematize student rule-breaking and frame disciplinary interventions in terms of building personal self-discipline (Millei 2010).

While practicality was the dominant reason given by students for rule-breaking, other related explanations also emerged, some of which reinforced explanations staff provided for why students break rules and some of which diverged. Some staff members argued that students break rules because they can, which was also a position that students raised in almost all focus groups, often in relation to practicality. In such cases, students broke rules because they thought they could get away with it. They found ways to 'get away with' skipping out of class, skipping detentions, skipping assemblies, and being in the halls when they were not supposed to. They also broke dress codes by hiding from the staff they knew would enforce them.

> JANICE: The spaghetti strap thing, I mean like, if it's a hot day I wear spaghetti straps, sometimes, you know and then just hope for the best.
> I: And what's 'the best'? That they won't notice or care?
> JANICE: Yeah, that they just won't [pause] see me.
> I: Right.
> JANICE: Yeah, and if I see the principal down the hallway I go the other way [laughs]. (Whitton FG 1)

Indeed, students narrated a whole series of ways that they succeeded in breaking the rules without getting caught.

Another explanation which resonated with staff views was raised by students in three Big City groups and one Whitton group who suggested that students have an inherent or natural desire to break the rules.

> LIZ: A lot of kids just don't like to be told what to do anyway, no matter what it is. If you're like 'go drink some water' and you're like 'no, I don't want to – because they told me to I don't want to do it.' It has to be your own idea and then you'll be like yeah. (Big City FG 2)

> JILL: Cuz like when they enforce the rules, it just makes us want to break them more. (Big City FG 7)

These comments support the position that people break rules out of defiance, either due to adolescent deviance or broader human nature. Similarly, one group's members directly stated that they break rules for fun. The members of Whitton FG 3 talked about creating an impromptu compost in a cupboard in their science classroom in the face of boredom, for instance.

Yet Whitton FG 3 was also the only one to overtly link such rule-breaking to the broader structural context of the school, a more politicized interpretation that staff were rare to articulate.

STEVE: Well this is my ideological suggestion, for that situation is that if they could make school a little more interesting you wouldn't be getting into these kinds of problems, like if people were actually paying attention everyday and you actually had things to talk about in class, this whole obsession with rules and everyone knowing that rules matter, well people would be 'like I am here to learn. (Whitton FG 3)

Steve's observation links issues of discipline to pedagogy, issues also raised in chapter 6 which addressed inequalities and discriminations that can alienate students from school. Another such intentionally political form of rule-breaking was articulated by Jeezy:

It happens in my school, it happens to me all the time. Every time I see somebody wearing a hat, I put on my hat. When they tell me to take off my hat, I tell them no. I say sorry, but my hat stays on my head just like his hat stays on his head [referring to a White student]. (Big City FG 6)

In this particular case Jeezy was motivated by concerns about what he felt to be differential enforcement of the hat rule based on race. Some students also said that they broke rules out of anger, a pattern that was particularly evident in Whitton FG 2 when students' responses to altercations with another student or a staff member would be with anger and aggression. For the most part these students experienced a lot of frustration with peers or the school and this frustration would burst out. Getting suspended, in turn, reinforced their anger at the school.

Finally, certain rules were considered to be less important, or unimportant, and the most direct way to challenge them was to break them. In fact, sometimes this non-compliance was observed to successfully put an end to an unwanted rule. In Big City FG 5, for example, Queen observed that a rule against going to lockers between classes failed because 'everyone goes anyways.' Janice (Whitton FG 1) described a system of hall passes that was introduced by a new vice-principal, effectively ignored by students and teachers, and soon dropped for being unwieldy. Anna-Holly (Big City FG 3) similarly described the fall of a computerized system for monitoring lates when students avoided it and teachers did not enforce it. The effectiveness of these last strategies was, of course, bolstered by the support of adults.

These are ways that students explained their own rule-breaking. While in some instances it was attributed to human nature or fun, practical reasons were more likely to be suggested and at times political explanations also arose, explanations that criticized the institution of the school or that were fueled by anger. Students rarely attributed their rule-breaking to their family backgrounds or personal histories but instead emphasized individual responsibility, a pattern noted elsewhere (Cothran, Kulinna, and Garrahy 2009).[2]

De-Problematizing Rule-Breaking

Resistance

If rule-breaking is conceptualized as a wilfull challenge to authority, deviance, or inherent, youthful rebellion, the problem is seen to be within the young people themselves and their challenges lack legitimacy. In contrast, by considering rule-breaking as resistance, young people become understood as subjects negotiating inequalities in ways that are available to them. This is a position discussed at length by Paul Willis in his classic text Learning to Labour (1977) but has also been adopted by other, more recent scholars (e.g., Apple 1995; Smith 2003). Willis suggests that the British working class lads he studied were inclined to break the rules because the rules represented the middle class values of the school. The rules therefore represented a way of life that was quite different from their own, and one in which they could not be successful. In seeing the deck stacked against them, the lads embraced the limited source of power that they had in working class masculinity and noncompliance. Willis lamented that this strategy, while understandable, ultimately reproduced these lads' own future economic marginality.

Since the publication of Learning to Labour the book has been used as a classic example of youth resistance, but it has also been severely criticized. For example, to some extent Willis interprets the lads' activities as resistant when the lads themselves did not necessarily explain or understand them as such. Further, as Angela McRobbie (1978) and others have contended, Willis's work neglected to consider intersections of gender and race in the working class lads' identities and often sexist, racist actions. Scott Davies (1994) draws on quantitative data on high school dropouts in Ontario to similarly argue that those working within resistance theory have underestimated the salience of gender and academic success, with underachieving boys as those particularly likely to challenge the rules; he also sees those working in critical pedagogy as exaggerating the link between working class culture and rule-breaking as resistance.

Indeed, McFadden (1995) reviews various studies which found student resistance to be less about directly challenging class inequality and more about trying to resolve their social and personal problems in the context of problematic pedagogy (problems which can both arise from and reproduce other forms of structural inequality, including class). Finally, as Tait (2000) argues, such subcultural positions tend to assume culture to be linked with class, with dominant culture reflected in broader ideology and working class culture as subordinate. Classes are therefore understood through a modernist lens that presents them as monolithic and inevitably incorporated into a hierarchy of power, with the ruling classes imposing power on the working classes and the working classes struggling against it. There is little room here, Tait contends, for more Foucauldian, governmental orientations towards power in which power is much more diffuse, productive, and exercised through practices.

Despite such critiques however, Willis's work offers us the important suggestion that rule-breaking in itself is not always about individual defiance, ignorance, or personal troubles but that it can reflect social structures and associated inequalities which permeate schools, a theme that has been extensively investigated through a number of studies in critical pedagogy (e.g., McLaren 1989; Giroux 1983; Apple 1995; Ferguson 2000) and which informed chapter 6. As we have seen in this book, school rules and consequences for their infraction do reflect certain values that are related to culture and class. Staff who create and in turn enforce these rules hold certain philosophies and backgrounds; and students do not leave the social patterns and inequalities of their communities behind them when they enter a school. Furthermore, we know that school disciplinary procedures do not unfold for students of all backgrounds in the same way. Marginalized students are more likely to be seen to be breaking the rules, more likely to get into trouble, and more likely to receive a harsher consequence for the same infractions than other students. As such, schools reproduce inequalities.

As Annette Lareau (2003) illustrates when discussing class and families' negotiation of the middle class elementary school, those without the cultural capital rewarded in schools are much less likely to flourish there. This position is also presented by Smith (2003), an ethnographer who argues that educators' attempts to teach dominant cultural capital to a group of young parolees actually fostered resistance, including disciplinary challenges such as pranks, disinterest, and dress code breaches, as the skills the youth already had were not valued. Dickar (2008) draws on James Scott (1990) to similarly suggest that students engage in infrapolitical resistance, quietly undermining authority rather than confronting it head on, in order to keep their community culture in the classroom – she discusses boys routinely wearing their hats in class as an example of this, for instance, forcing teachers to explicitly exercise their dominating power. Recall the discussion on fighting in chapter 3 in which certain marginalized students were more likely to debate the 'no fighting' rule. These discussions bring to mind Willis's work. By accepting physical mechanisms for dispute resolution, the participants in Whitton FG 2 potentially counter a more reserved, middle class dependence on verbal dispute resolution.

In addition to inequalities based on class, race, culture, and so forth, schools are structured within the context of age-based inequality. To some readers, this form of inequality may seem like a benign given: of course adults should have authority over young people because young people are still in the process of growing up; consequently they need adult guidance, which can include a firm hand. But we know that such authority is not always benign. Indeed, to prevent abuses of power, social protections are legislated. One such protection is the *UN Convention on the Rights of the Child* which states that in addition to rights to protection and provision of services such as education, children have the right to have a say in decisions that directly affect them. This protection is important because adults do not always know what is best for young people and frequently have alternative investments of their own. Young people's right to participation is one that is infrequently recognized in schools. It may, in part, be because of the compulsory nature of schooling and students' lack of involvement in school decision-making that student rule-breaking is so prominent as students try to live within the school's unbending, institutional structure (Raby and Domitrek 2007; Thornberg 2008a). For many students rule-breaking is the only evident way to challenge that structure, particularly for more marginalized students. Yet, like Willis's working class lads, such resistance often reproduces the very conditions of inequality students seek to challenge. Rather than creating change or solidarity when students challenge rules by breaking them, rule-breaking often raises safety concerns among other students as it perpetuates violence and harassment, confirms discourses of young people as unthinkingly rebelling, individualizes students and their grievances, and ultimately increases surveillance, rules, and the rules' enforcement. Despite these consequences, few of my own participants identified any other way to express their frustration with certain rules: the rules and their enforcement are 'just the way it is,' with rules either followed or broken.

There are various features of critical resistance theory that are quite valuable and compelling. Like our discussion of cultural capital in chapter 6, it reminds us that school rules are not outside of unequal value systems and in such a context, when some students challenge or break school rules, they may be participating in a political conflict of ideals. Yet there is much rule-breaking that does not easily fall into such an analysis. Also, this approach has not been without important critiques, some of which I have already discussed in reference to Willis. A key question is whether this perspective imputes more meaning to rule-breaking than is actually intended by students. This question raises the issue of member accounts, or the explanations given by participants themselves, and presumptions about young people. Must students articulate their behaviour as political or resistant in order for it to be so? Are students' accounts of their own motivations convincing? What does it mean for researchers to interpret young people's actions differently from how they interpret them themselves (Widdicombe and Wooffitt 1995)? I would contend that members' accounts are important to consider, and that political explanations are frequently there if researchers are willing to look – they are certainly present in comments within my own focus groups. The critical resistance approach also tends to frame the classroom as a site of two competing sets of values, disregarding the complicated interplay of class, gender, and racialized and cultural inequalities and differences, a problematic that is significantly complicated when we return to Foucault's engagement with power below. Finally, this approach tends to focus on structural causes of inequalities in school as well as outside of school, suggesting that there is little schools can do to address the situation (McFadden 1995) – McFadden counters this position by arguing that schools can create 'safe' spaces for change and challenge through shifts in pedagogical practices towards student participation in shaping pedagogical context and production of knowledge, a potentiality I contemplate in the following chapter.

Post-Structural Framing of Resistance and Contestation

As I have already described, a post-structural framework emphasizes the complex flows of power relations, and the fragmented and constructed nature of our subjectivities, contending that we are all produced through shifting discourses and historical contexts. Within the current regime of neoliberal governance, for instance, our selves are created through discourses of self-scrutiny, self-formation, and self-governance – as governmentality studies have explained (Rose 1990). Of course, if our very subjectivities (and experiences) are created by discourse, then how do subjects come to resist? Does the term resistance remain useful?

Post-structural understandings of resistance often point first to the work of Michel Foucault who understood power as operating at the most micro levels of interaction as people watch, assess, evaluate, and categorize each other, thus creating and reproducing certain beliefs or knowledge about them (Foucault 1977). At each of these points there is, at the same time, resistance to these manifestations of power (Foucault, 1978b). Foucault thus argued that power and resistance are always tangled together, with resistance about local, disruptive responses. What is opposed is less clear than it is within critical theory however, for power is enacted by all, and people occupy multiple subjectivities, or locations in relations of power. In this way resistance is understood to be much more scattered and less collectively political than it is in critical theory, although resistance can also manifest as a more pointed response to dominating power which attempts to limit the options of others. While a Foucauldian approach to understanding resistance does not present two clear sides in a conflicting battle of those with all-power and those without, it does open up opportunities to see how we all participate in producing certain forms of power and how resistance is always evident in even the most small-scale practices.

Various scholars have built on this understanding of power and resistance, including Laws and Davies (2000), whose work I discussed at the beginning of this chapter. In reflecting on several incidents within Laws' school for students with behavioural issues, Laws and Davies illustrate how students not only perform 'good student' but also use, negotiate, and reject dominant psychological discourses about themselves, often in ways that challenge the rules. In responding to such rule-breaking, staff can reinforce dominant discourses which individualize and problematize students; but they can also try to explore ways to change the script. Laws and Davies describe one example, in particular, where a student climbed onto the roof and yelled about how another student had been wronged. Laws's reaction was to affirm the student's sense of injustice rather than to demand obedience. In this way, she resisted dominant power relations by trying to interpret the student's behaviour through a different lens, to change the story and to produce a different (and more affirming) kind of student subjectivity.

Such challenges can emerge through a number of different features of the social fabric. I have already talked about the role practical need can play in challenges to dominant, school-based definitions of 'good student.' Such practical need can emerge through the body[3] (temperature), through the organization of school time and space (needs to eat outside of lunchtime, using backpacks because lockers too far away), social relations (emotion, such as heart-break), peer culture (note-passing, skipping), and so forth. In this sense practicality can be an example of contradiction, or tension, in needs or expectations. More academically, we can talk about 'discursive fissures,' where certain discourses (e.g., of the good student) conflict with others (e.g., the good friend or the masculine boy) to create gaps in the discursive fabric that students negotiate. Such gaps are even seen in the multiple understandings of students that we see illustrated in staff philosophies behind school rules and their understandings of student misconduct illustrated in chapter 4.

The concept of disidentification provides another lens through which to think about the disruptive potential of discursive fissures. José Muñoz's (1999) notion of disidentification draws on Judith Butler's work (1993) to argue that we are formed through our identifications with others, but that this identification is always partial and temporary. Because identifications are fragmented, and changing, we may partially identify and even counter-identify with a subject position. Thus a young person may partially identify with being a student, a boy, a Catholic, *etc.* and also counter-identify with being a teenager, all interlinked in a particular, contextual way. Muñoz was particularly compelled by the creative potential of *disidentification,* a process whereby subjects take up dominant roles, or discourses, but then deploy them in new ways that disrupt the dominant message, creating something previously unthinkable. Muñoz was interested in how such disidentification is conducted through art as a 'survival strategy' for people who are in marginal, or minority social positions. For instance, people in minority social positions might can take 'damaged stereotypes' and make them into powerful forms of self-creation, much like Judith Butler's observation that hate names such as 'queer' can be re-appropriated and redeployed as terms of celebration (1997). Disidentification thus recognizes that we are subjected through dominant structures, but that we can distort them and come away with something different at the same time.

While Muñoz focused on very specific moments of conscious performance, performance can be broadened to encompass our constant presentations of self, including young people's presentations and negotiations in school. For example, young people may take certain naturalized assumptions (e.g., that adolescence is a time of experimentation or rule-breaking) and work with them to engage in activities that are less available to adults (Raby 2002). As we saw in chapter 4, young people can mobilize age categories to warrant both breaking rules and following them. We heard Fernando (Whitton FG 8) talk about how 'they expect teenagers to be responsible enough to look at an agenda [book] .Yeah but I mean like, it's like – it's trying to do something that you can't do.' Through such strategies, young people do not necessarily accept these identifications (e.g., of disruptive teenager), nor do they reject them, but instead find a way to use them, e.g., to bring their 'street life' into the school.

Another strategic, partial identification was evident when some students argued that their compliance was a manoeuvre just to get through high school.

JOHN: But now that it's in the higher levels of high school, [parents] say, 'Yes we know this is wrong but you're almost out of there and teachers, they can determine if you're going to university or not,' because if they can give you really bad marks/

TINA: And they can give you bad reference letters.

JOHN: So, and it's not like they directly harm you [pause] so you can live with it for now.

TINA: Yeah that's like 'suck it up' [you have one year left].

I: [laughs]

JOHN: Well yeah I mean there's a reason for it, it's not/

I: It's strategic.

JOHN: Yeah. Yes, worth it.

NICOLE: That's the thing, you have to suck up to teachers in the senior grades because they're the ones giving your university references.

Tina: Yeah. (Whitton FG 4)

While these students did not necessarily agree with all the rules, they were sufficiently invested in their educational credentials that they saw breaking them as detrimental to themselves personally, since they might be labelled as troublemakers by teachers and thus potentially punished with bad grades and references. This pattern was also discussed by Thornberg (2008a) in presenting his ethnographic research with primary students. Because students would rarely talk about their criticisms of the rules with teachers, they commonly presented public compliance without privately agreeing, a 'false acceptance' that was reinforced through institutional pressure to comply. On the one hand this is an example of student compliance with the rules but on the other hand, these examples emphasize a consciousness about 'playing the game' which challenges staff goals of fostering self-regulation. Strategic compliance suggests that the rules have not been accepted or valued, that students have learned that there is little room for them to negotiate with teachers, and that students present merely the impression of acceptance of the rules. From the position of those working in moral education or classroom management, this suggests a failure to foster democratic engagement or an understanding of why certain rules might be considered important. It also suggests a failure to develop self-regulation that transcends the school environment. From another perspective, however, such 'face obedience' can be interpreted as a form of strategic, temporary, and conscious compliance and thus potentially a form of (rather impotent) resistance (Raby 2005).

From this post-structural perspective, young people, like all of us, are thoroughly enmeshed in the social fabric, both reproducing and disrupting it. This perspective opens up possibilities for us to see the myriad of contestations that occur across classrooms rather than only those that seem to reflect a deeper, more political challenge to the dominant cultural structure of the school. These smaller challenges maintain a political dimension through recognizing local productions of resistance and strategic identification although they can problematically shift us away from seeing more structural patterns of politicized resistance that are central to critical theory. Finally this position complicates the idea that the rules are a set of ordinances that reflect a coherent set of values that are then resisted *en masse* by students.

Rival Desires

One critique of post-structuralism has been in terms of its focus on the discursive rather than the body (Skott-Myhre 2008). Rather than theorizing rule-breaking as specific, politicized resistance to rules that represent a dominant order, or resistance as a response to dominating power, another approach can consider students' failure to abide by school rules not so much about young people responding to the rules themselves but about living their desires or their 'creative life force' which the rules attempt to contain but which are ultimately uncontainable (Skott-Myhre 2008). Tarulli and Skott-Myhre (2006) draw on Deleuze and Guattari to argue that creative life force (which is located in the body) will always overflow and consequently unsettle the social/institutional boundaries and binaries that try to categorize and contain people, including the boundaries that distinguish child and adult. From this perspective, desire is a celebrated source of disruption to order which cannot (and should not) be entirely contained, a position which directly counters Freud's contention that a child's socialization is about the necessary constraint of young people's desires and urges in order to secure civilized society. These ruptures are particularly likely among adolescents as they have been constructed to occupy a liminal space in which youth still have a degree of freedom in terms of their creative productions because they are not yet thoroughly subsumed by capitalist production. To Deleuze and Guattari (1983), manifestations of desire, or 'lines of flight,' poke through established capitalist order and structure (and the many inequalities and rigidities that are embedded in them) to disrupt and consequently change that order and structure.

School rules embody state practices of categorizing, limiting, and repressing possibilities. The immediacy of young people's desires, including their desires for touch, comfort, and peer relations counter the categorizing and containment that social structures reproduce, unsettling, disrupting, and changing them. By living in their immediate desires, young people are living in the present. Through instantiations of desire, or lines of flight, a way of being is produced that is outside the fixed endpoint of docile adulthood. From this perspective, it is the rules, not the youth, that are reactive, for the rules attempt to problematically contain young people and to impose order through categories such as 'responsible student,' 'future worker,' and 'independent adult.'[4]

Some of the students' explanations for rule-breaking support this conceptualization, when they emphasize bodily practicality or self-expression, for instance. However, when students draw on dominant categories such as 'adolescence' or 'self-respect' to explain their rule-breaking, or discuss breaking rules in order to serve other institutional ends (e.g., listening to music to do well in class), their motivations, or at least their explanations of their motivations, are reabsorbed into, or recontained within, order and categories. Skott-Myhre recognizes such continual containment of creative life force, for creative life force is only evident in its moment of being – as soon as we put it to language, even, we contain and order it. Deleuze and Guattari also refer to 'molecular segmentarity,' which recognizes that within rigid structures and fixed roles there is some disruption and modification but that these often remain more rigid than lines of flight. Certain student rule-breaking might thus be better understood as molecular segmentarity, as it remains embedded within more rigid structures. Of course, my data relies on student explanations rather than observations, which complicates these interpretations as well. Are respondents framing their explanations in the language of the institution because they are embedded within that language, or might it be strategic in the belief that their explanations will then be given legitimacy (by a teacher, or a researcher)?

Overall, while Skott-Myhre (2008) argues that a discursive analysis is important, he contends that it does not sufficiently address the body, specifically the creative life force within it. Furthermore, he argues that resistance, which he considers our creative life force, is not a reaction to dominant social structures but instead comes before them or exceeds them. It is the dominant social structures that respond to this life force, attempting to contain or control it. The challenge of schools rules, in this context, arises in that they are part of a larger system of structured ordering and containment. Some readers might hesitate to embrace this position, and at least two reasons come to mind. One is that it inherently problematizes order and structure as inevitably embedded in the containing dominations and hierarchies of capitalism – a position which might trouble those committed to certain modern, ordering ideals including ideals such as rights. The second, more post-structural critique is that it essentializes an elusive creative life force inside of us and attaches that life force to child-like or adolescent features, leading us to ask where such a life force might come from and how it might participate in producing romanticized ideals of what it means to be a young person. Despite these important critiques, however, the idea of a creative life force compellingly provides exciting possibilities for how we think about young people, and potential for creativity and change.

There are many reasons why students break school rules. A common adult interpretation of such rule-breaking is to see it as adolescent rebellion or defiance of authority. In this section I have drawn on several different but interrelated approaches to consider rule-breaking as quite distinct from disobedience or immature, youthful defiance. These positions also directly challenge a top-down conceptualization of socialization in which young people passively learn their culture. From these perspectives young people's rule-breaking can sometimes be about critically engaging with structural processes which attempt to contain or define them. In discussing these perspectives it is not my intention to romanticize students' rule-breaking but rather to consider perspectives that do not simply dismiss or undermine students' actions but to suggest that there are multiple ways in which students embrace, accept, and also contest the rules they encounter and to value their multiple motivations for doing so.

Other Forms of Challenge to the Rules

While students most commonly resorted to breaking the rules, a process which can clearly be understood through a wide range of possible lenses, both students and staff also discussed other ways that students addressed rules that they disagreed with or that did not work for them, primarily through negotiation but sometimes through overt, organized challenge.

A number of students were likely to discuss their concerns with teachers and even administrators when they did not appreciate a rule – this was particularly the case when a new rule was introduced and more likely at the classroom level, as students were inclined to discuss rules with the teachers to negotiate in-class concessions, for instance (e.g., being able to listen to a personal music device at certain times in class).

> MATTHEW: Yeah but you can discuss it with your teachers, right? [...] You know the teachers will sometimes say, 'You know what, since I'm done the lesson and we've got twenty minutes and you're going to be working on assignments, go ahead and listen to music, sound good?' kind of thing or you can ask a teacher if it's alright, you know it happens informally. (Whitton FG 1)

Students also sometimes approached administration with concerns about a rule or a particular incident. As Maggie explained in an example of overt criticism, after authorities took a friend's drawings from her locker and tore them up without her knowledge:

I went with her to the principal and we got in a big argument with him and he was like 'That's the school rules' and I was like 'I think it's not mandatory but I think it's more professional if you were to go get her in her classroom, because her friend told you her name and it was easy for you to find her but you didn't do it.' (Whitton FG 1).

At the classroom level, students frequently found such informal negotiations to be successful, particularly with certain teachers. In terms of higher or official influence, however, students were more discouraged. While administrators suggested that such discussions were often fruitful opportunities for students to have a say in school policy, as I address in the following chapter, students frequently felt that their voices accomplished little except when they were supported by either teachers or parents and were directed towards individual cases.

Yet students did narrate some notable instances when students initiated more organized, collective action, particularly during the Whitton focus groups. For example, in FG 1, a student described an incident with a visiting police officer:

MATTHEW: ... then they had this cop stand there and shout at us and talk about how when a cop tells you to do something, you do it and he pointed at somebody in the front row who had his feet up on his chair or the chair in front of him, whatever, and said 'Put your feet down right now' and I just remember simultaneously about fifty kids put their feet up on the chair in front of them all at once.

Matthew and Patricia also had a discussion about the need to sometimes challenge authority:

PATRICIA: Well, there is nothing wrong with like obeying the rules cuz they are there for a reason but – like nothing will just change and nothing will get better if no one stands up for themselves.
I: But do you think there is a certain kind of student who is more likely to follow rules?
MATTHEW: Students who are afraid of the authority and who are afraid of the consequences.
PATRICIA.: Ah – (thinking) I guess, yeah and people who do not know that they have a say, people that have just coasted along in life – they don't really know that they can do anything about it, they just accept everything.

Participants in Whitton FG 3 described an occasion where several of them refused to stand for the national anthem although in this instance their ultimate compliance was secured through the threat of suspension. These students also attempted to bring political debate to campus and confronted the administration when they were not allowed to put up posters about an up-coming political meeting. In Whitton FG 9, Allison provided a few other examples while talking about the value of student solidarity

> I know our school, a lot of the students, like either in your class or [the whole school] students are pretty cool. They notice the teachers being really stupid or there's a rule that you know, something is used against you that shouldn't be used against you. Like we had one teacher who used to always like – had a habit of, like we had a language closet where all the language books are kept. And one teacher had a habit, if a student disrupted [class], 'go to the closet!' You know you'd sit in there with all these language books and do nothing. So there'd be times where like she'd send one student to the closet and we'd be like, 'Oh can I come?! Can I come?!' and she'd be like, 'Fine get the other student out.' Just to be fair. So a student would beg to go and I know [pause] my grade 9 year, one guy as a joke wore a very, very flowy skirt and he just wore it to school and they tried to suspend him I think for three days. And the next day [...] I think 25 to 50 per cent of the males at our school the next day came to school wearing female skirts.

Finally, one teacher also discussed an example of students in the Whitton Catholic school board organizing to challenge a ban on cell phones.

Such examples of group resistance were far less evident within the Big City focus group, except for one example in FG 3.

> ANNA-HOLLY: Um, oh yeah, the hall pass rule because kids were like why, like there's no point, right? So many kids just leave and like skip class. There's no point in having a hall pass and I guess that was the idea
> I: So people just said 'why' and then like was it effective?
> ANNA-HOLLY: Um, I think that was like a debated rule, like before they put it out there, kids heard that they were thinking about it and then they brought it to the office and the office I guess lost interest in it because they thought there would be too much like opposition and I think some of the teachers didn't want to do it either because it was just too much of a hassle for them.

In each of these cases, as with many others, instead of simply breaking rules, students asserted themselves in the face of seemingly arbitrary authority and tried to participate in making change with limited resources. In this way students positioned themselves as political agents involved in wider social struggles – it was through locating themselves as involved and invested school participants that they acted on their concerns with certain rules.

As I have observed elsewhere (Raby 2008b), it is frequently when students considered themselves to be subjects in the present, particularly as rights-bearing subjects, that they were likely to question the rules rather than simply break them. This was especially the case when students drew on rights discourse around their freedom of expression. For example, five students referenced their individual rights to self-expression to challenge dress codes. Other students suggested that they had the freedom to carry cell-phones, to listen to music, and to go to the bathroom.

> TINA: Yeah some teachers – like if it's twenty minutes before class ends they'll say 'no, you're not allowed to go.' I think it's kinda rude cuz by the time you're like sixteen or in high school you should be able to decide when you have to go to the washroom. (Whitton FG 4)

Occasionally a more formal gesture to rights was made; for instance, Fernando (Whitton FG 8) argued that students should get a say, Patricia (Whitton FG 1) asserted that students are more likely to stand up for themselves and make change if they know their rights, and Whitton FG 8 referenced a case in which a Catholic student demanded his right to have 'unnaturally' coloured hair. Finally, rights were raised in the aforementioned example when some students refused to stand for the national anthem.

> We were deciding that if, if we, if we had the right to stand up to this national anthem or this national was like ah [2 second pause] something from an imperialist time really, nationalism and all that so that we decided that we would have the right not to stand up if we had the right to stand up.

When these respondents faced suspension as a result, they felt their rights to free speech were being violated.

It is interesting to note that such rights were invoked both to challenge the rules which infringed upon them, and to recognize the value of rules which were seen to protect personal freedoms by regulating the actions of others. Dress codes, in particular, led to contrasting views within focus groups about balancing between different people's freedoms. While some invoked freedom of expression to support various forms of dress, dress codes were also seen as protecting students from having to see others' outfits (or lack of outfits!). Personal autonomy was considered important, and a right, but most saw that certain limits are needed to ensure that the school space is pleasant for everyone. Students thus asserted their present rights to demand and accept rules to ensure their safety and to limit the actions of others, to defend some of the rules about maintaining the quality of the school, and to support the right to question others.

The language of rights has become quite prominent in the sociology of childhood and in advocacy by and on the part of young people, particularly as children's protection, provision, and participation rights are codified within the *UN Convention on the Rights of the Child*. Lack of student and staff familiarity with child rights (and concomitant responsibilities) in Canada and beyond has been of significant concern for many child rights advocates (e.g., see Covell and Howe 1999) and increased familiarity has the potential to shift students and staff towards negotiation (Carter and Osler 2000). The use of the language of rights draws attention to the value of fostering subjectivities that encourage a self-understanding as agentic either individually or collectively (Davies 1990). Among the focus groups in this study, a rights discourse was a powerfully accessible concept to students, yet overall rights seemed to be understood quite narrowly, primarily in terms of individual freedom of expression. Rights to collective participation were infrequently mentioned.

A rights discourse can be problematic as well, when it is thought to address weakness. In their study in a British all-boys secondary school, Carter and Osler (2000) found that a rights discourse was assumed by many staff and students to represent unmasculine weakness by asking permission (for rights) and protecting vulnerable people. The language of rights was also seen by teachers as a way for students to simply make demands. While these impressions may reflect a lack of understanding about how rights work, they also suggest challenges to using rights discourse as a primary avenue to address negotiation of rules and rule-breaking in schools. More broadly, the rights discourse tends to individualize concerns and can neglect much deeper structural inequalities – Fernando (2001) suggests that the discourse of child rights in particular can lead advocates to neglect pivotal class, gender, and racialized in-equalities. Finally, others have suggested that the sovereign language of rights suggests that participation is premised on state definitions of the role of subjects (Tarulli and Skott-Myhre 2006; Besley and Peters 2007) and consequently do not really address the depth of power rela-tions, within disciplinary and governmental power for instance (Ran-som 1997). I return to this question of rights, specifically participation rights, in the following chapter.

Ongoing Conflict

Young people's relationships to school rules are as complex and diverse as they and their lived experiences are. At the same time, most chal-lenge at least some aspect of the rules and all, at some point, have bro-ken them. It is primarily in the enforcement of 'smaller' school rules, especially dress codes, where students note inconsistencies, generate resentments, and push back. Students were likely to identify a number of these rules as pointless other than to allow administrators to exercise control, and consequently students did not acknowledge the legitimacy of such rules. They dealt with these frustrations primarily through rule-breaking. While codes of conduct and some staff comments suggest that school rules are about garnering obedience, research with students suggests that schools are often unsuccessful in such a venture. Students accept many of the rules, but this is often on their own terms, with dis-ruption, resistance, and/or hostile compliance. Students will wear the clothes they deem practical, even if this breaks dress codes, eat outside the cafeteria if they need a quick snack between classes, bring music players and cell phones even when they are banned, and break rules in order to make classes more interesting. As such, students participate in creating their school culture, although often in ways which frustrate teachers and ultimately reproduce students' own regulation through in-creased rules and rigid enforcement. For the most part students did not identify legitimate, established avenues through which to address their grievances with the rules. As such, rule-breaking can be understood as a form of resistance in the face of various forms of control, inequality, and oppression, including that between young people and adults.

The paradox that arises from students' wish to elude and negotiate school rules alongside their sense of powerlessness and their wish for certain rules to be in place (such as interpersonal and safety-related rules) is that it fosters an environment in which staff must focus significant time and energy on negotiating discipline, particularly 'petty polic-ing' of minor rules. Meanwhile, this focus frustrates students who are marginalized by differential discipline, reproduces assumptions that adolescents are inherently rebellious, and thwarts students who would prefer to effect change without rule-breaking. Students simply experi-ence the rules as top-down, arbitrary, and frequently unfairly applied.

In this chapter, critical and post-structural approaches have been prominent in reflecting on students' engagements with their school rules. These approaches illustrate a range of underlying structural and micro-level politics that circulate through the rules and their applica-tions; they also understand young people as legitimate, knowledgeable participants in these processes, whether creating the ordered class-room or disrupting it. Post-structuralism in particular makes it clear that these things are messy – we can both accept and challenge at the same time. While the emphasis on a creative life force suggests an es-sential undercurrent to human existence that sits uncomfortably with post-structuralism, I am also drawn to the idea of creative life force as it resonates so well with the regular, banal, daily attempts to order students' lived lives in school. Students' ongoing discussion of their practical lives as clashing with school structures may not be about a creative life force as Skott-Myhre describes it, but it is certainly about an everyday life force that resonates deeply for students. Finally, the approaches that have been reviewed in this chapter suggest that there is great value in considering why and how the rules are there in the first place and what they represent in terms of wider social structures.

There are also important occasions when students attempt to en-gage with the rule-making process by negotiating with teachers and administrators, instead of simply breaking the rules, in an attempt to become exempt from a rule or even to change it. These attempts seem most successful at the classroom level, even though staff concerns about inconsistency would suggest that such localized shifts in rules are problematic. Student attempts to change the rules reflect an incli-nation among a small number of students to think of themselves as individual rights-bearers; they also suggest that some students feel that they should have a say in how their school community is governed.

9 Students Having a Say

> It is ironic that in a society that sees itself as democratic, it would be taken for granted that children should be raised under conditions of virtual dictatorship. Giving children an equal right to participate in setting the standards and guidelines by which they will live seems necessary if they are to mature into adults that are capable of participating in a genuine democracy. Windsor House [a democratic school in North Vancouver] is hardly without rules; there are plenty. The important thing is that anyone who dislikes a rule is free to gather support to change it.
>
> (Hughes and Carrico 2008, 167)

As earlier chapters have indicated, school rules, their creation and enforcement are inevitably linked to deeper beliefs about human nature, growing up, and social ideals. This chapter engages with the wide body of literature which seeks to re-examine school disciplinary processes in the interests of democratic participation, with a specific focus on student involvement in school decision-making, including on the subject of school rules.[1] I then consider student participation as addressed in each facet of my data.

School is mandatory for most students, and they spend a significant portion of their lives there; yet overall few have any opportunity to be involved in developing or revising the immediate rules that govern them (Schimmel 2003). In my own study, I found that experiences of participation were very limited, and so it is not surprising that many students considered potential participation with scepticism. Staff generally spoke positively of student participation, although with few gestures towards concrete possibilities for what such student involvement might look like beyond the level of students' councils. Yet while there are various attitudinal and practical concerns that challenge student participation (Porter 1996), there are various examples of successful student participation in some schools and classrooms, several of which are described here. Finally, this chapter ends with an examination of some concerns that may be raised about such student participation, with particular reflection on one which arises through governmentality studies: does student involvement problematically deepen and obfuscate the regulation of young people?

Advocacy for Participatory Rights

Student participation can be valued for a focus on preparing young people to become democratic citizens in the future through training, practice, and moral education. Alternatively, student participation can be conceptualized through the lens of the present, in which young people have rights to have a say in decision-making that affects them, for example, or to be fully involved in actualizing themselves in interaction with others (Biesta 2007). These distinctions link back to conceptualizations of young people discussed in chapter 4: some consider young people primarily in terms of what they will become in the future, while others are concerned with them primarily as beings in the present. Beliefs about student participation also link to how concepts like democracy, citizenship, and rights are conceptualized, for these are contested concepts, especially when we are talking about young people (Alderson 1999; France 1998; Roche 1999; Taylor, Smith, and Nairn 2001; Imre and Millei 2010).

Currently, democracy is largely discussed in terms of citizenship rights and the expansion of such rights to children, including rights to protection, provision, and participation. *Protective* citizenship rights address safety from discrimination, abuse, and injustice. *Provision* rights address access to such things as health care, education, and recreation (Archard 2004). *Participation* rights are premised on rights to speech, representation, information, and participation in decision-making (John 1995; Hart 1992; Beauvais, McKay, and Seddon 2002; Lansdown 1994). Protective and provision rights can be considered 'passive' because those receiving such rights do not have to be the same people as those who advocate for them (Taylor, Smith, and Nairn 2001). Such rights, to a child's safety and to education, were occasionally referenced in my research, in codes of conduct and by staff. In contrast, participation rights are 'active' because they include the ability to realize these rights through direct, political, democratic engagement and must therefore be exercised by those who possess them (Archard 2004). These kinds of rights have been advocated by many who seek more democratic decision-making in schools and beyond. Within my research, however, such rights were rarely addressed.

Citizenship has been criticized for being an exclusive concept, since citizenship rights frequently divide the deserving from the undeserving (Plummer 2003) and have commonly been premised on a rational, autonomous individuality which has been ascribed to some people and not to others (Alderson 1999), or must be fostered over time through education. Not surprisingly, young people are commonly located outside the full umbrella of citizenship, based on their lack of this education, their lack of independence, and their developmental location (Beauvais, McKay, and Seddon 2002; Roche 1999). While many have nonetheless advocated for children's citizenship, Imre and Millei (2010) are concerned that such initiatives mask children's lack of access to the same kinds of participation rights as adults. Children thus have an ambiguous relationship to citizenship rights: they are both conceptualized as citizens and not quite citizens.

A *caretaker* approach makes the assumption that children should not have the same rights as adults, arguing that children must have their rights to decision-making exercised by an adult on their behalf (Archard 2004) and that the prevention of choice for children (e.g., through mandatory schooling and rules) will help children make reasoned choices when they become adults. Citizenship thus becomes a future orientation. Most codes of conduct and staff commentary on the rules themselves reflect this position, although as illustrated in chapter 4, some understand citizenship in terms of future obedience as adults rather than democratic participation.

In contrast, *liberationists* counter that children should not be denied the opportunity to show that they are capable of making reasoned choices for themselves and of developing the skills to do so (Archard 2004). This position assumes young people's right to participate in the present and asserts that young people should have the same rights as adults not just because they are able but because they are members of society (Johnny 2005). Roche (1999), Archard (2004), and Johnny (2005) all argue for a balance between these positions via 'partial citizenship,' which recognizes that as young people age their levels of maturity increase and so should their rights to self-determination, a position reflected in the *United Nations Convention on the Rights of the Child* (CRC). The CRC (which Canada has signed) ensures rights to freedom of expression (Articles 13 and 14), rights to be heard, and rights for children to participate in decision-making that affects their immediate lives (Article 12). However, it also includes a provision to address the increasing capacities of the child, with the premise that as young people age, they should have increasing involvement in decisions that affect them. Ironically, though, in schools the actual pattern is frequently the opposite of this ideal, with fewer opportunities for students to participate at the secondary than at the primary level (Lewis 1999a).[2]

Various scholars have drawn on the CRC to advocate student involvement in democratic participation in schools. Johnny (2005) argues that the spirit of the CRC suggests that children should have a say in matters that affect them, including in schools. Johnny also points out that while the Supreme Court of Canada has not treated the CRC as binding in terms of Canadian law, it has argued that the CRC's principles should be drawn on in decision-making and it should therefore be used as an increasingly important guide for schools.[3] Covell and Howe (2001) and Mitchell (2010) have similarly argued that the CRC is a vital tool that needs to be much better taught and implemented in Canadian schools.

Some such initiatives have been successful elsewhere. For example, Covell and Howe (2008) recently reported on an application of the Rights, Respect, and Responsibility (RRR) initiative, developed by Cape Breton University Child Rights Centre in Canada and applied by the Hampshire Education Authority in England in 2003. The RRR initiative is about implementing whole-school reform based on the tenets of the CRC. Fully participating schools developed higher levels of engagement and rights-respecting behaviour among students, as well as a greater understanding among students of rights and responsibilities than in regular schools and those that only partially participated. They also had less teacher burnout, due to better student behaviour and generally improved relations between students and teachers. In contrast, those schools using only partial implementation problematically taught that rights are contingent on responsibilities, taught about rights in only one or two areas of the curriculum, and/or used RRR as a tool for behaviour management. In such contexts, children came to see their rights as little different from rules (Covell and Howe 2008).

The RRR process was particularly effective in disadvantaged neighbourhoods. The project was also facilitated by the degree of school independence in the Hampshire Education Authority, so that individual schools could feel ownership of school reform and could vary their implementation. Success depended on the head teacher really embracing the initiative, a finding supported by Hannam in his review of student participation initiatives in British schools (2001).

Hannam's (2001) project took a very broad definition of participation, including such student involvement as committee work, peer education, and student-run groups to look at participatory schools. Despite this broad definition, only sixteen out of a long list of fifty British schools met the criteria, and only twelve ultimately participated. Hannam drew on questionnaires and interviews with staff and students, as well as whole-school examination, to find that student participation adds to student motivation, a sense of ownership, and a sense of being trusted, as well as an improvement in relations between students and teachers, a reduction in expulsions, and even a slight improvement in the attendance of potentially more alienated students.

Advocacy for Democratic Engagement

Rather than concentrate on young people as rights-bearers in the present, some advocates of student involvement emphasize the kind of student participation that shapes who they will become, arguing that it is valuable to teach participatory, democratic citizenship through hands-on participation to prepare students for the future (Dobozy 2007; Mitra 2008). From such a perspective, situating young people in the process of becoming future adults and citizens can also justify their active engagement within their schools. Mitra's work in a school in California foregrounds the importance of fostering student involvement in pedagogical rather than disciplinary school reform. She emphasizes the value of student involvement primarily in terms of 'positive youth development' for the future, as participating young people learn confidence, compassion, connection with others, competence, and character. She also argues that student involvement improves school policy. Dobozy, speaking on the Australian context, is similarly concerned that when schools themselves are not democratized, they are not sufficiently preparing students with the necessary skills for participating in Australia's democratic society. Whether or not young people are thought to be sufficiently able in the present to be involved in rule-making, there is something to be said for the argument that we must teach young people citizenship skills (Archard 2004; Covell and Howe

2001). But while many schools provide a degree of citizenship education for young people, rarely is such education considered something
which must be *practised* (Ruddock and Flutter 2000; Storrie 1997).

Furthermore, when the focus is solely on preparing young people for
the future, they are again reduced to 'becomings' and their lives in the
present are of less importance. Others advocate for students without
focus on the individualizing rights focus of the CRC and without an
emphasis on future democratic citizenry. These advocates argue that
schools must cultivate responsible, democratic citizenship and democratic self-respect among students in the present. For those seeking
participatory democracy, 'the rule of the people' (Osborne 1994, 417)
requires immediate active citizenship through social and political participation in decision-making at all levels of society. If participatory citizenship requires people who can engage in debate in ways that respect
rather than degrade 'the other' (Plummer 2003), inclusion, reflexivity,
and practice are essential. From this perspective, while young people
may not share adult styles of thinking, skills, and experience, they are
nonetheless invested in the organization of their immediate environments, have the creative skills to imagine ways to organize those environments fairly, and should have a say. DeRoma, Lassiter, and Davis
(2004) have found that teenagers feel better about their families and
themselves when they are involved in disciplinary decision-making.
Students, similarly, seek and value such participation in schools (Thorson 1996; Denton 2003). Rowe also points out that teachers and other
adults frequently underestimate even very young children's abilities
to grapple with such participation (Rowe 2006). Fallis and Opotow
(2003) believe that the only way that school rules such as those against
skipping can be effectively (and morally) addressed is through genuine engagement with what students have to say about their motives
and their experiences of the school. While it is not by any means the
most dominant approach in North America, many argue that children
have this legitimate say into the organization of their lives in the present (Schimmel 2003; Devine 2002; Roche 1999). These approaches have
gained much more ground in Britain and Australia, and more so at the
primary level.

In chapter 4, I discussed how our assumptions about adolescence
shape how adults and students think about their engagements with the
rules. Devine (2002) argues that our beliefs in young people as incomplete and at risk prevent us from seeing them as active citizens. Possibilities for young people to understand and be understood as having

a legitimate say are increased through deconstructing these and other essentialized assumptions about adolescence, including the belief that teenagers' challenges simply reflect an inherent rebelliousness, which delegitimizes their political positions (Raby 2002). Possibilities for students' democratic engagement may seem daunting, requiring significant energy and resources, but advocates argue that extraordinary time, energy, and resources go into top-down disciplinary processes as well. The extent of the rules and the amount of time spent enforcing them or arguing about them make it clear that student impotence does not necessarily mean obedience, respect, or efficiency. Kuhn (1996) suggests that only temporary compliance is attained through authoritarian methods, often with a struggle, and is devoid of deeper moral, ethical thinking. Schimmel (1997) draws on social psychological research to argue that when rules are autocratic and people have not been able to participate in creating them, they are less likely to be followed, will be broken without guilt, and will result, in fact, in less respect for those in authority. As I have argued in the previous chapter, students quickly learn that one of the few ways to deal with their frustration is simply to break the rules and many come to define such a response as inevitable due to their developmental location. Students' more democratic involvement in the school, in contrast, potentially allows them to flourish in decision-making, conflict-resolution, debate, and respect for others (Devine 2002).

Codes of Conduct

Student participation in schools can encompass a wide range of possibilities, from representation on key school committees to peer mediation, to widespread student involvement in school governance (see Table 9.1, p. 236). Ontario's *Code of Conduct* (2001), many school board policies, and many individual school codes state that student views must be considered in the construction and review of school rules. All school boards in Ontario must include (non-voting) student representation in the form of one or two student trustees. Some school committees or other rule-review bodies also include student representation but this is not mandatory, not widespread, and involves only a small number of students. In my interviews, several teachers spoke of occasionally involving their students in deciding on classroom rules, but these were in the minority. Overall, there is little room for most young people's widespread, frequent, institutionalized or consistent participation in

the making of rules, particularly as blanket school rules are increasingly made at higher levels of government such as the school board
or even the province. Only very rarely did a code of conduct mention
students' participatory rights or provisions for appealing disciplinary
decisions (Raby 2008b).

These patterns in the codes of conduct concur with those Covell
and Howe observe in Canada (2001), Lewis in Australia (1999a) and
Schimmel in the United States (2003). When students' rights are acknowledged in codes of conduct, focus tends to be on protective rights
(especially on safety from bullying and harassment) and provision
rights (e.g., education) rather than on the right to have a say. Moreover,
provision rights are occasionally linked to good behaviour or fulfill-
ment of certain responsibilities, suggesting that these rights are earned,
e.g., you have the right to an education if you are responsible and follow the rules. The implication is that if a student does not behave, she
or he forfeits this right.[4]

As I explored in chapter 4, most codes of conduct seem to engender
passivity premised on following the rules. Roche argues that 'the older
the child is the more objectionable it is to fail to consult or take into
account their wishes and feelings' (1999, 483) yet when young people
are closest to the age of majority, and presumably more experienced in
decision-making, they are less likely to be involved as *bona fide* participants in the organization of their schools (Lewis 1999a).

Students' Limited Experiences with Participation[5]

When asked, 'Have you ever helped create the rules at your school?'
students I talked to responded with a resounding 'No!' and felt the
possibility to be almost unimaginable. Students were familiar with students' councils, and occasionally mentioned that these councils play
some role in shaping school policy, yet overall students were quite critical of students' councils and dismissed them as pointless. As Fernando
(Whitton FG 8) stated, 'Students' council is garbage. They have no say
in anything.' Many noted that their students' council was ineffective
at addressing real student issues that related to rules, dress codes, or
various other aspects of student life. While students' council members
may be elected based on campaigns which include providing students
with a voice in rule creation or student activities, these are not seen
to materialize, particularly in the case of rules. In fact, students were
critical of the favouritism members of students' council seemed to

receive, especially as they were thought to more easily get away with breaking rules (see chapter 5). Meanwhile only four staff members even mentioned students' councils when asked about student involvement in creating or evaluating rules and consequences.

While involvement in students' council has been found to provide some slight practice in democratic citizenship and representative government, in their examination of students' council constitutions across a diversity of schools in the United States, McFarland and Starmanns (2009) found that these advantages are not shared equally among schools or students. Furthermore, schools often have certain requirements of council members: they must maintain a certain grade point average, for instance, which limits who can run and ensures that those who do are likely already invested in the school (McFarland and Starmanns 2009). Over a quarter of schools they studied had no students' councils and those tended to be the more disadvantaged schools. Among those with councils, disadvantaged, urban schools were more likely to have councils emphasizing social rather than political activities, to have less power to influence decision-making in the school, and to have more rules regulating who can run for office. Unfortunately no comparable data seems to be available on Canadian students' councils, although through a qualitative, questionnaire-based survey of ministries of education, school boards, school principals, and students across Canada, Critchley (2003) found some informative patterns. There were many opportunities for student representation on students' councils, a few provinces had student representation on provincial youth councils, and students were sometimes consulted via surveys and focus groups. Ontario was the only province with non-voting student trustees on school boards (Critchley 2003). Overall, however, Critchley found few consistent, formalized opportunities for students to shape school policies.

Beyond students' councils, some students in my study had a smattering of other experiences related to shaping school rules. In Whitton, while focus group respondents' experiences and knowledge of participation were generally dismal, a few examples arose. Nicole (FG 4) was once 'randomly' chosen to participate in a dress code discussion group, while Marjory and Betty (FG 5) had been allowed to vote on the potential introduction of school uniforms, although they did not know if their vote counted.[6] Carrie (FG 4), who was still in middle school, had an experience where her class had been made to create and sign their own rules as a punishment (!) for harassing a substitute, although most students signed with fake names and the new rules only lasted two days. John (FG 4) mentioned that he and some friends had made their own rules within the limited environment of a school club. Finally, Ferg and Liz (FG 7) had participated in a survey which they thought might influence school rules but which seemed really about student risk and resiliency.

Big City students had somewhat richer experiences. Some in FG 1 had participated in a rule-making activity in class at the beginning of the year, but students were then disappointed to learn it was simply a practice exercise for marks.

> I: And so you thought it was really going to be making a difference?
> JJ: Yeah, we all thought it was for real but it was a joke/
> MALE PARTICIPANT: But then she said no, it's just a dream.
> [General agreement]

A student in FG 2 had been asked for input on the name of a school team and Owen mentioned that his students' council had successfully lobbied for a minor change in the uniform at his private school. Students in FG 7 suggested that students can raise an issue with their parents who, if they are inclined and feel the sense of entitlement to do so, can then take it to a committee meeting where rules are evaluated. Students in FG 8, all in a school within the Catholic school board, had an experience of being asked to anonymously evaluate their teachers, which they appreciated. They also noted that sometimes a select group of students is consulted on an issue. Finally, students in FG 9, who attended an alternative school, discussed being consulted at the beginning of the year about appropriate rules.

The most exciting example of student involvement came from the student leadership group (Big City FG 3). These students were part of a larger organization whose aim was to provide students with a venue to voice concerns and influence policy at the municipal level, though this entity existed outside of schools and was not mentioned in any other group. Their organization's past campaigns included influencing the municipal budget, lobbying for youth outreach workers, and addressing homelessness. Students in this group were the most knowledgeable about children's rights and they suggested that students can and should lobby for themselves in school.

Despite this smattering of examples students experienced rules as being made by others – teachers and administrators in particular, even though many teachers are also uninvolved in creating school-wide rules – with very little attention being given to their own opinions. As I discussed in the previous chapter, occasionally students would mobilize in response to a particularly unpopular rule, usually approaching a teacher or administrator to complain. This tactic was seldom successful at the level of the school but could garner results when students negotiated with individual teachers for minor amendments to school rules within their classrooms. It was not only students' experiences of participation that were sparse. When asked if they could ever imagine being involved in the making of their school rules, some had trouble even considering the possibility, particularly in Whitton.

> JASON: But I think that if the students logically created the rules between them and followed those rules then/
> ALLISON: That's not going to happen.
> JASON: I know it's not. (Whitton FG 9)

> I: Have any of you ever been involved in actually getting to decide what the rules are in your classroom or in your school?
> [All chuckle]
> RAMONE: That's a miracle!
> [All laughter] (Big City FG 1)

Once prodded to exercise their imaginations, a number of respondents did suggest that it would be quite an opportunity, particularly those who had had some participatory experience already.

> BIBI: I think it's quite important because since these are the rules that affect us, we know better what consequences will be more effective and I think it's also a fact that we can give our opinions on what rules are just ridiculous and will not work. (Big City FG 3)

> ASH: Yeah, we should have an opinion on that.
> SALLY: Yeah.
> GREG: Yeah, because, like you know it's our school, like we're just going to be there like going there like all year, so … (Big City FG 9)

Big City participants Queen (FG 5) and Jane (FG 7) echoed several others in suggesting that student involvement would increase the likelihood of students following the rules. This argument is strongly supported by Schimmel who contends that such involvement improves the rules, increases self-discipline, and successfully fosters citizenship skills which remain after students graduate (1997). It is interesting that this was one reason staff also cited for student involvement – to encourage students to 'buy in.' I return to this hope for student involvement at the end of this chapter. A few respondents even suggested a need for compromise between various school stakeholders:

> SUZY: I just think that the, like, teachers and school board and us students should all kinda just go together and cooperate. Like, compromise with the rules and stuff. (Whitton FG 5)

But in the end most respondents agreed that such involvement will 'never happen' in their schools. As summarized by Saddam (Big City FG 4), 'It's never going to happen. They're never going to consult you. They'll never do it.'

Others were sceptical of the potential *success* of student participation. First, some students argued that hierarchies of physical size, age, and authority would always ensure that administration would prevail, or that administration would only consult favoured students:

> BACON BOY: Nobody, nobody will never accept the kids as the responsible ones. They'll be like 'I'm an adult, I'm more smarter than you. I've been here longer.' […] Yeah, it's like 'I'm older, I'm smarter, so listen.'
> FERG: 'I'm big, you're small and there's nothing you can do about it.' (Whitton FG 7)

Some suggested that principals might sometimes placate students, telling them something would be done, but then never follow up on the matter, a legitimate position supported by comments made by some administrators (see below).

Second, respondents doubted the interest or democratic skills of fellow classmates: either students would be too apathetic to participate or certain groups of students would force their will onto others.

> STEVE: It's easier just not to obey the ones you want, you know just doing what you were doing already, than to get involved in the process [laughs],

you know, which is the same thing with voting, which I wish I could. (Whitton FG 3)

MARJORY: But then again, like, it could backfire. Like, the little girls that wear/
BARB: Well yeah/
MARJORY: ... like short shirts and short skirts. They can all [say], like, 'oh that's a stupid rule! Let's gang up and get rid of that so we can wear these skirts.'
BARB: Yeah.
CATHY: Yeah, but I think there's, there's more people [pause] I think the majority would think that, that rule/
MARJORY: Is good/
BARBARA: is good rather than – but you never know! [chuckles] (Whitton FG 5)

CARMELLA: I think if you got students together to try and make up a set of rules, you would just end up with a lot of stupid rules, like people will want stupid rules to be okay.
I: Don't you think that you folks could come up with a good set of rules?
CARMELLA: I think if you, if enough people wanna do the right thing, then yeah. (Big City FG 5)

Of course, this concern touches on one of the challenges of participatory democracy in which accepting the process of participation means that there must also be acceptance of the results, at least until a weak decision can be overturned. In sum, students doubted that they would ever be consulted, that such consultation would be legitimate, and that students would even have the skills to successfully participate.

Finally, among the Big City participants there were also a few who argued against any kind of participation.

OWEN: Well I just rather the teachers make the rules because then it just makes it easy on us students, cuz we have less to worry about. (FG 3)

SADDAM: I say no. [...] Cuz I think that the teachers should handle it, and they're doing a good job. (FG 4)

JEEZY: No, I don't care personally, I just go there to get my credits and then boogie. (FG 6)

These three boys were comfortable with teachers doing the work of making the decisions due to disinterest, respect for teachers' expertise, and/or a utilitarian approach to the school. These last few comments may remind us of two things. First, as explored in chapter 6, students' cultural, class or family backgrounds may make them more or less inclined to favour a participatory approach. For example, in Dickar's ethnographic study (2008) she found that some students from the West Indies felt that the teacher is the one with authority and that authority needs to be respected. Cultural preferences for authoritarian teaching need not thwart students' democratic involvement, however, particularly if students have a say in the creation of rules that teachers enforce or a say in shaping curricula – the benefits of the latter engagement is seen in Mitra's work (2008). Second, these comments remind us that democratic involvement is not always easy. It takes time, energy, skills, and commitment to community that many students may not have, particularly if they feel disconnected from, or marginalized within, the school in the first place, if they are already inured to autocratic rule, or if they experience staff's commitment to democratic practices as false (Dickar 2008). This latter issue is of great concern to Rosalyn Black (2011) who notes that many participatory initiatives fail to include students from high poverty backgrounds and that such students are less likely to get involved in part due to their lack of faith in social institutions, lack of participatory skills and lack of sense of their own agency.

Lack of Appeal

A narrower avenue through which students may experience themselves as having a legitimate voice is access to appeal. Part of democratic citizenship, social participation, and the legitimacy of law is the right to give your side of the story, the right to a fair hearing, and the right to appeal (Pritchard 1990; John 1995; Covell and Howe 2001). Yet within Ontario, students' only formal access to appeal arises in cases of suspension and expulsion and unless the student is at the age of majority it must be his or her parent who appeals. Furthermore, in these cases, by the time the appeal process is complete most suspensions have already been served, although a successful appeal does result in a clean student record. Few codes of conduct inform students of this appeal process and no other formal or informal avenues for appeal are evident. It is not surprising then that few students had any sense of the option to appeal. Only Nicole (Whitton FG 8), who uniquely identified herself as a child-rights activist, once took an issue to the school board (to no avail) and Bibi, from the Big City youth leadership group, argued that you can take an issue to the school trustee:

> There's strength, there's complete strength in numbers, right? So if your class believes that [unfairness] is happening and they say that is happening, you can go and take it to your principal and your principal has no other option than to actually pay attention to it, and if they don't, you can completely talk to your school trustee and they will pay attention to it, right?

Several others mused on similar potential avenues for appeal:

> BETTY: I dunno, like, if I felt really [pause], if something was really gone awry I would definitely go all the way with it. Like parents, school board, whatever it took. (Whitton FG 5)

Maurice (Whitton FG 8) went beyond the institution of the school by suggesting police can be called in when a student is unfairly accused of breaking a rule. Otherwise, few had a sense that they may independently appeal an accusation and in any case, some groups suggested the futility of an appeal:

> ANGELINA: It depends what it is but, you, you can go to teachers, you can go like you can try to fight it but it's pretty much pointless.
> [Yeahs]
> ANGELINA: Like when vice-principals and the principal make up their mind, they make up their mind. There's no going back at all. Cuz if there's going back on it then it's like/
> KIERSTYN: They screwed up.
> ANGELINA: Yeah. They don't want to feel [pause] under/
> I: Undermined?
> ANGELINA: Yes. There you go. That's the word I was looking for. It's a whole power thing with them. (Whitton FG 6)

These students felt that a successful appeal was too risky for administrators as it would undermine their authority.

Participants similarly believed it would be very difficult to clear their names if they were inaccurately accused of breaking a rule. Often they felt that questioning authority would not be tolerated, bolstered by some codes of conduct which explicitly state that students should not challenge authority. Also, if a student was sent by a teacher to see the principal for an unfair reason, some students felt that occasionally principals punished the students in order to placate teachers:

> MARJORY: And the teacher who caught me was just really mad at me, and I was like 'whatever.' And the principal was, like, 'just to make him happy, just don't go to that period. Come to the office.' So/
> BARBARA: Yeah, that's what they did to me. To make the teacher happy they're like 'OK, well we'll suspend you [...] but [pause].' And it's like – they're just doing it to make him be quiet. (Whitton FG 9)

Students therefore doubted that administrators would take their concerns seriously because they saw administrators as being on the teachers' side, not theirs:

> SMEGAL: I go to talk to the vice-principal or the principal or somebody higher up, but half the time they're not kind of [pause] cuz they're a team right? The teachers and the staff and the vice-principal, they're all a team so they're all on the same side so what the teachers say to the vice-principal or whatever 'this is what happened' then that's what happened. They're not trying to hear your side of the story.
> MARIO: They're all against you.
> SMEGAL: Yeah, no matter what you try to say. (Big City FG 9)

With such a perception, even if teachers do treat a student unfairly, there is no official that students feel they can report it to. Two groups argued that if they said they were innocent they would not be believed unless they could prove their innocence. A few students even felt that if they complained they would just give themselves a bad reputation, so it wasn't worth it. Whether these perceptions are accurate or not, the important thing here is that students feel that there is little point in addressing a situation they feel is unfair. In contrast, two students who were part of the youth leadership organization mentioned that they felt comfortable voicing concerns to administrators because they were friendly with them. Such students were much more likely to talk informally, discussing issues with teachers, though they noted that this worked more for academic-related problems, such as turning in assignments late, than in cases of discipline.

Finally, students felt that their teachers often have relatively little power to change school-wide rules anyway and that they are unlikely to bring up student issues to higher-up administrators (or, if they do, students assume, sometimes quite rightly, that teachers are ignored).

In the end, for many, the only path they could imagine for successfully influencing the rules or addressing an unfair accusation was through their parents, a tactic also mentioned by some teachers. Students seemed to feel that parents were much more effective at making change than they were and cited moments when parents successfully changed a rule at the school. This was not always interpreted as fair, however. Shelina (Big City FG 7) argued that

> ... it's mostly the snotty rich kids that really go to their parents [...] and it's not really what, like, what most of the school population's um parents would say, it's just what those certain people would say [...] and a parent would come to the committee and like, say like something, 'Oh my son got beat up by a guy wearing, um, bandanas so bandanas is a gang and then they'll want to [ban them].

Additionally, a reliance on parents is less useful for individuals who do not have traditional parents or guardians, who may not have close relationships with their parents, or whose parents have limited cultural capital to draw on in making a complaint, as discussed in chapter 6. In any case, students generally felt that their parents were unfamiliar with their school rules, in agreement with them, and/or unlikely to fight on their behalf because it would be seen as pointless.

Overall students felt that they have little means of righting wrongs, of addressing the wider problems they may see with the rules themselves, or for advocating for themselves in any kind of institutionalized way. Only the few students with experience in student involvement, either within their school (Big City FG 9) or within a broader leadership group (Big City FG 3), were likely to consider such involvement as feasible.

The Mixed Feelings in Teachers' and Administrators' Commentary

While many staff spoke in favour of student participation, formalized input was more likely to be discussed in terms of parental involvement. Most staff referred to parent or school councils, through which parents can have input, with varying degrees of influence. Those working at

Spencer's school (Big City) spoke very highly of parent involvement and the extent to which it had been fostered at the school. Parents are invited to be on committees and there is significant parent outreach, outreach which Noonan, Tunney, Fogal, and Sarich (1999) consider vital to improve student discipline because it bridges the school and the community. Participants from several other schools also suggested that parents on school council have some capacity to make recommendations and a few even felt that parents have more power than they think, although for the most part, parent input seemed limited. Indeed, five countered that parents really have very little input and that only a select few parents become involved. Staff also had mixed feelings about the role of parents. A few spoke of involved parents as troublemakers – as pushy, demanding, privileged, and stuck in their ways – yet most wished for more parent involvement and appreciated those who are interested and informed about what is going on in the school and in their own students' school lives. Generally staff wanted and welcomed parent involvement, arguing that those in the home and those in the school need to work together.

Staff in both regions also favoured the idea of student involvement. In Whitton, many spoke positively about student involvement, although only four were interested in developing a formal system of student representation. Several others referenced the provincial procedures available to appeal a suspension, two referred to the students' council voice, and three said that they had involved students in the creation of classroom rules at some point in their teaching careers. In advocating student involvement, only Barb (Whitton teacher) and Tim (Big City teacher) presented the possibility that students might have some kind of immediate right to participation. Tim emphasized the need to educate students about their participatory rights and Barb suggested that students need to have a say if they are going to be asked to take responsibility:

> BARB (Whitton teacher): ... you know, we talk about social responsibility and taking responsibility for your environment and for yourself and for your friends and I mean how can we ask these kids to respect their area if they don't feel that they have any say in what's going on? You know?

Supporting a more future-oriented position, Whitton teachers Jen and Simon similarly felt that student participation is a valuable way for students to learn about law-making and community involvement to prepare for when they are adults.

Others cited more utilitarian reasons for student involvement. For example, three Whitton staff emphasized that students need to *feel* that they are being heard, even if it makes no difference to decision-making.

JACK (Whitton vice-principal): And a lot of times in the end, we will not agree and they know that I've gotta make a decision – but at least I've heard them and I've heard their point of view.

BILL (Whitton teacher): There was a little bit of take from them but not a whole lot. We didn't modify a ton of what we were doing. But it was important for them to hear [the reasons for the rule] and, after I recognized it was important to include [to have] representatives of the students along the way.

In related comments, others sought greater student compliance through student involvement. Three Whitton vice-principals and one Big City teacher all suggested that student involvement is valuable for student 'buy in' and consequent obedience, a position also argued by Porter (1996).[7]

Rather than advocating formal student involvement, Whitton staff were far more likely to endorse informal processes that are currently available to students, such as talking to teachers or administrators about their concerns. While informal involvement is valuable and Whitton staff frequently felt that 'open door' avenues are easily available to students, relying on informal procedures raises some concerns, however: such procedures are at the whim of specific teachers and administrators rather being institutionalized, they fail to directly address the unequal power relations that may prevent such informal feedback, and they are most available to those students who feel sufficiently confident and supported to approach a teacher or administrator. Recall, for instance, that some students commented that students' council members or those who are friends with teachers are more comfortable approaching staff.

Finally, some Whitton teachers did not support the idea of student appeal. Vice-principal Blair only mentioned appeals as something to be avoided through clear language in codes of conduct. Joe felt that appeal processes should not be explained to students as 'society doesn't work like that.' Further, at least three felt student involvement to be inappropriate, in part because students need to learn within parameters that are determined by teachers and administrators. Even though he would sometimes have his students create rules for his own class-room, for example, Joe felt that student involvement is unworkable on a larger scale because students do not understand the broader con-sequences of their decisions, they lack the expertise to create rules, and they need clear rules imposed from above in order to learn re-spect. Patrick supported the concept of student involvement but said that in practice students want and value clear rules and boundaries supplied to them by someone else. To Teacher X and Lana (Big City teacher), it is part of teachers' jobs to guide students about right and wrong.

Like those in Whitton, Big City staff also raised possibilities for stu-dents to address their concerns informally, although half also indicated that their students currently have representation on their school com-mittee that reviews school rules, and the rest argued in favour of such representation. Two discussed student surveys, which are becoming routinely used to seek student views on issues of safety in their schools, two others mentioned opportunities for students to draw on peer mediation, an option not mentioned in Whitton, and one discussed student-teacher mediation. Overall, processes for students' more for-mal involvement seemed much more available in Big City schools than in Whitton – a finding which may, in part, result from the limited and select nature of the Big City participant sample, although the more urban codes of conduct I reviewed also suggested greater diversity of approaches in urban areas, including those providing for student in-volvement.

In both districts, staff who agreed with the idea of increasing stu-dent involvement and those more resistant to the idea shared concerns over implementation. Resources and staff were seen as necessary but challenging to secure. Both these concerns are emphasized in research texts outlining concrete examples of student participation (see Mitra 2008; Blase and Blase 1997). Barb (Whitton teacher), for instance, was quite keen on student participation but noted that you would have to have the 'right administration' to even introduce it, and Robin was concerned about the resources needed to make such participation pos-sible. Reflecting some of the ambivalence that even supportive staff felt about the idea, Blair (Whitton vice-principal) was concerned that power struggles would need to be negotiated through a leadership fig-ure and that the ultimate decision-making would need to remain with the principal. Laura (Whitton teacher) was similarly concerned that a clear structure would be needed to prevent too much time being spent in endless debate. Like some students, staff were also worried about students introducing 'crazy rules.' Barb and Chicago (Whitton) and Sarah (Big City) all felt that there needed to be some kind of regulation to prevent students from introducing inappropriate rules and to ensure certain 'non-negotiables' would be in place. These concerns draw attention to legitimate questions about how to implement student participation, although it is interesting that these staff, like most students, had little sense of student participation as an integrated component of co-operative rule-making with staff, nor did they think that students' participation would include guidance and skill development. Some even seemed to assume that student involvement in rule-making meant that each student would independently decide whether or not to follow the rules, suggesting a lack of familiarity with principles of democratic, participatory decision-making.

Staff commentary reveals that overall, there is interest in opening up some decision-making to students, or at least support for this idea in principle; yet at the same time, many of the comments above underscore the challenges of achieving such a goal in any kind of significant way. This gap was supported by Lewis (1999b) in his survey of 294 secondary teachers in Australia in which he found that teachers who experience a gap between their desire for more student involvement and their daily practices which follow a more controlled orientation to discipline tend to experience stress. Lewis concludes that staff members need to talk more with each other about such issues but that they also need more direct professional development training in tactics for increasing student participation. Drawing on the same data, Lewis and Burman (2008) note that lack of administrative support, having too much to do, classroom size, and classroom layout all inhibit teachers from drawing on student voices. They hypothesize that stress may therefore be a key factor preventing teachers from learning about, and implementing, inclusion. Finally, Porter (1996) and Dickar (2008) raise the concern that broader educational policy creates obligatory rules that students can have no say in, undermining any democratic process.[8] Certainly provincial and school board stipulations prevent much genuine, local decision-making for students.

Alternatives

As I have illustrated, student participation in the area of school rules and discipline is sparse. With a generous interpretation of active citizenship, in my own data I have identified some jurisdictions where staff discussed participation and where opportunities for student representation were evident. Those schools that do provide greater possibilities for student involvement, or more egalitarian presentations of school rules, include student representation on committees, student surveys, student-led mediation for resolving disputes, and a grievance process that students may initiate. These possibilities seem most evident in urban schools.[9] While my research suggests that few schools have codes of conduct that make room for the cultivation of students' active citizenship, that few students have any experience with such involvement, and that such participation has mixed support from staff, wider research literature describes a range of possibilities for moving towards making schools more democratic.

Short of forms of enhanced participation and more radical deschooling that I will discuss below, there are tamer tactics listed in the range of participatory possibilities outlined in Table 9.1 that educators can, and yet rarely, employ when developing rules, tactics which gesture towards a more inclusive approach to rule making and enforcement. For instance, rules can address parents' and teachers' rights and responsibilities as well as students' (Lewis 1999a) in order to educate students about the mutuality of rights and to include all school actors within codes of conduct.[10] Similarly, codes can also explain students' rights, including right to participation, right to free expression, and right to appeal (Schimmel 2003). Codes can include pre-emptive, positive strategies which encourage cooperation, tolerance, self-esteem, and pride rather than only including punishments (Lewis 1999a), approaches Lewis found to be more likely in Australian primary than secondary schools. In my own study, overall only eight schools even mentioned that an intention of the code of conduct was to foster school pride or positive memories, as most were focused only on negative rules. Codes can also explain the rationale behind the rules, a gesture which is surprisingly rare.

Rule development itself can involve students in a wide variety of ways, including representation on rule review committees, asking for feedback, sharing interpretation of feedback, and formal negotiation with classes. In their surveys of Australian teachers, Lewis and Burman (2008) found that teachers are more willing to negotiate more conventional and teaching/learning issues with students than issues involving morality and safety. He concludes from this finding that inclusiveness does not have to be all or nothing, but can be partial, although his con-

Table 9.1 Degrees of democratic possibility within school rule design

Organization of the rules and their presentation	• Rules clear, enforceable, and to a minimum (Porter 1996) • Include rationale for rules and process by which rules created (Porter 1996) • Ensure an appeal process is available and notify students of it • Autonomy for students and teachers to determine classroom rules
Minimal, institutionalized student representation	• Student vote on a single issue, e.g., uniform • Student surveys • 'Town hall' meetings with students on a specific issue • Student council participation • Several student representatives on rule review committee • Student representatives occasionally consult with wider student body • Student representation at the school board and/or provincial ministry (Critchley 2003)
Comprehensive student representation and participation	• Student representatives with genuine, frequent role • Student participation in interpretation of student survey data • All students voice concerns at student committee which then takes concerns to staff committee (Sehr 1997); representatives have frequent, formal consultation with student body • Frequent student voting • Open committee meetings, e.g., in central student space • Student involvement in peer mediation.
Full student involvement	• All students eligible to participate through commentary, consensus and/or vote on the development of rules or schools' disciplinary strategy (e.g., Albany Free School) • Students also participate in curriculum development. • Student representation on school's disciplinary committee, e.g., students take turns, by lot, to sit as members of school's judicial committee, which makes disciplinary decisions (Sudbury Schools)

clusion counters Goodman's (2006b) recommendation that it is more important for students to be able to discuss and challenge issues of morality than issues of convention.

There are also many examples of much more involved participation, however, moving far beyond these tactics. I have already presented research by Covell and Howe (2008) and by Hannam (2001). In another study, Dobozy (2007) discusses five 'democratic' Australian primary schools. While different in terms of location and the socio-economic backgrounds of students, these schools shared three common traits. First, the principal of each school saw their school as 'out of the ordinary,' in that they saw their schools as supporting children's legitimate voice in decision-making and rights to dignity and respect. Second, while all agreed that rules are important for safety, order, and equal opportunity, they conceptualized rules as minimal statements of core principles, such as safety and respect, rather than lists of dos and don'ts. This strategy encouraged students to reflect on the core principles as they related to their own actions and to thus learn the more ethical dimensions of interpersonal relations. Finally, they did not attempt to treat all students equally, but instead overtly recognized the differing backgrounds of students in the enforcement of rules to consider the underlying issues behind problem behaviours, a practice which they communicated directly to the student body.

Mitra (2008) provides a detailed ethnography of student participation in school reform at an inner city school in California. Student focus groups identified issues to address and then acted on them. With adult guidance, student presenters eventually created a student forum, with regular meetings. This group focused first on developing membership and then on communication between students and teachers. The latter led to several key initiatives: teachers being taken on tours of students' neighbourhoods, 'ghetto forums' for student discussions of issues involving the wider student body, and some student input into a textbook adoption process. Overall the group succeeded in providing pedagogical feedback, bridging communication between staff and students, and helping students learn about the process of organizing, presenting, and arguing their concerns. Mitra found that the project required attention to group process, an adult advocate, support from those in power, and sustainable structures. For those students involved, the impact was exceptionally positive. In this example, the primary focus of student participation was on pedagogy not discipline, as we also see in Smyth and McInerney's study.

Smyth and McInerney (2007) sought to examine a school with external criteria that suggested it should have problems (e.g., low SES) but that was successful. Plainsville, a primary and public middle school, had an innovative student-centred approach, which they then studied ethnographically. Through the instigation of a new principal, the school gradually introduced learning teams, talking circles, student-developed individual learning plans, and a student-initiated curriculum. The teachers were considered resource people and students worked in clusters in open space areas. Students would generate ideas of what they would like to learn about, e.g., fishing, thus making the material relevant to their lives, including their cultural and class backgrounds. Through negotiation with an adult the project was shaped to extend their learning and to address the demands of the state curriculum. Each day, students registered where they would be in the school, and what they would be working on. The idea was to shift students towards making real, authentic decisions, not just about the organization of the school but about their learning. The students were represented on committees and had a central role in class decisions. Much of the process was tentative and provisional, yet the authors argue that the school is an example of successful student voice and power-sharing in decision-making rather than perpetuating a form of school organization which they felt blamed disadvantaged young people and therefore further marginalized them.

Exciting collaborative initiatives more specifically focused on rule-making have also been introduced in American schools. For example, Denton (2003) describes the ongoing Jefferson Committee, established in 1987 in Kingston High School, a public school in New York State. This committee, with representatives from various school stakeholders including student representatives from all classes, drafted a code of conduct which was then regularly reviewed and applied through an established committee, on which students (called citizens) hold the majority of votes. Included in the code were class meetings, a public meeting to which students at large could bring their concerns, and a process for students to provide their side of the story. Denton's article reports thoughtful, respectful engagement between committee stakeholders, and a greater sense of justice among students than at other schools. The Jefferson Committee process was challenged by high administrative turnover, lack of communication between the committee and the wider school that was linked to the size of the school, and disinterest from a number of students and teachers which was most commonly attributed to this lack of communication. However, even students peripheral to the committee felt that they could invoke the code of conduct and have access to an appeal process. A special issue of American Secondary Education (summer 2003) provides this and several other examples of such projects.

As part of his interest in moral education, Nucci (2001) also references several specific American school projects in which students and teachers as a whole developed school-wide codes of conduct. He recognizes that if such projects are going to work, they require commitment of energy and time, and they need to be kept alive over a number of years. He also cautions that such involvement must be genuine, ambitious, and open to the possibility that a genuine commitment to morality may require significant social change. I have already noted the extent to which such involvement requires resources and commitment. Local flexibility is also vital: as Blase and Blase emphasize, participation cannot be mandated from above but must be explored and embraced at the level of the school (1997).

The more political side of democratic initiatives is highlighted by Apple and Beane (1995) in their argument for democratic schools. They contend that such schools require not only direct participation in decision-making by all school members, but also participation in creating curricula, genuine room to explore critical thinking, and a reaching out from the school to foster democracy within larger surrounding communities, challenging the broader inequalities that manifest in schools. Their edited collection provides a further set of examples of democratic schooling in process.

Finally, the deschooling movement is premised on a belief that children should be free to learn as they wish, as children are innately predisposed to do, and to participate fully and equally in the structures that govern their lives (Hern 2008). From this perspective, compulsory schooling itself should be abolished as it is primarily about control and obedience, which sap young people of any inner motivation and desire to learn.[11] Reflecting the immanence of childhood so central to the work of Skott-Myhre in the previous chapter, deschoolers believe that schooling crushes the 'radical potential of childhood the moment it arises' (Piluso and Piluso 2008, 83). Deschoolers argue that the current institution of schooling is problematically based on force, bribes, and punishment in which students learn mainly to distrust authority and to resist rules. Instead, deschoolers advocate nurturing children's critical and negotiation skills, as well as their challenge to authority – not just in terms of schooling but in parenting as well.

The deschooling movement spans a wide range of schooling alternatives, from certain forms of non-authoritarian home-schooling to democratic schools. There are a number of examples of such democratic schools; for example, see www.educationrevolution.org/ as well as Hern (2008) and Mercogliano (1998). What these schools have in common is that classes are not compulsory, that there is much focus on play, and that students are equal participants in creating the rules that govern the community. Schools are also small, so that decisions can be made together. The most well-known example of such a school is probably Summerhill, a live-in school located in Britain, operating for most of the twentieth century and continuing today. At Summerhill, students are involved in any decision-making that is relevant to their days, with adults and children all having equal votes, making students the majority. Students also participate in deciding consequences when rules are broken. Through this process students are believed to become socially responsible and engaged (Neill 1992). Other examples include the Albany Free School, which operated from 1973 to 2007 in New York State and the Sudbury Valley Schools which can be found in the United States, Canada,[12] and beyond. Sudbury Valley Schools are low-cost, private day schools with no entry requirement, small student populations, many part-time staff, free association between grades, no curriculum, no graded work, and student-initiated learning. The schools are run through formal, voluntary school meetings which cover the entire running of the school. There is also a judicial committee for discipline made up of a cross-section of the school – a committee on which everyone eventually serves. Decisions by this committee can be appealed to the larger school meeting (Gray and Chanoff 1986). In the Albany Free School any school member could, at any point that they were feeling an injustice was taking place, say 'STOP!' at which point a school council would immediately be convened by everyone to address the issue (Mercogliano 1998). While these schools deepen student participation in ways that jar with traditional, institutional schooling, they successfully illustrate the capacity students have for significantly more discussion and involvement than they usually get.[13]

Concerns with Student Participation and Rights

Beyond some of the more practical challenges raised by the participants and that are also discussed by advocates of student participation, some readers might express more political or philosophical concerns with various forms of student participatory involvement. Those who believe that rule-breaking and defiance are inherent either in human nature generally, or in adolescence specifically, may counter that young people need to break the rules, whether they are involved in creating them or not, and therefore need imposed structure. Others may find that children's empowerment, particularly through rights discourse, is simply too threatening to adult authority (Devine 2002). Alternatively, like some of the students I interviewed, children's genuine involvement may be considered too impossibly elusive within current age-based in-equalities. As we saw in the previous chapter, young people's experience of success with such challenges commonly hinges on the support of other adults behind them, in particular, the support of parents.

Similarly, those drawing on more of a caretaker model of under-standing young people may feel that students' current impotence is quite appropriate due to their developmental location. In their view, students need to obey in order to learn the vital skills necessary to become successful adult members of society and to prepare young people for obedience in the future workplace, as suggested in some codes of conduct (Raby 2005) and by some of the staff I interviewed (see chapter 4). For them, it may seem almost cruel to suggest to young people that they can play a role in developing the current and future rules that govern them.

In the face of collective disenfranchisement within our globalized and neoliberal societies, participatory citizenship may indeed mislead young people about their futures. As Stasiulis (2002) argues, neolib-eral politics have eroded the opportunities for people to participate in decision-making within Canadian institutions. Even if we embrace children's right to have a say, this possibility is undermined by the more general erosion of democratic involvement for all Canadians (Stasiulis 2002). Yet such collective disenfranchisement may instead indicate why a reflexive, participatory citizenship is so necessary: di-verse people must come together to be involved in their communities (Ellison 1997) and must have the skills to do so. It is through such involvement that people become more equipped to challenge the neo-liberal shift away from democratic decision-making (Stasiulis 2002) and to reclaim a sense of community. This should not be up to schools exclusively, as Biesta (2007) emphasizes, but schools do need to be part of the process.

As I have illustrated, advocates for children's participation in decision-making within schools and elsewhere often consider this par-ticipation integral to young people's immediate rights and preparation for future democratic citizenship. In discussing democratic participa-tion in schools, I have also drawn significantly on the language of rights and citizenship, both in the present of young people's lives and also in their futures. The rights perspective, while a very useful tool, has also faced criticism, however, as mentioned in the previous chapter. For one, it is an individualistic approach to understanding democratic engage-ment, with the focus on individual democratic skills.

Biesta (2007) challenges this focus by drawing on John Dewey's position that we become thinking subjects through interaction with others, and on Hannah Arendt's (1998) work on the human subject in action. Biesta is drawn to Arendt's argument that we are subjects when our actions are taken up by others in an environment that allows for difference. Through action, we experience the freedom of creating what is uniquely new (e.g., in what we say), but part of this process is that someone else must respond from their own place of action. Biesta interprets Arendt as saying that if we try to control how others respond to us, we deny or eradicate their otherness and in doing so we prevent ourselves from becoming subjects From this perspective, democracy depends on a way of being together that is based on plurality. In her essay 'The Crisis in Education' Arendt (1961) argued that education should be held separate from politics because of children's developmental location and a distinct line of separation between adult and child. Beista (2010) counters this position, contending that the issue is not the difference between adults and children but how people come together to achieve action and freedom, which is only possible 'under the condition of *plurality*' (1 567, italics in original) where there is also deliberation, judgment and the capacity to see other's positions through one's own eyes. Schools, Biesta argues, are places of such politics, politics that are premised on interaction with others. Tarulli and Skott-Myhre (2006) have also challenged the focus on rights, drawing on Deleuze and Guattari (1983) to argue that rights are framed as bestowed upon us by government, but that really action and participation can be (and are) seized by people through our creative life-force, a force that rules attempt to contain. Finally, the concentration on individual rights is questioned by global scholars who argue that such individualism does not resonate within collectivist cultures (Burr 2004) or easily address underlying structures of inequality (Fernando). These positions suggest that the discourse of rights produces a fairly narrow understanding of democratic engagement and that much broader, more social, understandings are possible.

Governmentality studies add other important cautions regarding student participation which were introduced in the previous chapter; for rather than providing children with the freedom to shape their environments and escape the domination of others, children's participation, along with other techniques aimed to foster self-discipline, can be alternatively understood as a deeper form of young people's subjugation (Millei 2011; Pongratz 2007; Vandenbroeck and Bourverne-de-bie 2006).

Rather than being expected to obey or resist when told what to do and when, student involvement can be understood as a technique for facilitating the internalization of discipline, a shaping of the self to better comply through students' own self-regulation. Children's participation in shaping the rules that govern them can be seen as a technique of government that broadens young people's investment in their own discipline and conformity as they become 'responsibilized' (Stasiulis 2002). Pongratz further suggests that participation makes the individual into a co-producer of the control that is embedded in social arrangements (2007) – as they participate in creating rules, their resistance becomes difficult because structures of power are made diffuse and anonymous. This concern has been significantly developed by Millei (2007, 2011) in her examinations of guidance or humanist approaches to early childhood education. These disciplinary approaches are ones that aim to democratically share power with students by giving children choice. Children are understood to be competent and deserving of respect and are therefore active participants in negotiating classroom dynamics, which, in turn, it is hoped, will increase their investments in those dynamics. While these processes may create a sense of skill, autonomy, and freedom among children, Millei suggests that they also govern children's conduct as the choices are conscripted, and children are enlisted to construct themselves towards socially desired ends, masking ongoing relations of domination as their very inner worlds are regulated. Children are therefore governed through their freedom to act. This form of governance is particularly insidious as children learn they must express their thoughts and desires, and that these are, in turn, evaluated through a moral lens (2011).

Governmentality studies draw attention to the unforeseen complexities and possibilities of institutional and other governmental processes. They force us to constantly question assumptions of progress and efficiency in terms of the social relations and subjectivities that such processes may produce. I contend that such Foucauldian analysis does not preclude the possibility of students' participatory involvement in their schools, however. Foucault's later work on governmentality and on the care of the self argues that governmentality includes strategies which people may use in order to relate to themselves and to each other and thus to become self-determining agents who can resist domination through 'both technologies of the self and ethical self-constitution' (Besley and Peters 2007, 21). In this sense, 'conduct of conduct' is about control, but also about facilitating a variety of other ways of being, such as healthy, happy, virtuous, and so forth. These ways of being can facilitate 'the security of society' (Besley and Peters 2007, 22) and good governance, but they can also help us to invent ourselves, through self-reflection and self-mastery, and thus turn ourselves into subjects who can, in turn, challenge domination. Rather than seeing people as constituted through the law with rights or not, for example, Foucault's (2003) position attempts to constitute subjects as free to attempt to control *each other* through governmental strategies, strategies which require certain skills. Some may legitimately guide and teach others, for instance, but concerns arise for Foucault when in the process, authority is abused – then we need skills to respond effectively to such domination. While students' authentic participation may create a shared investment in certain rules governing the space in which learning takes place and hence their own governance, this governance may also be mobilized to challenge domination. When young people recognize themselves in discourses of agency, involvement, and democracy, as evident in more participatory approaches to classroom management (Lewis 2001), they become able, legitimate participants in the social realm, expecting consultation, input, and opportunities to challenge unfairness, potentially weakening the petty tyrannies of adult domination.[14]

Another concern is that involved young people may simply reproduce the *status quo*. Certainly, some have found that students can even advocate more rules than teachers do and be more authoritarian than adults. The experiences of democratic schools suggest that this can be the case but that students also quickly learn the effects of such authoritarianism and then seek to redress the situation by changing the rules. Students may also participate in ways that are unexpected. The techniques of governance and their agents which attempt to shape us are not unified or consistent, for example, creating fissures for the unexpected. Indeed, by opening opportunities for student involvement, quite new possibilities for school organization may arise. As we have explored in chapter 7, young people's actions already disrupt and challenge the dominant social organization of the school, even if such disruption is individualized, pathologized, and contained. By opening up the possibilities for youth to engage more formally as participants within their immediate social world, we do not necessarily invest them with reproducing a pre-established system, but rather one which they have played a role in creating.

As critical pedagogues point out, when students are marginalized within schools, fail courses, are expelled, or drop out, the cause is frequently from class- and race-based discrimination within schools, a mismatch between the habitus of the student and that of the school, and a hierarchical streaming process which disadvantaged students experience as simply increasing their disadvantage. Those working in critical pedagogy might thus be concerned that through student participation, such students become disciplined into a specifically middle class regime. For example, emphasis on self-discipline is sometimes linked to acquiescence, the suppression of emotion, and an emphasis on order (Porter 1996). In this vein, Vandenbroek and Bourverne-debie (2006) argue that an emphasis on negotiation is naturalized as universally good when it really reflects Western, middle class norms of autonomy. This is an important point, forcing us to ask about the assumptions and motivations behind all tactics, and the discourses that contain them. We need to ask what assumptions are embedded in specific forms of participation and how they are understood, for example. A related concern is that participatory approaches frequently fail to engage with more marginalized students (Black 2011) who are then punished for resisting participation.

However, genuine, widespread and bottom-up student involvement in creating the culture of a school – from regulations concerning discipline to the deeply inter-related area of pedagogy – can also mediate some of these issues by opening lines of communication between staff and students so that school cultures better fit with the lives of all the young people who attend them, across class and cultural difference. You may recall an example of this in Mitra's study where student participants designed community tours for their teachers in order to educate them about their neighbourhoods and the issues related to poverty within them (2008). I would also hesitate to suggest that either negotiation or collective, democratic involvement is primarily based on Anglo, middle class values: authoritarianism also has a strong tradition amongst Anglo, middle class people, although sometimes hidden behind a façade of civility; similarly, many other cultural traditions include community participation. These concerns are important to note, however: participation fails if it simply becomes another mechanism to perpetuate and reward middle class values.

Participation is hard work, requiring resources, local autonomy, staff and student commitment, and attention to concerns about student remarginalization. This commitment includes an ability to change traditions, a willingness to disrupt established hierarchies based on status and age, resources and skill development, an acceptance that not all students will want to participate, and the willingness of a staff to entertain genuine self-reflection on their disciplinary and pedagogical beliefs and practices. It also means facing potential tensions as anti-democratic ideas are introduced as part of the democratic process (Apple and Beane 1995). These are all significant challenges.

Committing to Student Voices

This book has described how school rules frequently attempt to foster self-discipline through punishment and exhortations to obedience (Raby 2005; Schimmel 1997), providing little room for the consideration of students as legitimate participants in creating the culture of their classrooms or schools. Students have a number of concerns about various rules and their enforcement, and yet, as this chapter has illustrated, they rarely have any say in the organization of their schools even in terms of consultation. But there are various child advocates and moral educators who have argued that such participation is vitally necessary. They believe such participation recognizes the legitimacy of young people's views and rights in the present as well as cultivating reflection on rules and future skills in democratic decision-making. This chapter has also explored whether such a say is possible, and I have drawn on significant evidence to conclude that it is, in a wide range of configurations and degrees. Yet we also need to ask whether such involvement is desirable when it may really be about increasing young people's self-regulation and acquiescence. I conclude that it is indeed desirable and important, but that for genuine involvement to occur staff, students, and parents must open themselves to possibilities for imagining quite different school structures, be willing to shift age-based relations of power and inequality, and commit the resources to making it happen.

10 Conclusion and Practical Implications

School rules are often framed as common sense, normal, inevitable, logical, and fair. Through examining the minutiae of codes of conduct, as well as student and staff engagement with them, I have troubled this characterization. The rules and their application are not always transparent, straightforward and benign but rather they reflect fundamental tensions in how we understand discipline, young people, and the role of schools. The rules and their application also reproduce beliefs that are embedded in various forms of inequality. Some may feel that despite flaws, current patterns of rule-creation, presentation and deployment work: they efficiently contain and guide most young people, ensure their successful education, and prepare them for future work.

And yet as I and many others have illustrated through a wide range of research, they do not really work. Tremendous school time and resources go into attempts to garner student obedience. Major and minor rules are often problematically equated, as are responsibility and obedience. Students feel that they have little choice but to break school rules when they feel the rules are unfair and to address practical needs. These patterns worry those working in the areas of moral education and democratic participation as they confuse moral issues and dampen students' sense of themselves as present and future participants in the society around them. Some forms of discipline can also leave educational and psychological damage (Jones and Jones 2007). Most significantly, large groups of students, especially minority students, become disconnected from the school and disenfranchised from their education as suspensions accumulate. Staff, in turn, become frustrated and burned-out from repeating themselves over and over again, feel anger at their colleagues for not enforcing the rules, and fear the eruption of potential danger.

In writing this book my primary goal has not been to offer easy solutions to these problems but instead to draw on a diverse range of data and theorizing to provide an in-depth examination of the complexity of issues related to school rules. Following Millei, Griffiths, and Parkes (2010), my goal has been to reflect on classroom discipline as an issue to be considered through new perspectives. It is hoped that readers, particularly those working, or intending to work, in education will take these complexities and perspectives into consideration when creating policy and engaging with students around school rules and their enforcement. More practically, I will end this concluding chapter with a consideration of recommendations on school rules, recommendations arising from my own and others' research. First, a brief review of some of the key observations, tensions, and contributions made within this book.

Observations, Tensions, and Contributions

School rules in themselves are complicated by the diverse and even contradictory intentions that are often behind them. They are developed in order to manage a large group of young people within an institutional space for a significant period of time; thus, many of the rules are conventional ones. Most school rules are, therefore, about immediate containment, although rules are also commonly framed within the language of developing the student into someone who is self-disciplined, respectful, and responsible. These two goals of containment and cultivation are not always complementary, however. The rule against coats, for example, is difficult to convincingly link to ideals of self-discipline or respect unless these are primarily framed in terms of obedience.

These goals of school rules are also set starkly against a backdrop of fear in which concerns about safety and litigation often trump all others. Within this context, almost any rule can be legitimized through recourse to worries about safety. In American schools, especially, the security industry has been profiting substantially from fears around school safety (Robbins 2008) and court decisions have increasingly favoured schools' curtailment of students' activities and rights (Gereluk 2010; Blankenau and Leeper 2003). The result is that students are constantly watched, their activities heavily regulated and civic engagement with the policies of their own schools prevented – this backdrop to their educational experiences has been normalized for them (Kupchik 2010).

Tensions behind the intent of rules reflect broader understandings of young people that are similarly complex. Young people are alternatively conceptualized as beings in the present, with concomitant needs, challenges, and even rights, and also as beings in the future. For some, these two conceptualizations may resonate well together: obedience in the present is hoped to prepare young people for obedience in the future. Others seek to cultivate self-discipline, a goal which the rules link to obedience but which others, such as moral educators, connect to moral discussion and participation. Emphasis on obedience in the present can also conflict with the goal of democratically engaged students. If we draw on discourses from child rights, the sociology of childhood, or democratic schooling, then we must consider the location of young people in the present, and the need (and skill) for these young people to have a say in decisions that affect them – a position that challenges traditionally sanctioned age-based hierarchies. Additionally, as illustrated in chapter 4, staff members understand young people's rule-breaking through a diverse array of lenses which capture the complexity of what we consider young people to be, e.g., they were discussed as temporarily caught in the vortex of unmanageable, irrational adolescence, as desiring structure, as embodying certain inherent human inclinations to both rational thinking and rule-breaking, and as contextually located within specific configurations of family, school, and rule-breaking moments. This mixed collection of characterizations includes those that dismiss irrational adolescents as unable to really know themselves and those that emphasize student rationality. They both essentialize and contextualize. This shifting terrain enables staff members to explain school rules and conflicts about them in ways that routinely put the onus on the student or his or her family while reinforcing staff authority (Millei and Raby 2010).

School rules are also located within the school itself, an environment guided by certain expectations of what it means to manage, to educate, and to cultivate a proper student. First, management of the school for containment and safety comes to be about keeping track of student rule-breaking, keeping watch for student rule-breaking, following rules that are made higher up (at the school board and provincial levels), and responding to community concerns. These goals remind us of the challenges faced by school administrators and staff as they are accountable, particularly in the short term, to deal with difficult students and to keep students safe. It makes sense in this context that staff are frequently concerned about the consistent enforcement of the rules. At the same time, mixed understandings of the rules, discipline, and young people themselves, examined above, complicate easy recourse to consistency, reflected in staff's ongoing, intended, or unintended accommodation of context in student infractions.

Second, chapter 3 began with a discussion of discipline and various ways it can be conceptualized. Almost all classroom management approaches agree that for education to happen, some kind of order must prevail, easily bringing to mind a classroom of desks in rows, students silently working. In this way, discipline is directly yoked with pedagogy: you must have discipline in order to facilitate pedagogy. And yet various scholars in classroom management suggest the converse, that excellent pedagogy facilitates discipline. It is also possible to open up our ideas of what studiousness looks like – to accept that a learning classroom is not always a strictly disciplined one.

Third, most staff members may understand, and attempt to cultivate, a proper student as one who cares about her or his grades, does her or his work, obeys the rules, sits a certain way, talks a certain way, and even dresses in a certain style, expectations that may not directly correspond with the beliefs or attitudes of other staff members, parents, or the students themselves. In this way, the rules and their enforcement also participate in producing an 'ideal' student against which other, 'problem' students are compared. Findings suggest that teachers often wish for investment in this kind of proper student role, including appropriate respect, before they are willing to invest their time in the student. And yet, ironically, findings also suggest that students need to see care and respect from the teacher in order to invest in their schooling, particularly for marginalized students (Hoy and Weinstein 2006).

Ideas of what schooling should look like in turn contribute to tensions between the school environment and certain configurations of peer and personal student culture. This tension is evident in various ways. As I pointed out in chapter 2, school rules often seek to distinguish between the school (which focuses on education or even business) and the 'street' or the 'beach.' This distinction is also made in rules against public displays of affection. Such language is a concrete application of the idea that students must shed their personal, peer, and community lives within the school. Staff understandings of the school itself as a unified geographical entity reinforce this idea as well. For example, when students must take off their hats when they enter the school, the message is that the entire school is distinct from personal and peer cultural space. Students in the meantime push up against these rules as for them the school is a multifaceted, mandatory space in which they have personal needs, and which they occupy with their peers. They become frustrated with rules that seem to regulate everyday practicalities of life, including features of peer cultural life such as dress or music. They also become frustrated with the treatment of the school as a homogeneous space when they see it as logically divided by different kinds of classes, the classroom versus the hallway, and class time versus free time. Most feel that it is appropriate to treat the classroom itself as an educational space but not the hall or the schoolyard. Finally, research literature points to the added tension between school culture and peer culture when there is a more profound lack of fit between the two: e.g., when peer culture is premised on challenging the school, as we see in terms of hegemonic masculinity (Meyenn and Parker 2001), when the habitus of students' community and peer cultures is not valued in the school (Morris 2005) and when students perceive school staff to be discriminating against them (Dei 1996).

My hope is that readers come away from this book recognizing that the rules and their enforcement are not quite as matter-of-fact as their everyday normalization suggests. It is not a surprise that staff often feel stress and frustration around this area of their work because it is so fraught with contradictory institutional and student goals. It is also not a surprise that students will chafe against the imposition of what they experience as sometimes petty, value-laden, and controlling rules and their unequal enforcement.

Possibilities for Doing Things Differently

While my primary intention is for readers to come away from this book with a grasp of the complexity of school rules and their enforcement, there are some concrete possibilities for doing things differently that emerged frequently in this work.

One prevailing message emerging from this study is that there is an urgent need to develop better lines of communication between all those involved in the school community – students, teachers, administrators, and parents – so that all understand and account for each others' concerns and needs, the reasons why particular rules exist, and how these rules can be revised given the changing concerns of all stakeholders. For example, many of the rules that students categorized as 'bad' were ones that they considered impractical within the school environment. They argued that there is a need to be able to carry a backpack, for instance, in order to haul heavy books, particularly when there is not enough time to get back to one's locker, which is located at the opposite end of the school. Students were also interested in having more refined rules, recognizing the spatial and temporal complexities of a school day, and in schools more overtly addressing such issues as bullying and racism. Is it possible to accommodate these student interests? To create compromises? Perhaps. If not, then at the very least students need to be better informed, with convincing reasons, as to why rules are organized as they are.

Of particular focus here has been the question of student participation in the creation and appeal of school rules, which is covered in chapter 9. This focus on participation arises from its frequent discussion in research literature, its links to the questions mentioned above of what we understand young people to be, both in the future and the present, and its potential to disrupt normalized conceptualizations of dominant, cultural capital, particularly if students also have input into pedagogy. Participation also has the potential to concretely change the dominant power relations reflected in school rules and naturalized understandings of young people as incompetent. Whether someone is an advocate of student participation or not, it must be acknowledged that there is a gap between the views and experiences of many staff members and those of a range students in southern Ontario secondary schools. This gap fosters conflict between students and staff, and the alienation of certain groups of students, some of whom invariably drop out – genuine student participation provides one powerful and compelling strategy to both erode this gap and to foster democratic citizenship. Other related strategies are also in need of attention across classrooms, schools and in broader policy in terms of school climate, the rules themselves and the consequences for breaking them.

The School Climate

Students spoke of their need to be actively connected with the school and kept occupied. Some students lamented that time spent in class is boring, uninteresting, and unproductive, and that more interesting topics and discussions would encourage their attendance and participation in classes. Students thus reinforced the link between high quality pedagogy and successful discipline in the broader sense. Others stressed the need to have extracurricular activities to feel involved and tied to the school community, including having art exhibitions or sports. These recommendations are supported within classroom management literature, but seem to get overlooked sometimes when educators are instead focused on containment, obedience, and standardized testing – particularly within a context of limited resources. Concrete suggestions include the following:

- Draw on preventative measures. Foster classroom management that actively demonstrates caring about students and fosters engaged teaching, ensure a meaningful curriculum, and provide extracurricular activities; skill training and resources must be available to support such initiatives (Hoy and Weinstein 2006; Valenzuela 2009).
- Improve collaboration and communication among stakeholders, and with other support systems in the community (Skiba and Rausch 2006). This can be accomplished through student, staff, and parental participation, explanations for rules and shared projects to improve the school environment. It is particularly important to involve all school stakeholders, including teachers, parents, and students in any decisions that may lead to the securitization of the school, such as installing metal detectors, police officers, security cameras, etc. (Dickar 2008). In general, securitization has been found to foster a top-down focus on obedience rather than student support (Kupchik 2010).
- Consider shifting school structures, e.g., creating smaller schools and classes (Lewis and Burman 2008) and lengthening blocks of time for specific secondary school classes in order to develop caring relationships between students and staff (Jones and Jones 2007). This tactic can also facilitate student participation.
- Foster and practice self-reflexive, culturally responsive, and anti-racist approaches to issues of school discipline and classroom management (Weinstein, Tomlinson-Clarke, and Curran 2004).

The Rules

As this book has described, students are commonly introduced to the rules from the very first day of school, through their handbooks and reviewing rules in class or assembly. The rules then produce beliefs regarding what school is and what students should be. The following recommendations are intended to counter the common listing of negative, top-down, unexplained and therefore seemingly arbitrary rules:

- Involve all members of the school community in the creation and review of school rules, including students. This means instituting genuine, formalized interest in what all students have to say.
- Seriously re-evaluate why a rule is there and whether a different tactic is possible so that the number of rules can be reduced and those in place can, in practicality, be enforced.
- Distinguish between school contexts in a way that makes sense to students, e.g., kinds of class, class time and non-class time, class-rooms, and hallways. This may mean leaving more rules to the discretion of the teacher. Teachers may find this difficult because it can be easier to refer to rules that have been imposed from beyond the classroom, but greater discretion provides room for shared rule-making in the classroom and also legitimizes the discretion that teachers often exercise anyway.
- With the goal of clear, transparent communication, clearly define the rules and provide convincing, legitimate rationales for them (Rowe 2006); frame them in terms of positive skills (Jones and Jones 2007).
- Recognize the distinction between different kinds of rules (e.g., conventional, etiquette, moral) (Rowe 2006; Thornberg 2008b), rather than equating minor and major rules; then ensure consequences are logically linked to their seriousness (Skiba and Rausch 2006).
- Seriously reconsider the concept of 'defiance of authority' as it is a very broad, indistinct category that is subject to interpretation and vulnerable to cross-cultural misunderstanding. The category tends to blur conventional rules, moral rules, and etiquette. It also problematically assumes that authority is always correct and that students must always obey.
- Consider rules and their rationales in terms of what they produce, e.g., particular student identities and social inequality: do they reflect class-based or gendered assumptions? do they contain specific features that discriminate against certain groups of students? discriminate based on the omission of certain kinds of information?
- Include a clear appeals process that students may follow if they feel that they have been wronged – for all disciplinary actions, not just for cases of suspension or expulsion.

Consequences

Finally, in terms of the application of rules, as previous chapters have already indicated, staff members tend to favour a consistent application of the rules for fairness and to increase compliance. Students also supported consistency when they were similarly troubled by examples of favouritism and also teachers failing to follow the rules expected of students. That said, in practice most staff attended to context. Students also sought a consideration of context in terms of specific student infractions. These findings suggest a need for more consistent and overt criteria for attention to context (Dobozy 2007), criteria which the Ontario 2008 *Safe School's Act* potentially begins to cover.

- Seek positive options for dealing with problematic behaviour (Skiba and Rausch 2006) and especially alternatives to suspensions. Such options can include conflict resolution[1] (Stinchcomb and Bazemore 2006), peer mediation (Rowe 2006), and/or restorative justice (Cameron and Thorsborne 2001). If out-of-school suspensions must happen, they need to be only for clearly defined, serious problems and provisions should be made to make them useful and educationally supported.
- Create early, positive relationships with parents so that their first contact with the school is not a disciplinary one (Kupchik 2010).
- List rights and responsibilities for staff members as well as students;[2] expect staff to follow the rules they expect students to follow unless there is a logical, professional reason for different rules related to staff duties (Weist 1999).
- Attend to the fine balance between recognizing context and applying rules consistently between students. It is important for students to see fairness, not favouritism or discrimination (especially along the lines of race/culture), but they can also understand that student situations and contexts of rule-infractions are not all identical.
- Genuinely listen to students' concerns and explanations of why they break, or disagree with, certain rules and act on these concerns (Fallis and Opotow 2003; Kupchik 2010). This does not mean foregoing consequences but hearing what students have to say and taking it into consideration as something to also address.
- Ensure that counselling and social work resources are available to students. Counselling personnel must be quite distinct from those involved in disciplinary or policing processes, and student rights to privacy respected (Gregory, Nygreen, and Moran 2006; Kupchick 2010).

Notes for Specific Readerships

How a person might incorporate these suggestions into practice will depend on her or his role in relation to the school. In the introduction I spoke directly to three specific groups of readers in terms of what they might gain from reading this book: pre-service teachers, in-service teachers, and administrators or policy makers. Many of the recommendations I have made in this chapter bridge these roles, but clearly each of these roles also has a unique relationship to questions of school structure and climate, rule-making, and rule enforcement.

Pre-Service Teachers

In reading this book some of your beliefs and assumptions about students, discipline, and the role of teachers may have been reinforced, while others may have been challenged. Clearly the beliefs that we hold will in turn shape our actions when it comes to being a teacher who is also expected to enforce, and sometimes create, school rules. Pre-service teachers are encouraged to think through their beliefs and how they will apply them before getting buried in the day-to-day details of being a teacher. Keeping these beliefs at the centre may require creating your own, clear 'teaching philosophy' as a guide to refer back to and alter as needed, but that is also distinct from the messiness of specific students and incidents. Pre-service teachers are also encouraged to remember the value of building positive relationships with students, even ones with a reputation for being 'trouble,' and to remember that students have certain rights, including a right to have a say in decisions that affect them. As a teacher you are not only teaching and structuring a class, but modelling what it means to be a student and a person. Those in moral education remind us that we also need to engage students in discussions of moral questions. Finally, it is hoped that pre-service teachers will endeavour to become teachers who are active in their school decision-making processes, through safety committees for instance.

In-Service Teachers

Those of you who have been in the classroom for awhile already will have a treasure trove of experiences and stories about classroom incidents, student behaviours, and both difficult and rewarding classroom dynamics. Perhaps in reading this book you have reflected back on these experiences, finding them confirmed, contradicted, or made more complicated. Reading this book may have affirmed your commitment to a certain style of discipline or encouraged you to shift in one way or another. Perhaps you have rethought some of your own school's rules. It is hoped that in the classroom in-service teachers will increase or solidify their commitment to teaching about rights as well as responsibilities, to involving students in discussions of rules, rule-making, and morality, and to recognizing how cultural, class, and student diversity may mean that rules are not always as transparent as we may often assume. Classroom management literature tends to focus on the classroom itself, but teachers also have a significant role in shaping beliefs about students and about discipline in the wider school through staff room discussion, conversations with principals and vice-principals, enforcement (or not) of hallway rules, and involvement in rule-making committees such as safety councils. This book raises a number of questions for teachers to bring to such wider school engagement, and strongly endorses teacher involvement in rule-based decision-making in the school.

Administrators and Policy-Makers

Administrators are often in the difficult position of both significantly shaping whole-school policy while tending to interact most frequently with students who are considered problems. Administrators are also caught between responsibility for making decisions that shape school climate while also being guided by school board and provincial policy which significantly delimits possibilities. Many of the suggestions above can be hindered or facilitated by administrators. Administrators can foster schools that reflect positive communication with all members of the school, support for teachers, and guidance for staff members on questions of discipline. They also set the tone for how students and their parents are conceptualized. For these reasons, while administrators are often bound by structure and tradition, they are also in a particularly important position to support many of the recommendations that are being made in this chapter: fostering genuine, widespread student involvement in decision-making, for instance, as well as staff participation, educating teachers about student and staff rights and responsibilities, and accounting for diversity in the student body.

Similarly policy-makers within school boards and provincial governments must seriously think about the underlying beliefs behind policy

rather than creating policy only in response to specific incidents or political climates. At all levels of administration and policy-making the
important pull towards consistent discipline must be counterweighed
by a thoughtful consideration of context and the situational need for
flexibility in the interests of fairness, acknowledging diversity of student backgrounds and experiences, and students, staff, and parents'
involvement in decision-making. This is a difficult tension to navigate
in order to have schools that are both strategically consistent in their
approaches to discipline and careful to attend to context. Recommendations for alternative practices also need to be supported through education, training, and resources.

Geographical Differences: Urban and Rural Schools

Research for this book also involved comparing rules and commentar-
ies on them in two distinct kinds of regions, metropolitan and rural.
Overall, it was found that the urban region was more likely to recognize
diversity, to be concerned with issues of security, and to provide opportunities for student involvement. This urban diversity may both open
and close opportunities for students. On the one hand, exposure to diversity among students, parents, and staff may increase receptiveness to
student participation, recognizing that the cultural values of the school
staff are not necessarily shared by all students. Urban codes of conduct
directly named issues of inequality and harassment, particularly racist and homophobic harassment. In this study, it was also in the urban
space that students were both more educated about zero tolerance and
also more concerned about it. However, it was in the Big City schools
that students most often cited examples of racism while staff felt that racism is not an issue, suggesting a need to better listen to, and address, students' experience. Furthermore, it is in these diverse urban landscapes
that concerns about security seem most prominent, particular in terms of
potential intruders. In fact a number of Big City schools now have uni-
formed police officers on campus. Concerns about increasing securitization and surveillance seem to be particularly relevant to urban schools.

   The semi-rural region was fairly conservative and homogeneous. It
is perhaps for this reason that rules were more likely to focus on restraint and obedience. It was only in semi-rural codes of conduct that
there were rules directly against public displays of affection, for example. Similarly, semi-rural rules and staff were less likely to overtly raise
issues related to diversity, such as racism or homophobia. The presump-

tion of homogeneity in student populations can possibly foster trust and agreement between students and between students and staff, but assuming shared positions on rules, or on what civility or good taste looks like, does not sufficiently recognize the diversity that does exist. While the region may feel homogeneous, it is not. Even in relatively homogeneous regions students encounter racism and homophobia; class differences can also shape how students engage with the school and interpret its rules. Semi-rural regions like the one I studied need to more carefully consider the relevance of diversity in their schools, not only to make schools more hospitable for LGBTQ students, students of colour, and those from poorer families, but also to educate the entire student population about accepting diversity within a democratic society. The semi-rural region under study is typical of many non-urban spaces in that it is less likely than urban spaces to be the focus of studies on discipline. Yet in this region students talked about the many skirmishes between staff and students over the enforcement of minor rules. It was also in this region that students were most expected to obey without question, and to lack a participatory voice. Perhaps non-urban educational spaces need to be the focus of more research, discussion, and innovation when it comes to the kinds of questions of discipline that this book has raised.

The Last Word

When I look at schooling from a distance, I see students being taught to follow orders without question; indeed, what they see as common sense questions or observations must be ignored. Courteous behaviors, such as greeting a friend, can only occur between classes. Acts of support, such as listening to a friend's problems, explaining a confusing idea, or sharing knowledge, are all discouraged, sometimes with punishment. Authentic adolescent problems, such as bullying, sexuality, and the meaning of life, are ignored. [. . .] Students are taught to conform to a predesigned norm, which may in fact conflict with their reality.

(Thorson 2003, 73)

Beyond practical tinkering, we need to ask broader questions about why we organize schooling as we do. Why are schools large-scale, rule-based, institutional settings premised on hierarchy and competition? Is it possible to imagine a different kind of school, as the democratic schools movement has done? What kinds of rules do we feel are necessary for young people and why? What unintended consequences arise from them? Why is it that certain young people just do not want to go to school and what can be done to better meet their needs?

While some of the above possibilities would be fairly easy to implement, e.g., clearer rationales for the rules that exist, many require greater resources, staff will, community support, and study of their effectiveness (Skiba and Rausch 2006). It is particularly challenging when proposed changes go against the traditional teacher role, including status hierarchies that emphasize teacher authority and student obedience to that authority (Print, Ornstrom, and Skovgaard Nielson 2002). Authoritarian approaches to discipline are often favoured politically as a 'get tough' approach to solve social ills, with variations from such an approach portrayed as 'going soft,' creating a challenging climate for those interested in imagining a different way to conceptualize school rules, their creation, and their application. Others argue that there is limited scope for equal relationships between students and teachers in schools, particularly as the tactics most intended to provide autonomy and self-discipline are those that most insidiously maintain the control of students (Millei 2010). While I too am wary of such processes seeking to govern the self, I also see value in countering possibilities for the abuse of power, and in cultivating young people's sense of themselves as legitimate participants in the more overt, hierarchical relations of power that structure the school and other social institutions.

This book has provided a primary focus on the rules themselves rather than on general issues related to classroom management or school administration that tend to receive the most study, although clearly the latter connect quite significantly to the former. I have drawn on diverse theoretical perspectives to foreground rules as both reflecting and producing social assumptions in an attempt to problematize what may often be taken for granted popularly, within the institutional culture of many schools, and within some classroom management literature. In particular, I have sought to contextualize rule-making and enforcement as cultural, and frequently grounded in unspoken assumptions linked to unequal relations of age, class, culture, race, and gender. Finally, while I have included consideration of the perspectives of various stakeholders in the school, including prioritizing the responsibilities of staff, I have attempted to centre young people and their voice. Contrary to those who believe that adults always know best for young people, I believe that we need to better listen to them, to respect them, and to involve them in thinking about how to best manage the school spaces they are required to attend.

Appendix A   Methods

My methodological approach is one that draws on more traditional forms of research collection, such as textual analysis and interviews, alongside a youth-centred approach enacted through conducting focus groups with young people. Research on schools frequently falls into one of two categories: quantitative research based on questionnaires and ethnographic research based on researchers' interactions and observations in schools. The former can provide a broad snapshot of a number of schools while the latter can provide rich, local detail about a specific site. This project involved a different series of data collection techniques, however, with the goal of examining school rules in a broad sense and through talking with diverse stakeholders, including students, whose voices on school policy are less frequently solicited than those of staff. As Eder and Fingerson (2001) suggest, we need to favour young people's own voices and interpretations, rather than rely only on the viewpoints of adults.

An understanding of policy was gained through examining codes of conduct. Focus groups with students were useful for learning what students from a variety of contexts generally think of the rules and to foreground their perspectives. Interviews with teachers and administrators provided an opportunity to learn about staff views, including beliefs about school rules, why they are needed and why students follow or break them. While these methods have provided this project with a unique, broad angle on school rules, they rely on text and on the viewpoints expressed by those involved, rather than researcher observations of the rules 'in action' in a high school context. For this latter viewpoint we must turn to ethnographies. There are many valuable, relevant, book-length ethnographies conducted at the secondary school level, including Paul Willis's Learning to Labour (1977), Peter McLaren's Schooling as a Ritual Performance (1986), Ferguson's Bad Boys: Public Schools in the Making of Black Masculinity (2000), Nancy Lesko's Symbolizing Society: Stories, Rites and Structure in a Catholic High School (1988), Maryann Dickar's Corridor Cultures: Mapping Student Resistance at an Urban High School (2008), and Aaron Kupchik's Homeroom Security: School Discipline in an Age of Fear (2010). Numerous articles also reflect ethnographic research, including work by Edward Morris; Kathleen Gallagher and Caroline Fusco; Robert Garot and Jack Katz; Robert Thornberg; and Frances Vavrus and Kim Marie Cole. In addition to my own data collection, I have drawn on a range of such ethnographic work, in order to take into consideration researcher observations of classroom dynamics and hallway interactions, as well as quantitative and other qualitative studies to bolster my own research.

Before discussing my methods in more depth, I must make a note on my choices regarding the regions under study. The codes of conduct were collected from secular[1] public schools in a non-urban, semi-rural farming area and from an urban centre. Interviews and focus groups were conducted in similarly distinct locations which I have named Whitton and Big City, both located in Ontario, Canada. An examination of the Whitton and Big City regions similarly contrasts two distinct populations: the Whitton region includes youth living in rural areas, small towns, and a few medium-sized cities. It should be noted that this region is primarily dedicated to agriculture, manufacturing, tourism, and commercial services. The region includes pockets of relative affluence alongside working class communities. People within this region are predominantly Canadian-born and of European descent (Canada 2006). Big City, in contrast, is a large metropolitan centre including an urban core and suburban sprawl. It is racially and culturally diverse. By choosing these regions this study provides a contrast between very distinct contexts, both under the umbrella of the same provincial legislation.

Codes of Conduct

The first area of data collection examined secondary school codes of conduct. These codes, which outline the school rules and sometimes consequences for their infraction, are created within a wider, structuring context. Part of this context is provincial as it is at this level of government that school curriculum and some school policy is set. Most notably for this project, as I have discussed in chapters 1 and 5, in 2000, the Ontario government introduced the *Safe Schools Act* to improve school safety and discipline (Safe Schools Act 2000), an *Act* that was to apply to all public school boards and schools in Ontario. The *Safe Schools Act* included a *Code of Conduct* which some have more colloquially understood to be a zero tolerance policy that requires suspensions and expulsions for rule infractions such as fighting or bringing a weapon to school. The *Code of Conduct* also outlined the roles and responsibilities for school boards, parents, volunteers, teachers, and administrators as well as students. Many features of this code are still in place although within a broader shift towards progressive discipline enacted by the Liberal government that won the provincial elections in 2003 and 2011. This government also introduced new measures to address bullying and harassment in schools.

Within this wider context, each school board also develops its own code of conduct, a code that must draw on Ontario's *Education Act* and the *Safe Schools Act*. Most board policies are developed in consultation with students, parents, teachers, and community members. In the semi-rural region where I collected codes of conduct, school board discipline policies were framed around the development of student self-worth and self-control, with an associated emphasis on rights and responsibilities for students, teachers, and parents. The board policy listed expected behaviour, unacceptable behaviour, and consequences for a number of areas, including dress, alcohol and drugs, attendance, punctuality, electronic devices, physical assault, respect for self and others, parking, vandalism, etc. Like many other school board policies, this policy referred to mandatory consequences outlined in the Ontario Schools *Code of Conduct*.

The urban district policy was based on key principles of respect, safety, and diversity. It emphasized safe schools, respect for human rights, and social justice, and included a comprehensive table of mandatory consequences for various infractions. The policy defined problematic behaviour, e.g., sending hate material, physical assault, harassment, and bringing replica firearms to school, and made reference to the *Safe Schools Act* and Ontario's *Code of Conduct*.

Finally, individual schools also have their own codes of conduct that reflect provincial and school board policy, although they have significant flexibility in how their codes are presented, what is presented, and the detail that is included. Chapter 2 lists common school rules – a generic list I compiled that is similar to many of the school rules examined in this book, although there is also a lot of variation between schools in terms of exactly what is included, what is highlighted, and how the information is presented. Local codes are also frequently reviewed and subjected to minor changes. Through the course of my research, for example, there was even a shift from talking about the regulation of Walkmans to mp3 players!

The codes of conduct examined for this book were collected during 2003, although as part of my research strategy I tried to collect all codes from both before and after the introduction of the 2000 *Safe Schools Act*. The final complement of codes under study in this book include conduct codes for all but one of the secular, public schools in the semi-rural region and 50 per cent of the secular, public schools in the urban region. The former Board treated my request for school policies as pertaining to the *Access to Information Act* and, for a fee, collected all school codes on my behalf from both before and after the introduction of the *Safe Schools Act*. The latter board recommended that I contact each school individually to request codes. Thirty current codes were found online and twenty-one codes were acquired through phoning, faxing, and emailing each remaining school (out of over 100 potential schools). Response (and failure of response) crossed all school sizes and areas of the city, except that response rates for alternative schools were very low. All schools are referred to in this book with a pseudonym.

The codes I collected were not consistent in length, completeness, or style of presentation: many schools sent their student handbooks and several their internal, administrative rules. Some codes were a number of pages in length and others involved a single paragraph. Presentation of rules ranged across diverse styles, although four schools in the semi-rural region had developed an identical code of conduct for their schools. Codes from the semi-rural schools showed far more homogeneity overall than those from the urban schools. Across both sites, more recent sets of rules tended to be more detailed and involved than earlier ones, with new aspects added and few deleted. In particular, over several years a number of urban schools had added sections introducing school identity tags, or elaborating the consequences of failing to wear these tags.

All codes were first read through several times to note recurring patterns in how the rules were presented and, when relevant, how they were justified. Noteworthy quotes were also isolated during this process. Beth, a research assistant, then formally charted all the codes in three forms, first to note changes in school rules since the introduction of the *Safe Schools Act*, second to note the prominence of certain rules and the relative rarity of others across schools, and third, to identify prominent themes across the codes of conduct. All codes were read through a final time in order to address negative or unusual cases that had been overlooked in the original searches for themes. Despite variation in the completeness of codes I examined, this textual data was rich due to the number and diversity of codes analysed and the extent to which clear patterns of similarity emerged across many of the codes.

Focus Groups

The second component of my data collection involved conducting focus groups with secondary students within Whitton and Big City.[2] After receiving the 'go ahead' from my university's research ethics board, focus groups were located primarily through directly contacting service organizations and asking if young people they worked with would be willing to participate. In Whitton, six groups were located primarily through approaching organizations: a Boys and Girls Club, an LGBTQ group, an arts group, a drop-in centre for homeless youth, a youth drop-in centre, and a new immigrant youth group. More informally, three groups were organized through word-of-mouth with students from a Catholic school, a French school, and from a political youth group. In Big City, seven groups were located through approaching organizations: an inner-city youth drop-in centre, a youth leadership group, a new immigrant youth group, a Boys and Girls Club, a youth shelter, a Catholic group, and a support group for native youth. Two groups were organized informally through personal contacts, an informal group of friends and a group of friends who shared an uncommon sport. See Appendix B for a list of groups and participants.

By drawing on such organizations, we ensured a wide diversity of participating students, a context away from the school for participants to talk about school rules, and a context where participants already knew each other, creating a familiar setting distinct from the school. However, this strategy also posed a challenge as we could not control when or where the groups would take place, what size the group would be, nor what to expect in terms of setting: in one group the TV was on in an adjoining space, in another friends kept looking in the window, in another the acoustics were very bad. We also had little control over how the project was presented to potential participants. Service organization personnel were gatekeepers. They determined whether their organizations would participate at all, who was encouraged to participate, and how information about the project was communicated. The pre-established culture of organizations was also something that we were unfamiliar with and may have affected participants' comments, if an organization was particularly rule-bound, for example. In contrast, the groups of friends who had been located through word-of-mouth tended to be smaller, more engaged, and more contained, although they also tended to be groups of young people who were relatively invested in school (and school rules).

Over the summers of 2004 and 2005 my research assistant Lori[3] and I conducted nine focus groups with secondary school students in Whitton, generally between ages fourteen and eighteen.[4] Lori was primarily responsible for coordinating the groups, transcribing as much as possible on-site during the focus group, and then filling in gaps in the transcription by listening to the digital recording afterwards. I facilitated the focus groups. Over the summer of 2006 two other research assistants, Agatha and Simone, coordinated nine focus groups with secondary school students in Big City. The first third of these were facilitated by me and the remaining groups were alternately facilitated by Agatha and Simone. In each region, eight of the groups were with students primarily from the non-Catholic school board and one had students primarily from the Catholic board.

For each location, potential participants were first sent parental and personal permission forms. These forms outlined the purpose of the research project, what participants could expect to happen in terms of the focus group and filling out the exit questionnaire, potential benefits from the study, assurances of confidentiality,[5] assurances that participants could withdraw from the project at any time without loss of honorarium, and information on what would be done with tapes, digital recordings, and transcripts after the completion of the research. These forms were usually distributed by a key person within the service organization, or by a key participant in the focus group for those groups organized outside of service organizations. Participants were then required to bring their signed parental participation form to the group if they were under eighteen years of age. In several groups some potential participants had to be turned away because they did not bring the form, although in each of these cases, the people were still welcome to share in pizza and pop at break time. In the two groups composed primarily of homeless youth, service organization staff signed the guardians' forms. Participants were also asked to sign personal permission forms of their own at the beginning of each focus group. Finally, all participants signed a group confidentiality form asking that they agree to keep confidential what was shared among them in the focus group.

Participants were provided with refreshments and a $10 honorarium. They were also given the option of choosing their own pseudonyms. The focus groups lasted about an hour and a half and ranged in size from three to an unwieldy fourteen. We asked what rules they had at their schools, if they felt that their schools' rules are fair, if they are fairly applied, which rules they would change, which rules they would keep, what recourse they have if they feel they have been unfairly accused of breaking a rule, and whether they could imagine students participating in the creation of school rules. All but the first three focus groups included the cue card activity described in chapter 2 in which participants were given cards with various rules written on them for them to sort into 'good rules,' 'bad rules,' and 'controversial, or debated, rules.' This activity was introduced quite early in the focus groups. At the end of each focus group participants were asked to fill out a short questionnaire which asked for some demographic information and provided an opportunity for participants to record any additional thoughts or points they did not feel comfortable communicating in the wider group.

Through our groups we attempted to talk with students from a wide range of social backgrounds. Focus groups were roughly transcribed on-site but also tape and digitally recorded for later, more thorough transcription. All transcripts were coded twice: I coded them on paper and Lori coded them directly into NVIVO, a software program to assist in qualitative analysis. Lori then added my own codes to NVIVO. This process allowed for both descriptive and abstract coding by two independent coders. I then refined these codes through merging and dividing them where relevant. Through NVIVO, codes were then organized into broad, recurring themes that provided the groundwork for several academic papers and then for this book. More descriptive themes were summarized in a report that was then sent to the relevant school boards and to all participating focus group members who had provided an address and expressed an interest in receiving results. In the interests of member-checking, we also asked for feedback on the report, but did not receive any, and, in fact, seven of the twenty-three reports sent to students in Big City came back to us as 'return to sender.'

Focus groups are valued for the rich interaction they provide (Kitzinger and Barbour 1999; Bloor et al. 2001; Smithson 2000). Researchers can see how meaning is made and negotiated through participants explaining and defending their positions (Warr 2005), challenging others' comments (Hyde et al. 2005), sharing excitement (Vaughn, Schumm, and Sinagub 1996), and teasing and joking (Kitzinger 1994). Focus groups also provide access to the culture and language of peer groups (Kitzinger 1994; Bloor et al. 2001; Morgan et al. 2002). Another advantage of these focus groups was that the young people within the groups were acquaintances and sometimes even friends, providing a comfortable, familiar setting that mediated the traditional balance of power in research somewhat in favour of the participants (Eder and Fingerson 2001; Wilkinson 1998; Kitzinger and Barbour 1999). Indeed, overall we found this interaction to be rich and generally student-led. My research assistants noted how familiarity between respondents led to playful teasing, finishing each other's sentences, and calling each other out, a pattern described in more detail in Raby (2010a).

Despite the synergy of the focus groups, in some of the groups a participant or two dominated and a few members were silent. We tried to address this issue when asking for additional feedback through short questionnaires at the end, although responses to these questionnaires rarely added new information to what was said the larger group. While students had this opportunity to make limited, written, private comments on a questionnaire, they did not participate in individual interviews even though that had been an original goal of the research. Time and resource limitations prevented such follow-up interviews from happening. As Hollander (2004) and Mitchell (1999) have observed, more personal stories and views do not tend to emerge in focus groups; thus details of individual engagements or even sympathy with some staff may have been less forthcoming in the focus groups than if we had also conducted interviews. That said, my primary interest in this project was on more public talk around school rules. Furthermore, there was sufficient repetition across focus groups to suggest the findings are reliable and informative in themselves.

There were several other weaknesses to using focus groups, however. Most important, focus groups frequently lead to partial, fragmented, and contradictory data, or what Kitzinger calls 'unruly' data (1994). One of the greatest challenges in these focus groups was the unruliness of the data emerging from our larger groups. We attempted to keep focus groups to four or five participants, but our reliance on service groups to provide a setting for the focus groups meant that we sometimes ended up with far more. Some focus groups were organized during a 'drop-in' time, for instance, so we needed to accommodate whoever came. Once there, participants were frequently friends or acquaintances and so they would easily interrupt each other, talk over each other, finish each other's sentences, and have side conversations. This made some focus groups difficult for the facilitator to manage and unfortunately we lost much of the banter because details could not be sorted from the din when it came to transcription. It was also more likely in larger groups that some students would remain silent, especially girls. Despite these challenges, I would argue that if the only way to access some groups of young people is through such large groups, then it is certainly worth conducting such groups. For example, it was in our two largest, most challenging groups (Whitton FG 2 and Big City FG 1) that we heard participants critically assess the rule against fighting, providing important data on student engagements with school rules. By leaving participants to talk among themselves the focus group more closely captures the participants' 'natural,' spontaneous interaction. Sometimes in our focus groups participants even seemed to forget they were in a focus group and these moments often proved very rich. The kind of interaction which yielded such important material may not have arisen if we had been more strict about structure, and yet also proved very difficult to transcribe.

Staff Interviews

For the final stage of data collection for this project, teachers and administrators were recruited from Whitton and Big City regions. The data collection process for both regions first passed through my university's research ethics board. In Whitton, teachers and administrators were recruited through the Whitten District School Board (WDSB). After receiving permission from the school board, letters were sent to all principals and vice-principals in the district, who were asked to contact the researchers if anyone on their staff had an interest in being interviewed. Some principals simply posted the request for participants in their staff rooms and others specifically asked teachers they thought would be interested in participating. This process led to the participation of five vice-principals and fourteen teachers, nine of whom were department heads and one of whom was a guidance counsellor (although I have grouped her with the teachers in order to preserve confidentiality). The staff represent twelve schools from across the Whitton region. Two remaining teachers from the parallel Catholic secondary school system were recruited informally. All individual and school names used here are pseudonyms. Interviews were typically conducted during teachers' free periods at their schools, and were recorded. (Two teachers requested that they not be recorded and notes were taken by hand in these cases.) (See Appendix C.)

Big City staff were much harder to access. After receiving permission from the Big City School Board to follow a similar process to that in Whitton, we sent letters to twenty, and then an additional ten, Big City school principals requesting that they contact the researchers if anyone on their staff had an interest in being interviewed. Schools contacted were chosen through a strategic random sample ensuring representation across school sizes, school concentrations (e.g., arts, technical, academic) and district area. This method yielded responses from two principals and three of their staff members. This lack of response may have been partly due to the timing of our project, as it was shortly after a very public, violent incident in a Big City school, an incident that left all Big City schools subject to scrutiny. It is also possible that the lack of response arose from the high number of research projects Big City schools are asked to participate in and their possible preference for projects originating from within their own district. In any case, upon recommendation from the school board, I then placed an advertisement in 'Update,' the Ontario Secondary School Teachers' Federation newsletter requesting participants. This tactic yielded two more participants. Through snowball sampling with these participants, I located three more, for a total of ten – two principals, two guidance counsellors, and six teachers (see Appendix C).

In both regions, the participants were self-selected in that they were people who chose to participate because of their interest in the project, including some who were specifically asked by their principal or vice-principal if they would be involved. The self-selection and administrative recommendation suggests that most of the participants were people who were invested in school rules generally, in the ways the rules were enacted in their specific schools or classrooms, or in ways they were seeking to change the rules.

Due to geographical distance, time, and budget limitations, all Big City participants were interviewed over the phone. While in-person interviews provide greater opportunity for gathering non-verbal data and building rapport (Shuy 2001), these advantages have not been shown to be large, and are also counter-balanced by the efficiency and flexibility of phone interviews (Knox and Burkard 2009). We did not observe a significant difference in the quantity or quality of material collected in phone versus in-person interviews, although it is interesting to note that within the ten Big City interviews, three at some point in the interview confirmed that the interview material would be confidential, in contrast to only one in Whitton. This difference may be a result of the interviewing format but could also be a result of the very different district climates between the two regions.

All teacher and administrator interviews were transcribed by research assistants. The Whitton interviews were transcribed by Lori, who also conducted the majority of the Whitton interviews. I conducted the bulk of the Big City interviews and I transcribed half of them while another research assistant, Trent, transcribed the second half. Much like the focus groups, all interview transcripts were read through at least twice by each of two coders, myself and either Lori or Trent. First readings included a process of descriptive coding; second and any later readings included abstract coding, identification of key quotes, and also identification of any material that seemed to disrupt or complicate earlier, developing patterns in the data.

Other Issues and Concerns

Parents

Readers may note that parents were not included among the stakeholders I talked with for this project. I did not talk with parents because I did not see them as the central participants to rule-making or secondary students' engagements with the rules as they were being examined for this specific project. This does not mean that parents are irrelevant, of course. Parents' own rules and discipline styles shape how students will engage with the rules and disciplinary approaches within the school, for instance, patterns that are studied elsewhere. Parents also influence school policies, either when they are representatives on committees or councils, or when they complain to school staff about specific rules or disciplinary instances. In chapter 2 I have discussed this parental involvement as it was raised by both staff and students. With the exception of staff from one school in this study, however, students and staff suggested that most parents currently play a minor role in the creation and deployment of school rules in the schools under study.

Changing Context

As I have mentioned, the provincial context changed over the course of this research, with first a Conservative and then a Liberal government introducing relevant changes to discipline policy in Ontario schools. The latter government has also solicited reports on bullying and on sexual harassment, gender harassment, and homophobia in schools, initiatives that have called for increased peer mediation, conflict resolution, and education regarding harassment. In sum, the overarching climate of school and classroom management changed somewhat over the course of this study. Codes of conduct were examined under the original *Safe Schools Act*. Student focus groups were conducted while the original *Safe Schools Act* was under review, as were interviews with Whitton staff. Interviews with Big City staff were conducted after the *Safe Schools Act* had been amended. Positively, this climate of change may have fostered deeper reflection about school discipline processes among staff members but the changing ground has also made it harder to compare comments between Whitton and Big City staff. Furthermore, the codes of conduct that were reviewed at the beginning of this project have not remained static but have undergone minor changes over the years that have not been documented here. It is interesting to note, however, that despite a fairly significant reframing of discipline policy in Ontario from the language of zero tolerance to that of progressive discipline, the codes of conduct that students encounter in their schools have changed little. In 2010 we conducted a brief review of 25 per cent of the codes of conduct that were studied for this book, only examining codes that were available online. Among the fifteen urban codes we examined, only two mentioned progressive discipline, three had expanded their range of consequences, and eleven had links to the school board's general safe schools policy or a policy addressing online conduct. Seven had added rules related to electronic devices. Among the five non-urban codes, none mentioned progressive discipline and they had all added more detailed language around dress codes.

Inside / Outside

One weakness of this project has been my own distance from schools. Unlike ethnographic researchers who are deeply embedded in the school, I did not observe students and teachers 'on the ground' in classrooms, hallways, and on school grounds. Furthermore, my focus groups were organized outside of schools and most staff were interviewed outside of schools. This distance from the school left me reliant on documents and on the comments and perspectives of participants. I was not able to observe classroom management 'in action,' nor conflicts between students and staff regarding discipline. For an analysis of such interaction, I have relied on the extensive classroom observations that have been conducted by numerous other researchers, but my own study certainly remains impoverished by this gap. There was one advantage to my distance from the classroom as well, however. In conducting focus groups, my research assistants and I had no preconceived notions of the participants, and the participants themselves did not have to wonder about our roles within the school.

My non-presence in the classroom also relates to questions of insider and outsider positioning, for I am not a teacher or school administrator. Much research on schools is conducted by teachers and other school staff who have insider knowledge of how schools work and what dynamics might develop with students. A study on school rules, particularly in terms of how they play out in the classroom or in the principal's office, can well benefit from such insider knowledge and may increase the legitimacy of the project through the eyes of other teachers and administrators who might be reading a book such as this one. However, staff status can also have its disadvantages. For example, it may be harder for someone who works as a teacher or administrator to try to see school rules through the perspective of a student; it may also be hard for them to step away from the day-to-day business of maintaining order to consider the ramifications of what are frequently taken-for-granted decisions and actions in the school.

Sometimes teachers and administrators even conduct research within their own schools. Dickar is one such researcher and she reflects on the possibility that her position, as a teacher within the school she was studying, created a 'dual-role conflict' which may have undermined her research and been unfair to participants. While she acknowledges that she found it hard to slip out of her teacher role and that she was known within the school as a teacher, she felt that her position also helped students to participate – because of her familiarity with them they had a ground of trust. She also believes that her teacher role helped her to gain insight into the school culture (Dickar 2008). Finally, Dickar contends that when the role of teacher-researcher is devalued, this simply widens the gulf between teachers and educational research. She asks why the outsider should be considered more objective.

From the other side, as an outsider, I do not consider my perspective to be more or less objective; it is simply another angle to look at questions of school rules, discipline, and classroom management. Through reviewing documents, talking to students and staff, and doing extensive reading, I may be able to identify patterns and problems that those who are working within the school system may be less likely to see. Conversely, I also may have missed some things that are important to school staff. As such I do not consider this study to be definitive. It is simply one more, grounded, informed, and concerned part of a larger conversation.

In addition to the professional differences, other kinds of identity were also relevant to this research, both in terms of facilitating focus groups and in conducting interviews with staff. For focus groups, Smithson (2000) suggests that it may be useful for the facilitator to have a similar background to the participants, for instance. As she notes, however, shared identifications are quickly complicated by the relevance of diverse, intersecting identifications: should researchers try to find facilitators that share a similar age, gender, race, or cultural background to the participants? One value of research assistants facilitating focus groups with teenagers is that they are often younger, although most advice on conducting focus groups emphasizes the need for someone who is experienced and skilled at facilitating (Bloor et al. 2001; Morgan et al. 2002), and other features of identity such as gender or race may be equally or more important. As discussed elsewhere (Raby 2010a), in later conversations with my research assistants, comments did not consistently support an ideal of shared identity. For example, while Lori is fifteen years younger than me, she felt that my presence would be less intimidating than hers. Agatha suggested that Canadian young people do not seem to have a problem being outspoken with adults, and certainly focus group participants did not seem to have trouble arguing with me!

My research assistants discussed rapport in terms of race and status as well as age. Simone assumed that perhaps Agatha would have been able to better establish rapport with a racially diverse group she facilitated (Big City FG 6) because Agatha is Black. Yet when discussing a group she found particularly challenging (Big City FG 7), Agatha noted that the racially diverse participants may have been *less* respectful of her due to her age, and may have adjusted their behaviour had I (a White professor) been there. In this case shared racial background and similarities in age were not seen to be useful for the facilitator. In fact, within this focus group several quite troublingly racist comments were made by participants about a teacher of African heritage, adding to a 'chilly climate' for Agatha's facilitation and providing an example of how the balance of power in focus groups can undermine a facilitator (Kitzinger 1994). In this particular study, I was not convinced that a facilitator's similar age or racial background necessarily drew more information from participants or led participants to feel more comfortable.

In terms of the interviews with teachers, questions of identity were again complicated. As mentioned above, most of the Whitton interviews with staff were conducted by my research assistant Lori. At the time, Lori had recently finished a Bachelor of Education degree and had just begun working as a substitute teacher, a job that provided her with some professional insider status. That said, she was also a research assistant in the project and so when several interviewees asked questions about the project, she suggested that they needed to talk to me. It was not clear how Lori's work status, age, or gender may have influenced the interview dynamic.

Distance from the Data

The final potential weakness of this study is my own distance from some of the data, particularly some of the Big City focus group data. The use of research assistants was valuable for many reasons: it widened the scope of how many interviews and focus groups could be completed, it supported undergraduate and graduate students while also providing them with valuable skills training, and, as discussed above, it potentially created opportunities for rapport, e.g., between Lori and other teachers, and, for focus groups, between younger researchers and participants. That said, in listening to the interviews with teachers, there were inevitably moments when I wished that certain follow-up questions had been asked, or a participant had been pushed just a little bit further on an issue. Similarly, there were several Big City focus groups that offered specific challenges that might have benefited from my presence, such as the one where Agatha had to negotiate a 'chilly climate.' I am not certain that I would have been able to draw more material out of these groups, but perhaps my greater facilitation experience might have allowed me to do so. Finally, when I have reflected on the groups I did not facilitate I have felt some disconnection – there is a certain texture to my sense of the focus groups that just is not there for these groups.

Concluding Thoughts

This study has been one conducted from the ground up in that I have relied on codes of conduct, focus group conversations, and open-ended interviews in order to gain a multifaceted perspective on school rules and how they are perceived, exercised, and experienced. The insight collected through this data is meant to add to a wide range of other research into questions of discipline and classroom management in secondary schools, research that has produced contrasting and often contradicting perspectives. I do not see such contrast and contradiction as a problem, however, but rather as pointing to a diversity of relevant material to consider when examining the very complicated issues involved in institutionalized schooling.

That said, a key component of my triangulated research has been an emphasis on student voice, gleaned through eighteen focus groups. Historically, students have often been marginalized or silent both in research about young people and in the construction and execution of school and classroom rules, and yet my focus groups suggest that they have a lot to say. While most teachers acknowledged the value of hearing from students, all did not see this as equally valuable. As one teacher asked, 'Why would you take the students' side first? Why did you interview all the students first? Do you think the students should have a right to define the discipline or the dress code policies?' My answers would be that it seemed vital to first hear from those for whom it is compulsory to be at school every day and who tend to remain unconsulted on disciplinary issues. And yes, students should have some say in how school discipline policies are created and executed. Such an emphasis reflects the sociology of childhood's call for young people's direct involvement in research about them (Christensen and James 2000) and with Articles 12, 13, and 14 of the United Nations *Convention on the Rights of the Child* that ensure rights to freedom of expression, rights to be heard, and rights for children to participate in decision-making that affects their immediate lives. Furthermore, as issues related to classroom management are often stated to be the most stressful parts of teaching (Lewis 1999b), it would seem imperative to talk to students about their views about how it is that issues of classroom and school discipline arise. Yet the importance of listening to students does not mean that their views are sufficient to an analysis of school rules and how their presentation and enforcement unfolds in schools, as my interviews with teachers and administrators make clear.

Appendix B   Focus Group Participants

Whitton

#1 Youth Centre

Youth centre in a mall in a small city.
Participants were White.
One participant self-identified as Jewish.
15–17 years; five females and two males.
Economic backgrounds unavailable.

#2 Street youth

Drop-in and shelter for street youth in a small city.
Participants were primarily White.
16–21 years; four females and ten males.
Economically marginalized youth.

#3 Political youth

Located through word-of-mouth, all participants involved in a leftist political group.
All participants were White
16–18 years; three males.
Middle to upper class, professional parents.

#4 Performing arts

Members of an organized performing arts group in a small city.
All participants were White.
One 13-year-old, the remaining members 16–17; three females, one male.
Middle to upper class professional parents.

#5 French group	Located through word-of-mouth, all at a public French school. All participants White. Aged 15–18; four females. Working class parents (trades and service industry).
#6 Catholic group	Participants located through word-of-mouth. All attending public Catholic school. All participants White. Aged 17–18; two females, two males. Middle class, professional parents.
#7 Boys and Girls Club	Drop-in centre for young people located in a small city. All participants White. Aged 13–16; four females, two males. Economically marginalized.
#8 New immigrant group	Weekly program for new immigrant youth in a small city. One participant Latin American, two from North Africa, one from East Africa, remaining three also non-White. Aged 15–18; two female, five male. Working and middle class parents
#9 LGBTTQ group	Weekly group for lesbian, gay, bisexual, transgender, two-spirited, queer and questioning teens. Seven White, one Black, one Asian youth. Aged 15-19; five male, four female. Across range of class backgrounds.

Big City

#1 Drop-in centre	Group conducted at a drop-in centre for inner city youth. Participants were primarily South Asian and Black. 14–18 years; two females and seven males. Economically marginalized youth.

#2 Informal group

Three friends
Two White, one Black.
14–15 years; two females and one male.
Professional parents.

#3 Youth leadership group

Part of a youth leadership organization.
Racially mixed group.
15–17 years; three females.
Professional parents.

#4 New immigrant youth group

Community group for young people from a specific African country.
All African, mostly Muslim.
14–18 years; four girls, three boys.
Mixed economic backgrounds.

#5 Alternative hobby group

Four friends involved in an alternative hobby group and also attending an alternative school.
Three white, one South Asian.
14–15 years; three females, one male.
Professional parents.

#6 Youth shelter

Group conducted at a homeless youth shelter.
Racially mixed group.
17–19 years; three females, two males.
Parental information unavailable. Currently economically marginal youth.

#7 Boys and Girls Club

Racially mixed group.
14–16 years; three females, four males.
Parental information unavailable.
Program directed at economically marginal youth.

#8 Catholic group

Group within an organization for Catholic youth.
15–18 years; three females
Racially mixed group.

Professional and working class
backgrounds.

#9 Native group   Youth group within a Native centre.
                         18–19 years; one female, four males.
                         Diverse economic backgrounds.

Appendix C   Staff participants[1]

Whitton

Participant	Number of years in schools	Position
Joe	11–15	Teacher, Department Head
Jen	6–10	Teacher, Department Head
Patrick	6–10	Teacher, Department Head
Dylan	11–15	Teacher, Department Head
Laurel	6–10	Teacher, Department Head
Gemini	16–20	Teacher, Department Head
Simon	16–20	Teacher, Department Head
Barb	over 20	Teacher, Department Head
Laura	11–15	Teacher, Department Head
Maria	under 5	Teacher
Iron	over 20	Teacher
Bill	11–15	Teacher
Glenn	11–15	Teacher
Martha	6–10	Teacher
Lurleen	6–10	Teacher
Teacher X	11–15	Teacher
Jack	11–15	Vice-Principal
Blair	16–20	Vice-Principal
Robin	over 20	Vice-Principal
Chicago	11–15	Vice-Principal
Mike	over 20	Vice-Principal

Big City

Participant	Number of years in schools	Position
Nicole	Over 20	Guidance
Brenda	16–20	Guidance
Louis	16–20	Principal
Spencer	over 20	Principal
Sarah	over 20	Teacher
Tim	11–15	Teacher
Lana	11–15	Teacher
Sandy	6–10	Teacher
Jim	6–10	Teacher
Monster	16–20	Teacher

Notes

1 Introduction

1 Ontario's publicly funded education system has two parallel school boards, one Catholic and one secular.
2 Teachers were advised by their unions not to suspend, however, which argued that the decision to suspend should be left up to administrators while teachers need to focus on teaching and learning and to avoid potential tension with parents following a student's suspension (Coad 2004).
3 Throughout this book the term 'race' will be used as a shifting social category that has been constructed based on physical differences that have been selectively prioritized, commonly in the interest of maintaining social inequality. While races are therefore socially created, they nonetheless hold meaning and consequence. I will also use the term 'racialized' to flag the creation of race as a process.
4 Subjectivity can be considered a sense of self, and a site through which we can understand our relation to the world around us (Brah 1996). It also frames the self as a subject who both acts and is acted upon.
5 Discourses can be considered culturally produced stories, beliefs, or representations that often act as truth statements (Burr 1995). Power relations are evident in the reproduction of discourses as they produce how we see, understand, and engage with the world around us.

2 'No hats!' and Other Conventional Rules

1 Please note the following transcription conventions:
[. . .] indicates missing text; square brackets are also used to indicate my own text or description. / indicates that speech was interrupted.

This excerpt provides a great example of how focus group participants built their conversations: disagreeing, adding to each others' comments, and sometimes shifting participants' views – indeed it is in conversations with others that viewpoints are often shaped and developed (see Appendix A).

2 I refer to 'minor' and 'major' school rules in order to distinguish between those that more locally address personal and conventional issues in the school and those addressing deeper, more moral issues such as those related to violence and/or those breaking established laws.

3 Uniforms are not the same as dress codes. A uniform policy requires that all students wear a variation of a similar style and set of colours. Dress codes, in contrast, provide guidelines for what is acceptable and unacceptable dress but within these guidelines students may wear what they wish. While I occasionally discuss uniforms in this book, I more frequently focus on dress codes.

4 The term 'ethnicity' can imply a degree of homogeneity to a group and yet it is useful to distinguish ethno-culture from other forms of culture such as class-based culture or youth culture and so I will be using it in this book.

5 A smaller later sampling of urban codes suggests that the urban codes were also more likely to reference changes in legislation towards progressive discipline (see Appendix A).

6 Please note that some of the following discussion draws on my 2005 paper 'Polite, well-dressed and on time: secondary school conduct codes and the production of docile citizens.'

7 This separation of school and street is reminiscent of the streetcorner state discussed by Peter McLaren (1993) in his ethnography of an urban, Catholic high school in Ontario, Canada. McLaren describes the streetcorner state as a time of peer-centred, free-flowing interactions, a physical, cathartic state where pent-up frustrations are released. The student state is more contained and subdued, based on the ethos of work.

8 The Big City school board to some extent recognizes how context varies across schools by acknowledging that specific school communities have their own standards of decency.

9 This discussion has been well-examined through the lens of Pierre Bourdieu's working concepts of habitus, field, and cultural capital (Bourdieu and Passeron 1977; Webb, Schirato, and Danaher 2002; Apple 1995), links I discuss in 'Polite, well-dressed and on-time' (Raby 2005) and also develop in chapter 6.

10 I do not focus on symbolic dress here, e.g., religious or politically significant forms of dress. Dianne Gereluk (2010) argues that symbolic dress is

important for ensuring diversity within schools, diversity which in turn contributes to civic conversation necessary for a sense of justice. By legislating against contentious issues related to symbolic dress, Gereluk argues, societies fail to foster attitudes that favour social justice. She suggests that criteria for banning dress should be limited to whether the dress can be shown by the school to be unsafe or unhealthy, hindering educational aims, or oppressive to self or others.

11 It is surprising then that so many school rules are not explained in student handbooks.

12 While the importance of removing hats as a traditional sign of respect was frequently mentioned in the rules themselves, by teachers and by students, it is interesting to note that in the West this tradition is commonly both a Christian and a gendered one. Historically in the West, it was men who needed to remove their hats indoors and in the presence of a woman, while for women it was considered appropriate to wear hats indoors, particularly in church. In contrast, within various other religions (e.g., Judaism, Sikh) boys and men are required to wear head coverings indoors and out.

13 Cell phones and the internet both also raise concerns about student conduct that expands well beyond the school: as cell phones have been used by students to record incidents in the school and then post them online, cell phones and the internet have been used in cyber-bullying, and personal online pages have posted material that some school authorities have deemed inappropriate. These issues raise new challenges and murkiness around the purview of the school in terms of whether it is necessary or appropriate to regulate what students do in cyberspace, questions that remain beyond the scope of this current text.

14 A very similar response is evident in Thornberg's interviews with primary students in Sweden (2008b). As one second-grade girl says, 'The thing about caps that [sic] actually don't disturb anyone and you don't start fighting because of them or anything' (45). Not only did Thornberg's respondents characterize such etiquette rules as pointless and unnecessary but also as insulting to them.

15 Throughout this book I will be referring to African American, African Canadian, Caribbean, and African students as 'Black' as I shift between research in the United States, Canada, and Britain, and I also wish to include new Black immigrants.

16 In some schools where the cafeteria is quite small student lunchtimes are staggered such that some students will be eating lunch in an earlier and some in a later block.

17 Backpacks are thought to be a tripping hazard, to invite theft, and to provide an easy place to hide such things as weapons.

3 Big Rules and Big Consequences

1 As a reminder, Whitton Focus Groups 1–3 were not among the six groups that participated in this exercise. Participants in FG 2, the street youth group, felt very differently about the 'no fighting' rule, which will be discussed shortly. Also, the more politicized participants in FG 3 did not feel the need for most edicts of school codes of conduct, including some of these 'major' ones, preferring instead the idea of simple, blanket rules such as 'use your best judgment and be nice.'
2 Disputes regarding the distinction between punishment and consequences are examined later in this chapter.
3 This observation, made within several focus groups, contradicts Nucci's (2001) suggestion that children would rather resolve their own moral disputes than seek the help of adults.
4 This section on fighting draws significantly on a portion of a previously published paper (Raby and Domitrek 2007).
5 When prodded to consider how they would address fighting if they were in the principal's seat, members of Whitton FG 2 argued that extracurricular activities, especially regulated physical alternatives to fighting such as boxing or football, would help them deal with their frustrations.
6 See Pascoe for a discussion of female masculinity in high school (2007).
7 Insolence can also be applied to other student actions in a murky, subjective manner. For example, some researchers have been concerned that it is through such an interpretive category as insolence or defiance that marginal students' behaviours are more likely to result in suspension than others', particularly under zero tolerance policies (Skiba and Rausch 2006; Robbins 2008). See chapter 6.
8 One Whitton staff member scoffed at this position, arguing that the only danger of an mp3 player is that it can damage hearing when played too loudly!
9 One Dallas school is even reported to be using electronic monitoring of individual students in order to combat chronic truancy (Kovach 2008).
10 This quote comes from a report created within the Toronto District School Board in Ontario in response to a school shooting (School Community Safety Advisory 2008). The report argues that zero tolerance and the dismantling of social supports have exacerbated a difficult climate of learning for marginalized youth. The report recommends regular student surveys,

culturally sensitive curriculum, increased staff supervision, community
outreach and other recreational activities, increased funding (especially for
social workers and counsellors), and some concrete interventions including uniforms, ID cards, a student equity committee, and an ombudsperson
office.

11 For reporting of suspensions between 2001 and 2008, see http://www.edu.
gov.on.ca/eng/safeschools/statistics.html (accessed June 7, 2010).

12 Information on race or ethnicity of those suspended was not available
in these documents, although others have contended that students of
colour were also disproportionately represented (e.g., see Bhattacharjee
2003).

13 Suspension rates are also somewhat problematic, however, as schools may
avoid suspension in order to elude negative suspension rates.

4 The Rules and Their Underlying Beliefs

1 See Porter (1996) for a comprehensive examination of a series of disciplinary approaches, including the underlying philosophies behind each of
them.

2 By agency I mean our ability to make change in the social world around
us. It is often conceptualized only in relationship to resistance but can also
be understood more broadly. To Watkins (2010), agency arises when subordination is used for productive purposes, but resistance is only one form
that this productivity can take. Bronwyn Davies's (1990) conceptualization
of agency is broader still, and more interactive. Her position is that a person is a person through shared discursive practices. Within this context we
must make ourselves knowable, speak for ourselves, and have responsibility for ourselves – and this is agency.

3 Lewis finds that parents are also most inclined to support such a 'teacher-
oriented' approach (1991).

4 In their typology of forms of discipline, Hoy and Weinstein (2006) also
argue that a minority of teachers believe their role is to teach students to
challenge inequalities and protect the rights of the powerless, and so their
intent is to prepare students to act morally and justly. From this approach,
children are considered neither inherently good nor bad but shaped by unequal forms of social power. In my interviews only one respondent came
close to this position. The authors also introduce the *laissez-faire* position
which emphasizes children's goodness, inner harmony, self-discipline,
freedom, and fulfilment, although they did not find any teachers supporting this position, and neither did I.

5 The lack of focus on future citizenship through a more democratic lens can be considered a disappointing consequence of neoliberal individualism and portrayals of people as taxpayers and consumers rather than citizens. Young people's present (as opposed to future) citizenship is also contested. Some advocate that children be considered as citizens in the present. Imre and Millei (2010) problematize the idea of student citizenship in the present due to children's exclusion from political discourse and practice. They argue that because children cannot be full citizens, attempts to define them as such are really about deepening their self-governance. Others counter that it is through recognizing students as citizens and democratic participants that they will be empowered (Roche 1999; Devine 2002).

6 These patterns are also likely gendered. In reviewing previous studies and in conducting their own interviews with sixteen male and female principals in Israel, Oplatka and Atias (2007) find that men tend to focus on ensuring a classroom conducive to learning through control, obedience, hierarchy, prohibitions, teacher professionalism, and good teaching, while women tend to focus on socializing students in interpersonal relations and fostering a positive school climate through involving students and parents in showing caring, warmth, and love. Overall they argue that gender plays an important role in how principals orient themselves towards school discipline. Men's approaches tend towards management, rationality, hierarchy, formality, authority, objectivity, power, prohibition, assertiveness, and purpose. Women's approaches tend towards collaboration, positive emotion, caring, collegiality, awareness of context, tolerance, subjectivity, informality, and relationality. This suggested pattern could do with more study. See also chapter 7.

7 Levinsky interviewed principals and examined codes of conduct in Toronto, Ontario, to argue that zero tolerance constructed students as rational actors with the freedom to make good or bad choices. The disruptive student was then at fault for not making the right choice.

8 There was only one instance where a staff member specifically referred to students as adults. Jack mentioned that when he sees a student in his office he'll say, 'I'm talking to you like an adult and as adults we communicate and hopefully that solves the problem.' While Jack may hope to draw the student into a category of increased responsibility or problem-solving skills, the student is in the ironic situation of having to act like an adult in following rules that specifically govern the behaviour of teenagers.

9 Of course, some people are not comfortable with this leeway granted to young people on the basis of their developing maturity, as we see in calls for stricter discipline in schools and debates about legislation for young

offenders. While some believe that teenage young offenders should be treated as developing children in the court of law, for example, others contend that their crimes require them to be treated as adults – a position comprehensively reviewed and challenged by Bischop (2000).

10 Some students identified certain rules as unenforceable due to human nature as well. Some students argued that it is human nature to want to break rules or that sometimes rule-breaking 'just happens' when they are not thinking about it, such as swearing. For Elizabeth (Big City FG 4), for example, spreading rumours is inherent to all of us, not just teens: 'It's an [unreasonable] rule. It'd be hard not to. Like people do it unconsciously. People talk about someone and you don't realize that you're gossiping, but you are, I mean it's human nature [laughs].'

11 Conversely, Whitton teachers Joe, Luraleen, Simon, and Patrick suggested that students may follow rules because they know that the rules are right or reasonable, a position supported by many students who found most rules beneficial.

12 When Gregory and Mosely conducted interviews with nineteen teachers in an American high school, asking what led students to disobedience, adolescence was the most prominent response, with students thought to be fighting for autonomy, rebelling against authority, and lacking self-control.

13 See Millei and Raby (2010) for a close reading of staff commentary that illustrates these embodied logics at work, despite the more coherent understandings of young people that are described in theories of discipline.

14 Fallis and Opotow (2003), concerned with the extent and consequences of cutting classes, talked to students about their motivations for skipping out. Students said boredom, but with more probing it became clear that boredom stood in for much more: unengaged classes, disappointment with the course material or pedagogy, teacher absences without appropriate replacements, selective attention to students (e.g., strong ones ignored, disruptive students prioritized), and inequalities between schools contributing to comparatively limited course selection and extra-curricular activities.

15 The belief that it is emancipating to embrace young people as agentic, rights-bearing individuals in the present is potentially challenged by concern that young people have been abandoned because they are no longer seen as important resources for the future (Giroux 2003). Without this future-orientation, Giroux argues, young people, particularly minority youth, have been cast aside as irrelevant and therefore unworthy of various resources, including those that would ensure their education.

5 Consistency and Context

1 Gender and sexuality can also play a role in non-enforcement of certain dress codes. I address this in chapter 7.

2 As an interesting side note, Tamura (2004) found in her research in Japan that staff similarly felt that minor rules provide students with something to rebel against but that they also act as a kind of 'canary in the mineshaft' – they allow staff to catch personal problems early – so a student changing her hair could be a sign of bigger problems, for instance.

3 Dickar (2008) provides a nice description of students' attempts to hold on to hallway time as long as possible before having to commit to being in the classroom.

4 This may, in part, be a consequence of how the focus group questions were asked. There was a specific one on whether students tended to be treated unequally but no questions on whether there were occasions in which students *should* be treated unequally.

5 In their research, Kupchik and Ellis (2008) found that students involved in extracurricular activities and with higher grades perceived more school fairness in terms of the rules and their application. They suggest that this finding results from students' school bonds yet the students' comments examined here illustrate that favouritism towards such students may also play a role in their perceptions of fairness.

6 Thornberg found a very similar pattern in his research with primary school children in Sweden. The students noticed when teachers did not have to follow the same rules as the students and felt this to be both inconsistent and unfair (2008a).

7 One disciplinary strategy that raises a number of similarly problematic concerns about consistency and context is when a teacher or administrator will punish a group of students for the behaviour of some, e.g., keeping the whole class in detention because a number of students were rowdy or cancelling prom for the school because of a number of disciplinary incidents. The students I talked to generally resented suffering the negative consequences of the actions by others and considered it to be unfair.

8 Large scale legislation does not always translate into changes at the local level, of course. If deterrence was a central feature of zero tolerance, the lack of awareness of the policy among Whitton students suggests that it was not really communicated as expected at the ground level, perhaps in part because various Whitton administrators did not really see the 2002 *Safe Schools*

Act as offering anything really new. Indeed the language of both zero toler-ance and, later, progressive discipline, often does not seem to make it into school codes of conduct that students see. For a thorough study of how a large scale discipline policy did not come to pass on the ground level, see Brieschke (1989/90).

9 It has similarly been found that in the United States, zero tolerance ap-proaches are more likely to be evident within urban, inner-city, and pre-dominantly Black schools (see Robbins 2008).

10 One Ontario school board policy I reviewed included a number of 'extras' including suspension for persistent opposition to authority and acts considered 'injurious to the moral tone of the school' as well as expulsion for a student's persistent resistance to changing his or her behaviour.

11 Whitton staff interviews were conducted before progressive discipline was introduced, Big City interviews afterwards.

12 Note that in 2010 the Ontario government introduced new legislation to require that all potentially suspendable incidents, including bully-ing, must be reported by school staff members to the principal or the staff would face sanctions. This new legislation may address some teachers' concerns about consistency although it also raises ques-tions related to interpretation (e.g., what 'counts' as bullying or sexual harassment).

13 I discuss this pattern further, along with staff discussions of suspensions and social responsibility, in 'The intricacies of power relations in dis-courses of secondary school disciplinary strategies' (Raby 2010c).

6 The Contexts of Class, Ethnicity, and Racism

1 A further injustice is that they were considered too 'loud,' even when their loudness actually served them well academically.

2 I have used the term 'Native' as this is the term that was used by the in-digenous focus group participants. Please interpret this term to include all indigenous peoples of Canada, including Métis.

3 Kupchik expected similar findings in his comparison of four diverse American schools but actually found that all were equally focused on a top-down disciplinary style of 'teaching to the rules.' That said, he did find unequal applications and effects of the rules within all four schools, ac-cording to class and race (2010).

4 One teacher, when told of this example, suggested that there is some logic to administrative discomfort with students speaking their native

languages because they cannot be understood and so therefore 'it puts you at a disadvantage.'

5 Clearly, these comments are also addressing homophobia, which may be Jack's primary concern here. We will return to this issue at the end of the next chapter.

6 In their interviews with sixteen staff members from a mid-sized Ontario city on the topic of the *Safe Schools Act*, Daniel and Bondy's (2008) findings were similar to some of these comments. In discussing the *Safe Schools Act*, none of their participants felt that the *Act* had been used to unfairly target certain groups and certainly not at their own schools, despite observations by others, such as the Ontario Human Rights Commission, that the *Act* had discriminatory effects (Bhattacharjee 2003). Staff recognized the relevance of wider social issues in student behaviour, such as family problems, mental health, media influences, and so forth, as well as schools' lack of resources to appropriately help these students, but still ultimately focused on the individual offenders as the problem, potentially feeling this was the only area in which they could have any control or influence.

7 Cultural capital itself can come in various forms. The *'embodied state'* addresses forms of cultural capital that are dispositions within a person, such as certain knowledge or skills. The *'objectified state'* addresses forms of cultural capital embodied in objects or art, although this form of capital is created and interpreted through embodied cultural capital. The *'institutionalized state'* addresses the ways in which certain credentials are created and bestowed through institutions, and how these credentials then grant status.

8 One focus group moment illustrated the values embedded in such assertions about clothing. In this group, the values of the focus group resonated with those reflected in the school:

> MARJORY: I don't wear, like, skanky clothing or . . . I wear appropriate clothing [. . .]
> BETTY: I follow the dress code, but that's just the way I dress, so it's not like I'm doing it intentionally or anything.

Marjory defines her own dress as appropriate in contrast to 'skanky' clothing, thus defining herself as normal. Betty gestures towards the familiarity of a habitus which matches her school's.

9 Similarly, stereotypes about Black, Hispanic, or Native students and related assumptions about gang activity are influenced through representations of race that prevail in the popular media, representations which also play out in how certain students dress and act, and how their dress

and actions are, in turn, interpreted by school staff (Garot and Katz 2003; Ferguson 2000).

7 Regulating Sexualized and Gendered Bodies

1 Corrigan and Sayer (1985) focused on moral regulation as part of state formation and therefore exercised through state practices. As state institutions, moral regulation through schools can be understood as part of these processes. Instead, however, I am inclined to draw on work by Hunt (1999) and also by Brock (2003) to accept that moral regulation is evident within both state and non-state practices. Linking certain dress to self-respect as school rules do, for example, is linked to interpersonal processes whereby young people regulate girls' behaviour through the controlling insult of 'slut,' for instance.

2 While I asked about philosophies of discipline, and whether the rules are applied in the same way for all students, unfortunately I did not ask directly how students or staff understood gender to be relevant to school rules and their enforcement.

3 However, Barb (Whitton teacher) told of an incident where a girl reported to her that a new male teacher was flirting too much with his female students. Barb did not accept this girl's contention, countering with, 'I'm sure he isn't flirting as badly as you think he is, you know?'

4 Pomerantz contends that dress codes only became a serious concern since the 1990s around a rising moral panic in response to girls' new, revealing fashions (2008).

5 Of course, if girls are not supposed to be sexual for fear of being stigmatized as sluts (Tanenbaum 1999; Tolman 2002), then one way to avoid framing clothing choices in terms of sexuality is to emphasize the practicality of these choices. This pattern resonates with Gleeson's observations that girls explain their clothing choices through the language of personal taste rather than sexual attractiveness because 'being explicit about sexual intentions is inherently fraught' (2004, 103).

6 A case in Langley, British Columbia, revolved around this very issue. A young woman was sent home for wearing an 'inappropriate' tank top. The principal and various reporters noted, however, that this top was particularly revealing on this specific girl because of her breast size. Pomerantz (2007) critically examines this case, discussing how such dress codes patrol the borders of femininity and delineate acceptability. Pomerantz astutely observes that this was not a dress code violation but a corporeal violation.

7 As briefly mentioned in chapter 2, most urban schools specify that religious headgear is exempt from the rule against hats but such exceptions are less likely to be stated in semi-rural codes.

8 Age may also be relevant here. Within my focus groups, age was raised in two groups, with the suggestion that it is in middle school that there is more pressure to dress provocatively to be cool, while it is in the older grades of secondary school that those who dress provocatively are criticized. Some of these girls' comments may thus in part be about them locating themselves as more mature – an ironic position when provocative dress is so often a concern to commentators because it is considered too adult.

9 For other examinations of intersections between class and gender among high school girls, see Hey (1997), and for a discussion of similar intersections at the elementary level, see Renold (2005).

10 Students were similarly dismissive of potentially racist comments if they were playful and between friends.

11 Homophobia is also linked to the escalation of infractions such as fighting. Two focus groups narrated incidents wherein a student insulted another through the use of homophobic language, directly resulting in a fight, with the recipients of homophobic bullying defending themselves..

12 This pattern is potentially changing as 2010 legislative amendments now include racism, homophobia, and sexist behaviour as potentially leading to suspension.

13 Several teachers talked about the value of having an 'out' teacher in the school as this was then thought to increase both student and teacher awareness.

14 Of course mentioning homophobia in the school codes of conduct does not end the practice. One teacher was particularly vocal about what he felt to be the institutionalization of homophobia in Big City schools, for instance. He cited an example of a teacher actually leaving the school due to homophobia and a lack of administrative support and another of bringing a student to the office for homophobic comments and having the vice-principal ignore the problem.

8 Acceptance and Challenge

1 Several parts of this chapter draw on 'Slippery as fish but already caught? Secondary students' engagement with school rules' (Raby and Domitrek 2007) and 'What is resistance?' (Raby 2005).

2 Cothran et al. (2009) note that both teachers and students need to own the problem of misbehaviour in the classroom. While students have trouble

seeing the relevance of their family backgrounds, teachers fail to consider the curriculum or instructional practices. They contend that 'this self-serving bias is important because if one feels that they are not responsible then there is little reason to attempt to change behaviours' (165).

3 Foucault also suggested resistance through biopower, or through reinventing the body via new forms of desire or pleasure (Best and Kellner 1991), or through 'limit experience' (Foucault 1965; Jay 1998) wherein insight can be gained by pushing the body into new experiences to disrupt the self and potentially create insight into the workings of power. The ability to transform such experiences into resistance may depend on available resources and dominant, containing discourses, however. It is possible to consider the adolescent body, in itself, to be a disruptive kind of limit experience but significant academic and popular work has been invested in containing and explaining the bodily changes associated with adolescence.

4 As we will explore in the following chapter, in some ways this approach resonates with certain perspectives within the deschooling movement which contend that children should be free to pursue their own innate curiosities, for instance, and that it is schools' attempts to impose order and regulation that foster an antipathy to learning (Neill 1992; Hern 2008; Mercogliano 1998).

9 Students Having a Say

1 The democratic participation of teachers, while not the focus of this study, is also relevant. A North American group focusing on the participatory involvement of teachers is the League of Professional Schools, an American organization dedicated to fostering teachers' involvement in democratic decision-making in schools. For a detailed examination of how principals can better involve teachers, see Blase and Blase (1997). For profiles of eight such democratically organized schools see Blase, Blase, Anderson, and Dungan (1995). Others also advocate for the participation of parents (Noonan et al. 1999).

2 Furthermore, many who have advocated young children's participation contend that children's abilities to participate, and investment in doing so, are evident even among very young children (Hall and Rudkin 2011).

3 In Canada, the *Charter of Rights and Freedoms* is also a relevant document for considering the rights of children in schools as they relate to rules. Some have been concerned that the *Charter* has the potential to undermine the operation of schools through recourse to students' rights (Dennis 1996; Harte and McDonald 1996). To date, however, courts have ruled that educators

will sometimes need to infringe on student rights to maintain order and control (Dennis 1996). Such infringement has been supported in cases of search and seizure when there is a reasonable ground for suspicion of a school violation and in a case of detention, for example. Harte and Mc-Donald (1996) argue, however, that due to the *Charter*, school officials need to demonstrate that a school rule is reasonable, necessary, and legitimate. Rules must be clear and linked to an educational and/or disciplinary rationale, and students need an opportunity to provide their side of the story (Harte and McDonald 1996).

4 Based on his research with working class youth in Britain, France (1998) raises a concern with this approach. He found that the young people often felt no sense of community obligation or responsibility due to their surveillance and exclusion. They were assumed to be social problems and therefore had little stake in the community. These young people needed to experience themselves as having rights *in order to* feel a sense of responsibility.

5 Note that some portions of this section draw on 'Frustrated, resigned, outspoken: students' engagement with school rules and some implications for participatory citizenship' (Raby 2008a).

6 The *Safe Schools Act* (2000) includes a provision for parents, but not students, to vote on introducing school uniforms.

7 Others similarly noted that by having students educate each other about the rules, the rules are more likely to be followed.

8 In the New York city school Dickar studied, police officers were even introduced into the school despite significant community, staff, and student opposition.

9 They particularly seem more prevalent in alternative schools, which are likely to be found in urban centres, where students have more say and there is less focus on the detailed, top-down rules common to many regular schools. There were few codes of behaviour for alternative schools represented in the sample of school codes of conduct which I studied. However, in Gagne's (1996) review of Contact School, an alternative school for marginalized youth in Toronto, Ontario, he notes that one part of the school's success was that norms of behaviour are developed rather than imposed, with students involved in decision-making processes.

10 In Ontario, such guidelines are included in the *Safe Schools Act* but rarely in individual school conduct codes.

11 With compulsory education it is not only compulsory for children to attend, but also compulsory for parents to send them, a factor which I have not found addressed in the democratic school literature.

12 Another example of a democratic school in Canada is Windsor House in North Vancouver.
13 Gray and Chanoff (1986) conducted a follow-up study of graduates of Sudbury Valley Schools, some of the few ongoing, democratically run schools without academic requirements (which Chanoff participated in founding). Their findings suggested that almost 50 per cent of the sixty-nine respondents had completed college and six had either completed or were enrolled in advanced degrees. Students were involved in a wide range of career choices, with many self-employed, and many particularly successful in the arts. Graduates felt handicapped through a lack of transcripts and a lack of certain academic skills but they also talked about having learned motivation, responsibility, self-direction, a lack of fear of authority, a feeling of freedom, a tolerance of diversity, confidence, and how to overcome personal problems. The authors suggest that even if students at Sudbury Valley Schools are generally middle class students who might otherwise be inclined towards success anyway, their data makes it clear that such students can do well in society without coercive schooling. Furthermore, many of the students who had been latecomers to the Sudbury Valley Schools had had serious problems in the regular school system, with rebellious behaviour, learning disabilities, and/or anxiety and depression.
14 Of course this is within a broader discursive context in which young people are positioned as inferior and insufficiently skilled.

10 Conclusion and Practical Implications

1 In his ethnographic work, Kupchik (2010) observed that conflict resolution can simply end up reproducing an emphasis on obedience, however. In one school it ended up being used to extract the story of what happened from a student, which was then used to legitimize the punishment.
2 Such listing is evident in the Ontario *Code of Conduct* and emerges in a minority of school codes of conduct.

Appendix A Methods

1 Ontario is one of only two provinces in Canada with two parallel public school boards, secular and Catholic. While there are various points in this study where the Catholic system is discussed, it was not formally studied for this research project as the religious dimension of the Catholic system differently inflects a discussion of discipline, rules, and rule-breaking.

Clearly such a study would be valuable, particularly in comparison to a study of secular boards.

2 Part of this reflection on focus groups draws on Raby, 'Public selves, inequality, and interruptions: the creation of meaning in focus groups with teens' (2010a).

3 In this section, I have referred to all research assistants by pseudonyms to maintain confidentiality.

4 There were two exceptions. Whitton FG 2 included several young people who were over 18 and not in secondary school while Whitton FG 7 included three participants in middle school (grades 7–9) who were not yet 14.

5 Except to note that we would not be able to maintain confidentiality of any reported child abuse.

Appendix C Staff Participants

1 Listed positions were current at the time of interview. Many participants also had previous experience in other positions, schools, and school boards. The number of years presented reflects respondents' total number of years working in schools.

References

Adams, Mary Louise. 1997. The Trouble with Normal: Postwar Youth and the Making of Heterosexuality. Toronto: University of Toronto Press.

Albright, Julie M. 2009. You can't be hugging and hitting at the same time, or why allowing hugging in schools is smart policy. Teachers College Record, 21 July.

Alderson, Priscilla. 1999. Human rights and democracy in schools: do they mean more than 'picking up litter and not killing whales'? International Journal of Children's Rights 7:185–205.

Alladin, Ibrahim. 1996. Racism in Canadian Schools. Toronto: Harcourt Brace Canada.

Allen, Louise. 2009. 'The 5 cm rule': biopower, sexuality and schooling. Discourse: Studies in the Cultural Politics of Education 30 (4):443–56.

Amit-Talai, Vered. 1995. The waltz of sociability: intimacy, dislocation and friendship in a Quebec high school. In Youth Cultures: A Cross-Cultural Perspective, edited by V. Amit-Talai and H. Wulff, 144–65. London: Routledge.

Anderson, Wendell. 2002. *School Dress Codes and Uniform Policies*. Eugene, OR: ERIC Clearinghouse on Educational Management. See http://eric.uoregon.edu/publications/policy_reports/dress_codes/intro.html.

Apple, Michael W. 1990. Ideology and Curriculum. New York: Routledge.

– 1995. Education and Power. 2nd ed. New York: Routledge.

Archard, David. 2004. Children: Rights and Childhood. 2nd ed. London: Routledge. Original edition, 1993.

Archer, Louise, Sumi Hollingworth, and Anna Halsall. 2005. 'University's not for me – I'm a Nike person': urban, working-class young people's negotiations of 'style,' identity and educational engagement. Sociology 41 (2): 219–37.

Arendt, Hannah. 1961. *Between Past and Future: Six Exercises in Political Thought*. New York: Viking.

– 1998. *The Human Condition*. 2nd ed. Chicago: University of Chicago Press.

Beane, James A. and Michael W. Apple. 1995. The case for democratic schools. In Democratic Schools, edited by M.W. Apple and J.A. Beane, 1–25. Alexandria, VA: Association for Supervision and Curriculum Development.

Beauvais, Caroline, Lindsey McKay, and Adam Seddon. 2002. A Literature Review on Youth and Citizenship: Executive Summary. CPRN Discussion Paper. Canadian Policy Research Networks. Available from www.cprn.com/cprn.html.

Besley, Tina (A.C.), and Michael A. Peters. 2007. Subjectivity and Truth: Foucault, Education, and the Culture of Self. New York: Peter Lang.

Best, Amy. 2000. Prom Night: Youth, Schools and Popular Culture. New York: Routledge.

Best, Steven, and Douglas Kellner. 1991. Postmodern Theory: Critical Interrogations. New York: Guilford Press.

Bettis, Pamela J., and Natalie G. Adams. 2003. The power of the preps and a cheerleading equity policy. Sociology of Education 76 (April):128–42.

Bhattacharjee, Ken. 2003. The Ontario *Safe Schools Act*: School Discipline and Discrimination. Toronto: Ontario Human Rights Commission.

Biesta, Gert. 2007. Education and the democratic person: towards a political conception of democratic education. Teachers College Record 109 (3): 740–69.

– 2010. How to exist politically and learn from it: Hannah Arendt and the problem of democratic education. *Teachers College Record* 112 (2):556–75.

Bischop, Donna M. 2000. Juvenile offenders in the adult criminal justice system. Crime and Justice 27:81–167.

Black, Rosalyn. 2011. Student participation and disadvantage: limitations in policy and practice. *Journal of Youth Studies* 14 (4):463–74.

Blankenau, Joe, and Mark Leeper. 2003. Public school search policies and the 'politics of sin.' The Policy Studies Journal 31 (4):565–84.

Blase, Jo, and Joseph Blase. 1997. The Fire Is Back! Principals Sharing School Governance. Thousand Oaks, CA: Corwin Press.

Blase, Joseph, Jo Blase, Gary L. Anderson, and Sherry Dungan. 1995. Democratic Principals in Action: Eight Pioneers. Thousand Oaks, CA: Corwin Press.

Blatterer, Harry. 2007. Coming of Age in Times of Uncertainty. New York: Berghahn Books.

Bloor, Michael, Jane Frankland, Michelle Thomas, and Kate Robson. 2001. Focus Groups in Social Research. London: Sage.

Bodine, Ann. 2003. School uniforms and discourses on childhood. Childhood 10 (1):43–62.

Bonilla, Josh. 2001. Dress codes interfere with our freedom of expression. Toronto Star, 20 March, D1.

Bourdieu, Pierre. 1984. Distinction: A Social Critique of the Judgement of Taste. Translated by R. Nice. Cambridge, MA: Harvard University Press.

– 2001. The forms of capital. In The Sociology of Economic Life, edited by M. Granovetter and R. Swedberg, 96–111. Cambridge, MA: Westview Press.

Bourdieu, Pierre, and Jean-Claude Passeron. 1977. Reproduction in Education, Society and Culture. London: Sage.

Bowditch, Christine. 1993. Getting rid of troublemakers: high school disciplinary procedures and the production of dropouts. Social Problems 40 (4): 493–509.

Bowles, Samuel, and Herbert Gintis. 1976. Schooling in Capitalist America: Educational Reform and the Contradictions of Economic Life. New York: Basic Books.

Brah, Avtar. 1996. Cartographies of Diaspora: Contesting Identities. London: Routledge.

Brieschke, Patricia. 1989/90. The surprise side of policy analysis: a case study. Policy Studies Journal 18 (2):305–23.

Brock, Debi. 2003. Making Normal: Social Regulation in Canada. Toronto: Nelson.

Brophy, Jere. 2006. History of research on classroom management. In Handbook of Classroom Management: Research, Practice, and Contemporary Issues, edited by C.M. Evertson and C.S. Weinstein, 17–44. Mahwah, NJ: Lawrence Erlbaum.

Brown, Enora R. 2003. Freedom for some, discipline for 'others.' In Education as Enforcement: The Militarization and Corporatization of Schools, edited by K.J. Saltman and D.A. Gabbard, 127–50. New York: Routledge.

Brown, Lyn Mikel. 2003. Girlfighting: Betrayal and Rejection among Girls. New York: New York University Press.

Burman, Erica. 2008. Deconstructing Developmental Psychology. 2nd ed. London: Routledge.

Burr, Rachel. 2004. Children's rights: international policy and lived practice. In An Introduction to Childhood Studies, edited by Mary Jane Kehily, 145–59. Maidenhead: Open University Press.

Burr, Vivien. 1995. An Introduction to Social Constructionism. London: Routledge.

Butler, Judith. 1990. Gender Trouble: Feminism and the Subversion of Identity. New York: Routledge.

– 1993. Bodies that Matter. Routledge: New York.

– 1997. The Psychic Life of Power: Theories in Subjection. Stanford, CA: Stanford University Press.

Cameron, Lisa, and Margaret Thorsborne. 2001. Restorative justice and school discipline: mutually exclusive? In Restorative Justice and Civil Society, edited by H. Strang and J. Braithwaite, 180–94. Cambridge: Cambridge University Press.

Canada, Government of. 2006. Innovation in Canada.

Caputo, Virginia. 1995. Anthropology's silent others. In Youth Cultures: A Cross-Cultural Perspective, edited by V. Amit-Talai and H. Wulff, 19–42. London: Routledge.

Carter, Charlotte, and Audrey Osler. 2000. Human rights, identities and conflict management: a study of school culture as experienced through classroom relationships. Cambridge Journal of Education 30 (3):335–56.

Carter, Prudence L. 2003. 'Black' cultural capital, status positioning, and schooling conflicts for low-income African American youth. Social Problems 50 (1):136–55.

CBC. 29 August 2003. Zero Tolerance. Documentary. The Current. Canada.

– 2008. The Suspect Society. Documentary. Ideas. Canada.

Chambers, Deborah, Estella Tincknell, and Joost van Loon. 2004. Peer regulation of teenage sexual identities. Gender & Education 16 (3):397–415.

Christensen, Pia, and Allison James. 2000. Research with Children: Perspectives and Practices. London: Falmer Press.

Coad, Lindsey. 15 October. 2004. Teachers don't want the power to suspend. Centretown News Online.

Codjoe, Henry M. 2001. Fighting a 'public enemy' of Black academic achievement: the persistence of racism and the schooling experiences of Black students in Canada. Race, Ethnicity and Education 4 (1):343–75.

Connell, R.W. 1996. Teaching the boys: new research on masculinity, and gender strategies for schools. Teachers College Record 98 (2):206–35.

Corrigan, Philip, and Derek Sayer. 1985. The Great Arch: English State Formation as Cultural Revolution. Oxford: Blackwell.

Cosaro, William. 1997. The Sociology of Childhood. Thousand Oaks, CA: Pine Forge Press.

Cothran, Donnetta J., Pamela Hodges Kulinna, and Deborah A. Garrahy. 2009. Attributions for and consequences of student misbehaviour. Physical Education and Sport Pedagogy 14 (2):155–67.

Covell, Katherine, and Brian R Howe. 1999. The impact of children's rights education: a Canadian study. International Journal of Children's Rights 7:171–83.

– 2001. The Challenge of Children's Rights for Canada. Waterloo, ON: Wilfrid Laurier University Press.

– 2008. Rights, Respect and Responsibility: Final Report on the County of Hampshire Rights Education Initiative. Children's Rights Centre. Sydney, N.S., Cape Breton University.

Critchley, Stuart. 2003. The nature and extent of student involvement in educational policy making in Canadian school systems. Educational Management and Administration 31 (1):97–106.

Daniel, Yvette, and Karla Bondy. 2008. Safe schools and zero tolerance: policy, program and practice in Ontario. Canadian Journal of Educational Administration and Policy 70:1–20.

Dannefer, Dale. 1984. Adult development and social theory: a paradigmatic reappraisal. American Sociological Review 49:100–16.

Davies, Bronwyn. 1989. Frogs and Snails and Feminist Tales: Preschool Children and Gender. Sydney, Australia: Allen and Unwin.

– 1990. Agency as a form of discursive practice: a classroom scene observed. British Journal of Sociology of Education 11 (3):341–61.

Davies, Scott. 1994. In search of resistance and rebellion among high school dropouts. Canadian Journal of Sociology 19 (3):331–50.

Dei, George J. Sefa. 1996. Black/African-Canadian students' perspectives on school racism. In Racism in Canadian Schools, edited by I. Alladin, 42–61. Toronto: Harcourt-Brace Canada.

– 2008. The social construction of a 'drop-out': dispelling the myth. In Daily Struggles: The Deepening Racialization and Feminization of Poverty in Canada, edited by M.A. Wallis and S. Kwok, 263–74. Toronto: Canadian Scholars Press.

Deleuze, Gilles, and Guattari Felix. 1983. Anti-Oedipus: Capitalism and Schizophrenia. Minneapolis: University of Minneapolis Press.

Delpit, Lisa. 2006. Other People's Children: Cultural Conflict in the Classroom. New York: The New Press.

Dennis, Andrew. 1996. Student discipline and the charter. The Canadian School Executive 15 (8):13–17.

Denton, Paula. 2003. Shared rule-making in practice: The Jefferson Committee at Kingston High School. American Secondary Education 31 (3):66–96.

DeRoma, Virginia M., Kerry S. Lassiter, and Virginia A. Davis. 2004. Adolescent involvement in discipline decision-making. Behavior Modification, 28 (3):420–37.

Devine, Dympna. 2002. Children's citizenship and the structuring of adult-child relations in the primary school. Childhood 9 (3):303–20.

Dickar, Maryann. 2008. Corridor Cultures: Mapping Student Resistance at an Urban High School. New York: New York University Press.

Dobozy, Eva. 2007. Effective learning of civic skills: democratic schools succeed in nurturing the critical capacities of students. Educational Studies 33 (2):115–28.

Domitrek, Julie, and Rebecca Raby. 2008. Are you listening to me? Space, context and perspective in the regulation of mp3 players and cell phones in secondary school. Canadian Journal of Educational Administration and Policy 81:1–33.

Driscoll, Catherine. 2002. Girls: Feminine Adolescence in Popular Culture and Cultural Theory. New York: Columbia University Press.

Duits, Linda, and Liesbet van Zoonen. 2006. Disciplining girls' bodies in the European multicultural society. European Journal of Women's Studies 13 (2):103–17.

Dunbar, Jr., Christopher, and Francisco A. Villarruel. 2002. Urban school leaders and the implementation of zero-tolerance policies: an examination of its implications. Peabody Journal of Education 77 (1):82–105.

Durkheim, Emile. 1973. Moral Education: A Study in the Theory and Application of the Sociology of Education. London: The Free Press.

Dyer, R. 2000. The matter of whiteness. In Theories of Race and Racism: A Reader, edited by L. Black and J. Solomos, 539–48. London: Routledge.

Eder, Donna, and Laura Fingerson. 2001. Interviewing children and adolescents. In Handbook of Interview Research: Context and Method, edited by J.F. Gubrium and J.A. Holstein, 181–98. Thousand Oaks: Sage.

Effrat, A., and D. Schimmel. 2003. Walking the democratic talk: introduction to a special issue on collaborative rule-making as preparation for democratic citizenship. American Secondary Education 31(3):3–15.

Egale. 2008. First National Survey on Homophobia in Canadian Schools. Available from http://www.egale.ca/index.asp?lang=&menu=1&xitem=1401.

Ellison, Nick. 1997. Towards a new social politics: citizenship and reflexivity in late modernity. Sociology 31(4):697–717.

Emmer, Edmund T., Carolyn M. Evertson, and Murray E. Worsham. 2003. Classroom Management for Secondary Teachers. 6th ed. Boston: Allyn and Bacon.

Erikson, Erik. 1963. Childhood and Society. 2nd ed. New York: Norton.

Fallis, R. Kirk, and Susan Opotow. 2003. Are students failing school or are schools failing students? Class cutting in high school. Journal of Social Issues 59(1):103–19.

Fendler, Lynn. 2001. Educating flexible souls: the construction of subjectivity through developmentality and interaction. In Governing the Child in the

New Millennium, edited by K. Hultqvist and G. Dahlberg, 119–42. New York: RoutledgeFalmer.

Fenning, Pamela A., and Jennifer Rose. 2007. Overrepresentation of African American students in exclusionary discipline the role of school policy. Urban Education 42:536–59.

Ferguson, A.A. 2000. Bad Boys: Public Schools in the Making of Black Masculinity: Ann Arbor: University of Michigan Press.

Ferguson, Bruce, Kate Tilleczek, Katherine Boydell, and Anneke Rummens. 2005. Early School Leavers: Understanding the Lived Reality of Student Disengagement from Secondary School. Toronto: Community Health Systems Resource Group.

Fernando, J.L. 2001. Children's rights: beyond the impasse. The ANNALS of the American Academy of Political and Social Science 575 (8):8–24.

Fine, Michelle. 1991. Framing Dropouts: Notes on the Politics of an Urban Public High School. Albany: State University of New York Press.

Foucault, Michel. 1965. Madness and Civilization: A History of Insanity in the Age of Reason. New York: Random House.

– 1977. Discipline and Punish: The Birth of the Prison. London: Penguin Books.

– 1978a. Governmentality. In The Foucault Effect: Studies in Governmentality, edited by G. Burchell, C. Gordon, and P. Miller, 87–104. Chicago: University of Chicago Press.

– 1978b. The History of Sexuality. Volume 1, An Introduction. New York: Vintage Books.

– 2003 (reprinted from 1994). The ethics of the concern of the self as a practice of freedom. In The Essential Foucault: Selections from Essential Works of Foucault, 1954–1984, edited by P. Rabinow and N. Rose, 25–42. New York: The New Press.

France, Alan. 1998. Why should we care? Young people, citizenship and questions of social responsibility. Journal of Youth Studies 1 (1):97–111.

Frosh, Stephen, Ann Phoenix, and Rob Pattman. 2002. Young Masculinities: Understanding Boys in Contemporary Society. Houndmills, Basingstoke, Hampshire: Palgrave.

Gabor, Thomas. School Violence and the Zero Tolerance Alternative. Solicitor-General Canada 1995. Available from http://www.sgc.gc.ca/epub/pol/e199567/e199567.htm.

Gaetz, Stephen. 2004. Safe streets for whom? Homeless youth, social exclusion and criminal victimization. Canadian Journal of Criminology and Criminal Justice 46 (4):423–55.

Gagne, Antoinette. 1996. Success at contact: the argument for alternative schools for at-risk youth. The Alberta Journal of Educational Research 42(3):306–24.

Gallagher, Kathleen, and Caroline Fusco. 2006. I.D.ology and the technologies of public (school) space: an ethnographic inquiry into the neoliberal tactics of social (re)production. Ethnography and Education 1 (3):301–18.

Garot, Robert, and Jack Katz. 2003. Provocative looks: gang appearance and dress codes in an inner-city alternative school. Ethnography 4 (3):421–54.

Gartrell, D. 1998. A Guidance Approach for the Encouraging Classroom. Albany, NY: Delmar.

Gatehouse, Jonathon. 1998. Codes of conduct debated: flap over blue hair highlights, how different schools treat dress rules. The Gazette, Montreal, 23 April, A5.

Gereluk, Dianne. 2008. Symbolic Clothing in Schools: What Should be Worn and Why. London: Continuum.

– 2010. Children's autonomy and symbolic clothing in schools: help or hindrance? In Philosophy of Education in the Era of Globalization, edited by Y. Raley and G. Preyer, 198–211. New York: Routledge.

Gilbert, Rob, and Pam Gilbert. 1998. Masculinity Goes to School. London: Routledge.

Giroux, Henry A. 1983. Theories of reproduction and resistance in the new sociology of education. Harvard Educational Review 53 (3):257–93.

– 2003. Racial injustice and disposable youth in the age of zero tolerance. Qualitative Studies in Education 16 (4):553–65.

Gleeson, Kate, and Hannah Frith. 2004. Pretty in pink: young women presenting mature sexual identities. In All About the Girl: Culture, Power and Identity, edited by A. Harris, 103–14. New York: Routledge.

Goodman, Joan F. 2006a. School discipline in moral disarray. Journal of Moral Education 35 (2):213–30.

– 2006b. Students' choices and moral growth. Ethics and Education 1 (2):103–15.

Gordon, Colin. 1991. Governmental rationality: an introduction. In The Foucault Effect: Studies in Governmental Rationality, edited by Graham Burchell, Colin Gordon, and Peter Miller, 1–52. Chicago: University of Chicago Press.

Gottfredson, Denise C., Gary D. Gottfredson, and Lois G. Hybl. 1993. Managing adolescent behavior: a multiyear, multischool study. American Educational Research Journal 30 (1):179–215.

Gray, Peter, and David Chanoff. 1986. Democratic schooling: what happens to young people who have charge of their own education? American Journal of Education 94 (2):182–213.

Gray, Steven. 2007. Where students can't hug. Time Magazine, 13 November.

Gregory, Anne, and Pharmicia Mosely. 2004. The discipline gap: teachers' views on the over-representation of African American students in the discipline system. Equity and Excellence in Education 37 (1):18–30.

Gregory, Anne, Kysa Nygreen, and Dana Moran. 2006. The discipline gap and the normalization of failure. In Unfinished Business: Closing the Racial Achievement Gap in Our Schools, edited by P.A. Noguera and J.Y. Wing, 121–52. San Francisco: John Wiley & Sons.

Griffin, Christine. 1993. Representations of Youth: The Study of Youth and Adolescence in Britain and America. Cambridge: Polity Press.

Grossberg, Lawrence. 2001. Why does neoliberalism hate kids? The war on youth and the culture of politics. The Review of Education/Pedagogy/Cultural Studies 23 (2):111–36.

Gurian, Michael. 2002. Where it all begins: the biology of boyhood. In The Jossey-Bass Reader in Education, 101–24. San Francisco: Jossey-Bass.

Hall, Ellen Lynn, and Jennifer Kofkin Rudkin. 2011. Seen and Heard: Children's Rights in Early Childhood Education. New York: Teacher's College Press.

Hand, Jeanne Z., and Laura Sanchez. 2000. Badgering or bantering? Gender differences in experience of, and reactions to, sexual harassment among U.S. high school students. Gender and Society 14 (6):718–46.

Hannah-Moffat, Kelly. 2000. Prisons that empower: neoliberal governance in Canadian women's prisons. British Journal of Criminology 40:510–31.

Hannam, Derry. 2001. A Pilot Study to Evaluate the Impact of the Student Participation Aspects of the Citizenship Order on Standards of Education in Secondary School: Report to the Department for Education and Employment, London England.

Harris, Anita. 2004. Future Girl: Young Women in the Twenty-First Century. New York: Routledge.

Hart, R. 1992. Children's Participation: From Tokenism to Citizenship. Florence, Italy: UNICEF International Child Development Centre.

Harte, Austin J., and Kent McDonald. 1996. Implication of the charter for school discipline. Canadian School Executive 15 (7):3–6.

Harvard Civil Rights Project. 2000. Opportunities Suspended: The Devastating Consequences of Zero Tolerance and School Discipline. Cambridge, MA.

Hebdige, Dick. 1979. Subculture: The Meaning of Style. London: Routledge.

Hern, Matt, ed. 2008. Everywhere All the Time: A New Deschooling Reader. Oakland, CA: AK Press.

Hey, Valerie. 1997. Company She Keeps: An Ethnography of Girls' Friendships. Buckingham: Open University Press.

Hollander, Jocelyn A. 2004. The social contexts of focus groups. Journal of Contemporary Ethnography 33 (5):602–37.

Hoy, Anita Woolfolk, and Carol S. Weinstein. 2006. Student and teacher perspectives on classroom management. In Handbook of Classroom Management: Research, Practice and Contemporary Issues, edited by C.M. Evertson and C.S. Weinstein, 181–219. Mahwah, NJ: Lawrence Erlbaum.

Hughes, Meghan, and Jim Carrico. 2008. Windsor House. In Everywhere All the Tme: A New Deschooling Reader, edited by M. Hern, 165–70. Oakland: AK Press.

Hunt, Alan. 1999. Governing Morals: A Social History of Moral Regulation. Cambridge: Cambridge University Press.

Hyde, Abbey, Etaoine Howlett, Dympna Brady, and Jonathan Drennen. 2005. The focus group method: insights from focus group interviews on sexual health with adolescents. Social Science and Medicine 61:2588–99.

Imre, Rob, and Zsuzsa Millei. 2010. Citizenship? What citizenship? Using political science terminology in new discipline approaches. In Re-theorizing Discipline in Education: Problems, Politics and Possibilities, edited by Z. Millei, T. Griffiths, and R.J. Parkes, 131–45. New York: Peter Lang.

James, Allison. 2004. Understanding childhood from an interdisciplinary perspective: problems and potentials. In Rethinking Childhood, edited by P.B. Pufall and R.P. Unsworth, 25–37. New Brunswick, NJ: Rutgers University Press.

James, Allison, and Alan Prout, eds. 1990. Constructing and Reconstructing Childhood: Contemporary Issues in the Sociological Study of Childhood. London: Falmer Press.

Jay, Martin. 1998. Cultural Semantics: Key Words of Our Time. Amherst: University of Massachusetts Press.

Jay, Timothy. 1997. Improving School Conduct Codes: Clarity about unacceptable speech. http://www.eric.ed.gov:80/ERICWebPortal/search/detailmini.jsp?_nfpb=true&_&ERICExtSearch_SearchValue_0=ED408684&ERICExtSearch_SearchType_0=no&accno=ED408684

Jenks, Chris. 1996. Childhood. London: Routledge.

John, Mary. 1995. Children's rights in a free-market culture. In Children and the Politics of Culture, edited by S. Stephens, 105–40. Princeton, NJ: Princeton University Press.

Johnny, Leanne. 2005. UN Convention on the Rights of the Child: a rationale for implementing participatory rights in schools. Canadian Journal of Educational Administration and Policy (40):1–20.

Jones, Helen M.F. 2002. Respecting respect: exploring a great deal. Educational Studies 28 (4):341–52.

Jones, Vern, and Louise Jones. 2007. Comprehensive Classroom Management: Creating Communities of Support and Solving Problems. 8th ed. Boston: Pearson.

Katz, Susan Roberta. 1999. Teaching in tensions: Latino immigrant youth, their teachers, and the structures of schooling. Teachers College Record 100 (4):809–40.

Kelly, P. 2003. Growing up as risky business? Risks, surveillance and the institutionalized mistrust of youth. Journal of Youth Studies 6 (2):165–80.

Kemshall, Hazel. 2002. Effective practice in probation: an example of 'advanced liberal' responsibilisation? The Howard Journal 41 (1):41–58.

Kennedy, Mike. 2004. Providing safe schools. American School and University. Overland Park, KS: Penton Media, 1 January.

Kimmel, M. 2004. 'What about the boys?' What the current debates tell us – and don't tell us – about boys in school. In The Gendered Society Reader. 2nd ed. Edited by M. Kimmel and A. Aronson. New York: Oxford University Press.

Kindlon, Dan, and Michael Thompson. 2002. Thorns among roses: the struggle of young boys in early education. In The Jossey-Bass Reader on Gender in Education, 153–81. San Francisco: Jossey-Bass.

Kitzinger, Jenny. 1994. The methodology of focus groups: the importance of interaction between research participants. Sociology Health and Illness 16 (1):103–21.

Kitzinger, Jenny, and Rosaline S. Barbour. 1999. Introduction: the challenge and promise of focus groups. In Developing Focus Group Research: Politics, Theory and Practice, edited by R.S. Barbour and J. Kitzinger. London: Sage.

Knight, Melanie. 2008. 'Our school is like the United Nations': an examination of how discourses of diversity in schooling naturalize whiteness and white privilege. In Educators' Discourses on Student Diversity in Canada: Context, Policy, and Practice, edited by D. Gerin-Lajoie, 81–108. Toronto: Canadian Scholars' Press.

Knox, Sarah, and Alan W. Burkard. 2009. Qualitative research interviews. Psychotherapy Research 19 (4–5):566–75.

Kohn, Alfie. 1996. Beyond Discipline: From Compliance to Community. Alexandria, VA: Association for Supervision and Curriculum Development.

Kovach, Gretel. 2008. To curb truancy, Dallas tries electronic monitoring. New York Times. 12 May

Kupchik, Aaron. 2010. Homeroom Security: School Discipline in an Age of Fear. New York: New York University Press

Kupchik, Aaron, and Nicholas Ellis. 2008. School discipline and security: fair for all students? Youth and Society 39 (4):549–74.

Land, Deborah. 2003. Teasing apart secondary students' conceptualizations of peer teasing, bullying and sexual harassment. School Psychology International 24 (2):147–65.

Lansdown, Gerison. 1994. Children's rights. In Children's Childhoods: Observed and Experienced, edited by B. Mayall, 33–44. London: Falmer Press.

Lareau, Annette. 2003. Unequal Childhoods: Class, Race and Family Life. Berkeley: University of California Press.

Laws, Cath, and Bronwyn Davies. 2000. Poststructuralist theory in practice: working with 'behaviourally disturbed' children. Qualitative Studies in Education 13 (3):205–21.

Leck, Glorianne M. 2000. School uniforms, baggy pants, Barbie dolls, and business suit cultures on school boards: a feminqueering. In Thinking Queer: Sexuality, Culture and Education, edited by S. Talburt and S.R. Steinberg, 177–200. New York: Peter Lang.

Lee, Nick. 2001. Childhood and Society: Growing Up in an Age of Uncertainty. Buckingham: Open University Press.

Lesko, Nancy. 1988. Symbolizing Society: Stories, Rites and Structure in a Catholic High School. London: Falmer Press.

– 1996a. Denaturalizing adolescence: the politics of contemporary representations. Youth and Society 28 (2):139–61.

– 1996b. Past, present and future conceptions of adolescence. Educational Theory 46 (4):453–72.

– 2001. Act Your Age! A Cultural Construction of Adolescence. New York: Routledge.

Levinsky, Zachary. Unpublished paper. 'Not bad kids, just bad choices': negotiating school safety and (re)posing students under a zero tolerance policy.

Levinson. 2009. The war on hugs. Review of Reviewed Item. Teachers College Record, http://www.tcrecord.org/Home.asp. ID Number: 15603, Date Accessed: 5/5/2009.

Levy, Ariel. 2005. Female Chauvinist Pigs: Women and the Rise of Raunch Culture. New York: Free Press.

Lewis, Ramon. 1991. The Discipline Dilemma. Hawthorn, Victoria: The Australian Council for Educational Research Ltd.

– 1999a. Preparing students for democratic citizenship: codes of conduct in Victoria's 'schools of the future.' Educational Research and Evaluation 5 (1):41–61.

– 1999b. Teachers coping with the stress of classroom discipline. Social Psychology of Education 3:155–71.

– 1999c. Teachers' support for inclusive forms of classroom management. Inclusive Education 3 (3):269–85.

– 2001. Classroom discipline and student responsibility: the students' view. Teaching and Teacher Education 17 (3):307–19.

Lewis, Ramon, and Eva Burman. 2008. Providing for student voice in class-room management: teachers' views. International Journal of Inclusive Education 12 (2):151–67.

Loredo, Carren, Anne Reid, and Kay Deaux. 1995. Judgments and definitions of sexual harassment by high school students. Sex Roles 32 (1/2):29–45.

Lynch, Kathleen. 1989. The Hidden Curriculum: Reproduction in Education, a Reappraisal. London: One Falmer Press.

MacDonell, Allan J., and Wilfred B.W. Martin. 1986. Student orientations to school rules. The Alberta Journal of Educational Research 32 (1):51–65.

McCarthy, John D., and Dean R. Hoge. 1987. The social construction of school punishment: racial disadvantage out of universalistic process. *Social Forces* 65(4):1101–20.

McFadden, Mark G. 1995. Resistance to schooling and educational outcomes: questions of structure and agency. British Journal of Sociology of Education 16 (3):293–308.

McFarland, Daniel A., and Carlos Starmanns. 2009. Inside student government: the variable quality of high school student councils. Teachers College Record 111 (1):27–54.

McLaren, Peter. 1986. Schooling as a Ritual Performance: Towards a Political Economy of Educational Symbols and Gestures. London: Routledge.

– 1989. Life in Schools: An Introduction to Critical Pedagogy in the Foundations of Education. New York: Longman.

– 1993. Schooling as Ritual Performance: Towards a Political Economy of Educational Symbols and Gestures. 2nd ed. New York: Routledge.

McMurtry, Roy, and Alvin Curling. 2008. Roots of Youth Violence. Toronto: Queens Printer for Ontario.

McRobbie, Angela. 1978. Working class girls and the culture of feminism. In Women Take Issue: Aspects of Women's Subordination, edited by C.C.S. Women's Studies Group, 96–108. London: Hutchinson.

Mercogliano, Chris. 1998. Making It Up As We Go Along: The Story of the Albany Free School. Portsmouth, NH: Heinemann.

Meyenn, Bob, and Judith Parker. 2001. Naughty boys at school: perspectives on boys and discipline. In What About the Boys? Issues of Masculinity in Schools, edited by W. Martino and B. Meyenn, 169–85. Buckingham: Open University Press.

Middleton, David. 2004. Why we should care about respect. Contemporary Politics 10 (3–4):227–41.

Milgram, Stanley. 1963. Behavioral study of obedience. Journal of Abnormal Social Psychology 67:371–8.

Millei, Zsuzsa. 2007. Controlling or guiding students – what's the difference? A critique of approaches to classroom discipline. New Zealand Association for Research in Education and Australian Association for Research in Education Conference. Freemantle, WA.

– 2010. Is it (still) useful to think about classroom discipline as control? An examination of the 'problem of discipline'. In Re-theorizing Discipline in Education: Problems, Politics and Possibilities, edited by Z. Millei, T. Griffiths, and R.J. Parkes, 13–26. New York: Peter Lang.

– 2011. Thinking differently about guidance: power, children's autonomy and democratic environments. Journal of Early Childhood Research. Published online. 1–12.

Millei, Zsuzsa, Tom Griffiths, and Robert John Parkes. 2010. Continuing the conversation about discipline as a problem: a conclusion. In Re-theorizing Discipline in Education: Problems, Politics and Possibilities, edited by Z. Millei, T. Griffiths and R.J. Parkes, 175–80. New York: Peter Lang.

Millei, Zsuzsa, and Rebecca Raby. 2010. Embodied logic: understanding discipline through constituting the subjects of discipline. In The Politics of Classroom Discipline: Power, Freedom and Pedagogy, edited by Z. Millei, 27–42. New York: Peter Lang.

Mitchell, Lynn. 1999. Combining focus groups and interviews: telling how it is; telling how it feels. In Developing Focus Group Research: Politics, Theory and Practice, edited by R. S. Barbour and J. Kitzinger, 43–58. London: Sage.

Mitchell, Richard. 2010. Who's afraid now? Reconstructing Canadian citizenship education through transdisciplinarity. Review of Education, Pedagogy, and Cultural Studies 32 (1):37–65.

Mitra, Dana L. 2008. Student Voice in School Reform. Albany: State University of New York Press.

Moore, Oliver. 2007. Halifax school drops hoodie ban. Globe and Mail, 6 September.

Morgan, Myfanwy, Sara Gibbs, Krista Maxwell, and Nicky Britten. 2002. Hearing children's voices: methodological issues in conducting focus groups with children aged 7–11 years. Qualitative Research 2 (5):5–20.

Morris, Edward W. 2005. 'Tuck in that shirt!' Race, class, gender and discipline in an urban school. Sociological Perspectives 48 (1):25–48.

Muñoz, José Estaban. 1999. Disidentifications: Queers of Colour and the Performance of Politics. Minnesota: University of Minnesota Press.

Myhill, Debra, and Susan Jones. 2006. 'She doesn't shout at no girls': pupils' perceptions of gender equity in the classroom. Cambridge Journal of Education 36 (1):99–113.

Neill, A.S. 1992. Summerhill School: A New View of Childhood, Revised and Expanded. New York: St Martin's Griffin.

Nelson, R.W. 1996. Deviance and discipline in the classroom. In Social Control in Canada: A Reader on the Social Construction of Deviance, edited by B. Schissel and L. Mahood, 373–402. Toronto: Oxford University Press.

Noguera, Pedro A. 2003. Schools, prisons, and social implications of punishment: rethinking disciplinary practices. Theory into Practice 42 (4):341–50.

Noonan, B., K. Tunney, B. Fogal, and C. Sarich. 1999. Developing student codes of conduct: a case for parent-principal partnership. Social Psychology International 20:289–99.

Nucci, Larry P. 1981. Conceptions of personal issues: a domain distinct from moral or societal concepts. Child Development 52 (1):114–21.

– 2001. Education in the Moral Domain. Cambridge: Cambridge University Press.

Oakes, Jeannie. 1985. Keeping Track: How Schools Structure Inequality. New Haven, CT: Yale University Press.

Ogbu, J. 2003. Black American Students in an Affluent Suburb: A Study of Academic Disengagement. Mahway, NJ: Lawrence Erlbaum.

Olafson, Lori, and James C. Field. 2003. A moral revisioning of resistance. The Educational Forum 67 (2):140–7.

O'Malley, P., L. Weir, and C. Shearing. 1997. Governmentality, criticism, politics. Economy and Society 26:501–17.

Ontario, Government of. 2001. Code of Conduct. Toronto: Queen's Printer of Ontario.

– 2010. Safe Schools: Suspension and Expulsion Facts, 2006–07, edited by Ministry of Education. Toronto: Queen's Printer of Ontario.

– 2011. Education Act. Toronto: Queen's Printer of Ontario.

Oplatka, Izhar, and Miri Atias. 2007. Gendered views of managing discipline in school and classroom. Gender and Education 19 (1):41–59.

Osborne, Ken. 1994. Teaching for democratic citizenship. In Sociology of Education in Canada: Critical Perspectives on Theory, Research and Practice, edited by L. Erwin and D. MacLennan, 417–42. Toronto: Copp Clark Longman.

Page, Shelley. 2002. Shame, shame on who? School dress controversy reflects adult fear of girls burgeoning sexuality. Star – Phoenix, 22 April, D1, Front.

Parkes, Robert John. 2010. Discipline and the dojo. In Re-theorizing Discipline in Education: Problems, Politics and Possibilities, edited by Z. Millei, T. Griffiths, and R.J. Parkes, 76–90. New York: Peter Lang.

Pascoe, C.J. 2007. Dude, You're a Fag: Masculinity and Sexuality in High School. Berkeley: University of California Press.

Pasko, Lisa. 2006. The wayward girl revisited: understanding the gendered nature of juvenile justice and delinquency. Sociology Compass 2 (3):821–36.

Payne, Monica A. 2009. 'Teen brain' science and the contemporary storying of psychological (im)maturity. In Times of Our Lives: Making Sense of Growing Up and Growing Old, e-book edited by H. Blatterer and J. Glahn, 55–68. Oxford: Inter-disciplinary Press.

Piluso, Gus, and Geraldine Lyn-Piluso. 2008. Challenging the popular wisdom. In Everywhere All the Time: A New Deschooling Reader, edited by M. Hern, 82–90. Oadkland: AK Press.

Plummer, Ken. 2003. Intimate Citizenship: Private Decisions and Public Dialogues. Montreal & Kingston: McGill-Queens University Press.

Pomerantz, Shauna. 2007. Cleavage in a tank top: bodily prohibition and the discourses of school dress codes. Alberta Journal of Educational Research 53 (4):373–86.

– 2008. Girls, Style and School Identities: Dressing the Part. New York: Palgrave.

Pongratz, Ludwig. 2007. Freedom and discipline: transformations in pedagogic punishment. In Why Foucault? New Directions in Educational Research, edited by M.A. Peters and T.A.C. Besley, 29–42. New York: Peter Lang.

Porter, L. 1996. Student Behaviour: Theory and Practice for Teachers. St Leonards: Allen & Unwin.

– 2003. Young Children's Behaviour: Practical Approaches for Caregivers and Teachers. 3rd ed. Marrickville, NSW: Elsevier Australia.

Print, Murray, Susanne Ornstrom, and Henrik Skovgaard Nielson. 2002. Education for democratic processes in schools and classrooms. European Journal of Education 37 (2):193–210.

Pritchard, BW. 1990. Fundamental justice in student discipline. The Canadian School Executive 9 (9):3–5.

Raby, Rebecca. 2002. A tangle of discourses: girls negotiating adolescence. Journal of Youth Studies 5 (4):425–50.

– 2004. 'There's no racism at my school, it's just joking around': ramifications for anti-racist education. Race, Ethnicity and Education 7 (4):367–83.

– 2005a. Polite, well-dressed and on time: secondary school conduct codes and the production of docile citizens. Canadian Review of Sociology and Anthropology 42 (1):71–92.

– 2005b. What is resistance? Journal of Youth Studies 8 (2):151–71.

– 2008a. Frustrated, resigned, outspoken: students' engagement with school rules and some implications for participatory citizenship. International Journal of Children's Rights 16 (1):77–98.

– 2008b. Rights and responsibility: secondary school conduct codes and the production of passive citizenship. In Children's Rights: Theories, Policies and Interventions, edited by T. O'Neill and D. Zinga. Toronto: University of Toronto Press.

– 2010a. Public selves, inequality, and interruptions: the creation of meaning in focus groups with teens. International Journal of Qualitative Methods 9 (1):1–15.

– 2010b. 'Tank tops are OK but I don't want to see her thong': girls' engagements with secondary school dress codes. Youth and Society 41:333–56.

– 2010c. The intricacies of power relations in discourses of secondary school disciplinary strategies. In Re-theorizing Discipline in Education: Problems, Politics and Possibilities, edited by Z. Millei, T. Griffiths, and R.J. Parkes. New York: Peter Lang.

Raby, Rebecca, and Julie Domitrek. 2007. Slippery as fish but already caught? Secondary students' engagement with school rules. Canadian Journal of Education 30.

Raffaele Mendez, L.M., and H.M. Knoff. 2003. Who gets suspended from school and why: a demographic analysis of schools and disciplinary infractions in a large school district. Education and Treatment of Children 26:30–51.

Ransom, John S. 1997. Foucault's Discipline: The Politics of Subjectivity. Durham: Duke University Press.

Reay, Diane. 1995. 'They employ cleaners to do that': habitus in the primary classroom. British Journal of Sociology of Education 16 (3):353–71.

Reid, Rebecca. 2002. 'Fashions happens,' teens shrug. The Ottawa Citizen, 13 April, A4.

Renold, Emma. 2001. Learning the 'hard' way: boys, hegemonic masculinity and the negotiation of learner identities in the primary school. British Journal of Sociology of Education 22 (3):369–85.

– 2005. Girls, Boys and Junior Sexualities: Exploring Children's Gender and Sexual Relations in the Primary School. London: RoutledgeFalmer.

Robbins, Christopher G. 2008. Expelling Hope: The Assault on Youth and the Militarization of Schooling. Albany: SUNY Press.

Robinson, Kerry. H. 1992. Class-room discipline: power, resistance and gender. A look at teacher perspectives. Gender & Education 4 (3):273–88.

– 2005. Reinforcing hegemonic masculinities through sexual harassment: issues of identity, power and popularity in secondary schools. Gender & Education 17 (1):19–37.

Roche, Jeremy. 1999. Children: rights, participation and citizenship. Childhood 6 (4):475–93.

Roher, Eric M. 2008. Progressive discipline: totally rethinking safe schools. Principal Connections 11(3):18–19.

Rollock, Nancy. 2007. Legitimizing black academic failure: deconstructing staff discourses on academic success, appearance and behavior. International Studies in Sociology of Education 17 (3):275–87.

Roman, Leslie G. 1993. White is a color! White defensiveness, postmodernism and anti-racist pedagogy. In Race, Identity and Representation in Education, edited by C. McCarthy and W. Crichlow, 71–88. London: Routledge.

Rose, Nikolas. 1990. Governing the Soul: The Shaping of the Private Self. London: Routledge.

– 1999. Power of Freedom: Reframing Political Thought. Cambridge: Cambridge University Press.

Rowe, Don. 2006. Taking responsibility: school behaviour policies in England, moral development and implications for citizenship education. Journal of Moral Education 35 (4):519–31.

Ruck, Martin D., and Scott Wortley. 2002. Racial and ethnic minority high school students' perceptions of school disciplinary practices: a look at some Canadian Findings. Journal of Youth and Adolescence 31 (3):185–95.

Ruddock, Jean, and Julia Flutter. 2000. Pupil participation and pupil perspective: 'carving a new order of experience.' Cambridge Journal of Education 30 (1):75–89.

Runions, Dave. 2002. Living by a code. Standard – Freeholder, 31 Jan., 14.

Russel, Rachel, and Melissa Tyler. 2002. Thank heaven for little girls: 'girl heaven' and the commercial context of feminine childhood. Sociology 36 (3):619–37.

Sadker, Myra, and David Sadker. 2002. The miseducation of boys. In The Jossey-Bass Reader in Education, 182–203. San Francisco: Jossey-Bass.

Saltman, Kenneth J., and David A. Gabbard, eds. 2003. Education as Enforcement: The Militarization and Corporatization of Schools. New York: Routledge.

Sandals, Liz, Leeanna Pendergast, Stu Auty, Inez Elliston, Ray Hughes, Debra Pepler, and Lynn Ziraldo. 2008. Shaping a Culture of Respect in Our Schools: Promoting Safe and Healthy Relationships. Ministry of Education: Ontario Government.

Schalet, Amy. 2004. Must we fear adolescent sexuality? Medscape General Medicine 6 (4).

Schimmel, David. 1997. Traditional rule-making and the subversion of citizenship education. Social Education 61 (2):70–4.

– 2003. Collaborative rule-making and citizenship education: an antidote to the undemocratic hidden curriculum. American Secondary Education 31 (3):16–35.

Schmuck, Richard A., and Patricia A. Schmuck. 1989. Adolescents' attitudes toward school and teachers: from 1963 to 1989. ERIC Document Reproduction Service No. ED 316 381.

School Community Safety Advisory, Panel. 2008. The Road to Health: A Final Report on School Safety. Toronto: Toronto District School Board.

Scott, James C. 1990. Domination and the Arts of Resistance: Hidden Transcripts. New Haven, CT: Yale University Press.

Sehr, David T. 1997. Education for a Public Democracy. New York: SUNY.

Shalit, W. 2007. Girls Gone Mild: Young Women Reclaim Self-Respect and Find It's Not Bad to Be Good. New York: Random House.

Shannon, Mary M., and Douglas S. McCall. 2003. Zero tolerance policies in context: A preliminary investigation to identify actions to improve school discipline and school safety. http://www.schoolfile.com/safehealthy-schools/whatsnew/capzerotolerance.htm.

Sheets, Rosa Hernandez, and Geneva Gay. 1996. Student perceptions of disciplinary conflict in ethnically diverse classrooms. NASSP Bulletin 80:84–94.

Shuy, Roger W. 2001. In-person versus telephone interviewing. In Handbook of Interview Research: Context and Method, edited by J.F. Gubrium and J.A. Holstein, 536–54. Thousand Oaks: Sage.

Siegel, Carol. 2005. Goth's Dark Empire. Bloomington and Indianapolis: Indiana University Press.

Simpson, Brenda. 2000. Regulation and resistance: children's embodiment during the primary-secondary school transition. In The Body, Childhood and Society, edited by A. Prout, 60–78. Hampshire, UK: Macmillan.

Skiba, Russell J., and M Karega Rausch. 2006. Zero tolerance, suspension, and expulsion: questions of equity and effectiveness. In Handbook of Classroom Management: Research, Practice and Contemporary Issues, edited by C.M. Evertson and C.S. Weinstein, 1063–89. Mahway, NJ: Lawrence Erlbaum.

Skott-Myhre, Hans. 2008. Youth and Subculture as Creative Force. Toronto: University of Toronto Press.

Smetana, Judith G., and Bruce Bitz. 1996. Adolescents' conceptions of teachers' authority and their relations to rule violations in school. Child Development 67:1153–72.

Smith, Anne B. 2002. Interpreting and supporting participation rights: contributions from sociocultural theory. International Journal of Children's Rights 10:73–88.

Smith, Brian J. 2003. Cultural curriculum and marginalized youth: an analysis of conflict at a school for juvenile parolees. The Urban Review 35 (4):253–80.

Smithson, Janet. 2000. Using and analysing focus groups: limitations and possibilities. International Journal of Social Research Methodology 3 (2):103–19.

Smyth, John, and Peter McInerney. 2007. 'Living on the edge': a case of a school reform working for disadvantaged adolescents. Teachers College Record 109 (5):1123–70.

Sprick, Randall S. 2006. Discipline in the Secondary Classroom: A Positive Approach to Behavior Management. 2nd ed. San Francisco: Jossey-Bass.

Stanley, S.M. 1996. School uniforms and safety. Education and Urban Society 28 (4):424–35.

Stasiulis, Daiva. 2002. The active child citizen: lessons from Canadian policy and the children's movement. Citizenship Studies 6 (4):507–38.

Steinberg, Laurence. 2007. Risk taking in adolescence: new perspectives from brain and behavioral science. Current Directions in Psychological Science 16 (2):55–9.

Stewart, Eric A. 2003. School social bonds, school climate, and school misbehavior: a multilevel analysis. Justice Quarterly 20 (3):575–604.

Stinchcomb, J.B., and G. Bazemore. 2006. Beyond zero tolerance. Youth Violence and Juvenile Justice 4 (2):123–47.

Storrie, Tom. 1997. Citizens or what? In Youth in Society, edited by J. Roche and S. Tucker, 52–60. London: Sage.

Such, Elizabeth, and Robert Walker. 2005. Young citizens or policy objects? Children in the 'rights and responsibilities' debate. Journal of Social Policy 34 (1):39–57.

Sughrue, Jennifer A. 2003. Zero tolerance for children: two wrongs do not make a right. Educational Administration Quarterly 39 (2):238–58.

Tait, Gordon. 2000. Youth, Sex and Government. New York: Peter Lang.

Tamura, Yuichi. 2004. Illusion of homogeneity in claims: discourse on school rules in Japan. The High School Journal (Oct/Nov):52–63.

Tanenbaum, Leora. 1999. Sluts! Growing Up Female with a Bad Reputation. New York: Seven Stories Press.

Tarulli, Danny, and Hans Skott-Myhre. 2006. The immanent rights of the multitude: an ontological framework for conceptualizing the issue of child and youth rights. International Journal of Children's Rights 14 (2):187–201.

Taylor, Nicola, Anne B Smith, and Karen Nairn. 2001. Rights important to young people: secondary student and staff perspectives. International Journal of Children's Rights 9:137–56.

Thomson, Graham. 1998. Anything doesn't go at Ottewell junior high. Edmonton Journal, 4 May, B1, Front.

Thomson, Rachel, and Janet Holland. 2002. Young people, social change and the negotiation of moral authority. Children and Society 16:103–15.

Thornberg, Robert. 2006. Hushing as a moral dilemma in the classroom. Journal of Moral Education 35 (1):89–104.

– 2008a. 'It's not fair!' – voicing pupils' criticisms of school rules. Children and Society 22:418–28.

– 2008b. School children's reasoning about school rules. Research Papers in Education 23 (1):37–52.

Thorson, Sue. 1996. The missing link: students discuss school discipline. Focus on Exceptional Children 29 (3):1–12.

– 2003. Listening to Students: Reflections on Secondary Classroom Management. Boston: Pearson Education.

Tolman, Deborah. 2002. Dilemmas of Desire. Cambridge, MA: Harvard University Press.

Transitions Committee. 2003. Transitions: Youth Homelessness in Lanark County. Smith Falls, Ontario.

Trépanier, Jennifer E. 2003. Student Discipline: A Guide to the Safe Schools Act. Markham, ON: LexisNexis Butterworths.

Tupper, Jennifer A., Terry Carson, Ingrid Johnson, and Jyoti Mangat. 2008. Building place: students' negotiation of spaces and citizenship in schools. Canadian Journal of Education 31 (4):1065–92.

Valenzuela, Angela. 2009. Subtractive schooling, caring relations, and social capital in the schooling of U.S.-Mexican youth. In The Curriculum Studies Reader, edited by D.J. Flinders and S.J. Thornton, 336–47. New York: Routledge.

Vandenbroeck, Michel, and Maria Bourverne-de-bie. 2006. Children's agency and educational norms: a tensed negotiation. Childhood 13 (1):127–43.

Vaughn, Sharon, Jeanne Shay Schumm, and Jane Sinagub. 1996. Focus Group Interviews in Education and Psychology. Thousand Oaks: Sage.

Vavrus, Frances, and KimMarie Cole. 2002. 'I didn't do nothin'': the discursive construction of school suspension. The Urban Review 34(2):87–111.

Verdugo, Richard R. 2002. Race-ethnicity, social class, and zero tolerance policies: the cultural and structural wars. Education and Urban Society 35 (1):50–75.

Wald, Johanna, and Michal Kurlaender. 2003. Connected in Seattle? An exploratory study of student perceptions of discipline and attachments to teachers. New Directions for Youth Development 99 (fall):35–54.

Walkerdine, Valerie. 1993. Beyond developmentalism? Theory and Psychology 3 (4):451–69.

Wallace, John M., Sara Goodkind, Cynthia M. Wallace, and Jerald G. Bachman. 2008. Racial, ethnic and gender differences in school discipline among U.S. high school students: 1991–2005. The Negro Educational Review 59 (1–2):47–62.

Warr, Deborah J. 2005. 'It was fun but we don't usually talk about these things': analyzing sociable interaction in focus groups. Qualitative Inquiry 11:200–25.

Watkins, Megan. 2010. Discipline, diversity and agency: pedagogic practice and dispositions to learning. In Re-theorizing Discipline in Education: Problems, Politics and Possibilities, edited by Z. Millei, T. Griffiths, and R.J. Parkes, 59–75. New York: Peter Lang.

Webb, Jen, Tony Schirato, and Geoff Danaher. 2002. Understanding Bourdieu. London: Sage.

Weinstein, Carol S., Saundra Tomlinson-Clarke, and Mary Curran. 2004. Toward a conception of culturally responsive classroom management. Journal of Teacher Education 55 (1):25–38.

Weist, Lynda R. 1999. Practicing what they teach: should teachers 'do as they say'? The Clearing House 72 (5):264–8.

White, Emily. 2002. Fast Girls: Teenage Tribes and the Myth of the Slut. New York: Scribner.

Widdicombe, Sue, and Robin Wooffitt. 1995. Youth subcultures and sociology. In Language of Youth Subcultures, edited by S. Widdicombe and R. Wooffitt, 7–25. New York: Harvester.

Wilkinson, Sue. 1998. Focus groups in feminist research: power, interaction, and the co-construction of meaning. Women's Studies International Forum 21 (1):111–25.

Williams, Mary M. 1993. Actions speak louder than words: what students think. Educational Leadership 51 (3):22–4.

Willis, Paul. 1977. Learning to Labour. Farnborough, England: Saxon House.

Wotherspoon, Terry. 1996. The hidden curriculum. In Social Control in Canada: Issues in the Social Construction of Deviance, edited by B. Schissel and L. Mahood, 335–51. Toronto: Oxford University Press.

Youdell, Deborah. 2003. Identity traps or how black students fail: the interactions between biographical, sub-cultural, and learner identities. British Journal of Sociology of Education 24 (1):3–20.

Index

and victims, 179–80. *See also* harassment

sexuality, 14, 20, 60–1, 160–1, 167–85

Skott-Myhre, H., 204–6, 212–13, 239, 242

social contexts, 57, 63, 91–2, 126

socialization theories, 189–90, 192

staff, 4–20; and authority, 11, 83, 110, 113, 162, 194; and beliefs, 85, 101; and classroom management, 76; and consequences, 66–8, 102–3; and consistency, 107–36; and context, 90, 100; and discipline, 80, 91; and discrimination, 20, 134, 154–5, 251; educational, 72, 89, 105, 163; and gender, 161–86; as guides, 77; and no hats, 22–48; and human nature, 91; and major rules, 73; and minor rules, 47; and morality, 54, 59; and obedience, 80; and power, 193; and racism, 144–59; and repeat offenders, 58–9; and respect, 96–7, 99; and responsibility, 103, 194, 260; and rights, 257; and risk, 61; and rule-breaking explanations, 193–213; and safety, 61, 63, 74, 79; and student participation, 214–15, 218, 222, 229–45; and suspensions, 68–73; and teenagers, 94; and zero tolerance, 83–4. *See also* administrators; teachers

staff philosophies, 85, 91, 104–5, 202

status hierarchies, 86, 91–2, 96–7, 100–1, 103, 123

student councils, 118, 215, 221–3

student involvement, 21, 53–4, 214–18, 220–36, 243–5, 257–8

student participation, 21, 191–2, 214–20, 230–45, 252–3. *See also* decision-making, and students

student representation, 220, 222, 231, 235–6

students of colour: and inequality, 137–49, 157, 259; and zero tolerance, 130

suspensions, 7, 66–73; and appeals, 227, 231, 254; and authority, 33, 58; and Black students, 137–8, 154; as deterrent, 209; and fighting, 57; in-school, 68–71; and marginalized students, 129; and minority students, 12, 147; out-of-school, 68, 70–1, 73, 255; and parents, 46; and progressive discipline, 130–1; rate of, 7, 68; and teachers, 7; and zero tolerance, 85, 142. *See also* expulsions; zero tolerance

teachers, 3–22; and adolescence, 93, 95; Australian, 167, 235; and authority, 58–72, 188–213; and beliefs, 76–88; and bullying, 53; and consistency, 107–34; female, 161, 166, 168; and gender, 160–87; and no hats, 22–37; and inequality, 135–59; male, 77, 161, 163–4, 168; pre-service, 17, 256; primary school, 90; and respect, 96–105; and rule application, 41–8; and student participation, 217–45. *See also* staff

teenagers, 42, 89, 93–5, 202–3; beliefs about, 83–103; as hormonal, 94–5, 175, 179; and resistance, 219–20. *See also* adolescence; youth